LEARNING LEADERSHIP

From the Scriptures

12 PRACTICES FOR

Building Leadership Effectiveness
Based on Timeless
and Eternal Principles

SHAWN D. MOON

CFI
AN IMPRINT OF CEDAR FORT, INC.
SPRINGVILLE, UTAH

Other books by this author

Leading Loyalty: Cracking the Code to Customer Devotion

Talent Unleashed—3 Leadership Conversations to Ignite the Unlimited Potential in People

The Ultimate Competitive Advantage: Why Your People Make All the Difference and 6 Practices You Need to Engage Them

Building a Winning Culture in Government: A Blueprint for Delivering Success in the Public Sector

On Your Own: A Young Adults' Guide to Making Smart Decisions

Bill's Christmas Legacy

PRAISE FOR

Learning Leadership from the Scriptures

"*Learning Leadership from the Scriptures* is a rare book that follows the what, why, and how of leadership. Far from being a theoretical approach, this book by Shawn Moon provides a practical guide that easily applies to youth, adults, family, group think, and business interests whilst challenging us to 'up our game' individually and collectively. Rather than a textbook approach, this read is more akin to a personal conversation with the writer himself. His book is easily the most practical leadership book I have encountered."

—LARRY GELWIX, former Highland Rugby head coach, highlighted in *Forever Strong* movie, and "Winningest Coach in America"—*Fox News*

"This volume distills major leadership doctrines and principles in an engaging manner with clarity and conversational ease, while conveying the Spirit. How can we help everyday individuals see themselves as leaders and then act on correct principles? This volume directly addresses that need in a way that is extremely accessible, interesting, and motivating. Everyone will find value in the teachings of this book. It is principle based, scripture focused, clear, and action oriented. It is filled with foundational principles, stories and examples to help individuals in their personal, family, and church leadership roles."

—TIMOTHY L. TAGGART, director audio visual department, The Church of Jesus Christ of Latter-day Saints (retired)

"Every woman should read *Learning Leadership from the Scriptures.* This book gives women a foundational understanding of leadership that is tied to our divine identity as leaders and influencers. Seeing our many leadership roles through the framework of this book can encourage us to accept and seek opportunities to influence and 'bring illumination and leadership to a dark and desperate world' and increase our impact for good in our personal, family, and church lives."

—ANN TAKASAKI, board chair, Big Ocean Women

"I see the need for leadership in every facet of life—in our work, at home, in our communities, and in our service. *Learning Leadership from the Scriptures* highlights that need and provides powerful examples and practical counsel for any leader of any age."

—DANNY AINGE, CEO Utah Jazz

"Leadership is the most important of all the arts because it enables every other art. It's also essential. Effective leaders build trust—in their own lives and in their work with others. Shawn Moon brilliantly addresses the vital leadership principles needed to do just that, providing immense practical advice and inspiration. Whether we're in a formal leadership role or seek to have informal influence with others, this book is an important addition to any library—and one we'll want to both read and apply, again and again."

—STEPHEN M. R. COVEY, *New York Times* and
#1 *Wall Street Journal* best-selling author,
The Speed of Trust and *Trust & Inspire*

"Every church, community, and family leader needs Shawn Moon's latest book, *Learning Leadership from the Scriptures: 12 Practices for Building Leadership Effectiveness Based on Timeless and Eternal Principles.* The close connections with scripture and the authentic counsel of latter-day prophets adds an unparalleled dimension of relevance to Shawn's principles for focus and direction as a leader. His personable writing style is accessible and compelling. Leaders in every chapter of life, and in all settings, will enjoy this timely and valuable collection of best practices from effective leaders all over the world. Through decades of community and church service, and as the eldest of seven siblings in a family of 40 grandchildren and 116 great grandchildren, I am always on the lookout for new insights on leadership that work! This book provides today's generation of leaders with the tools and dispositions for success. The world could use a giant dose of Shawn's clear thinking and dynamic strategies for 21st century influencers. I recommend this volume to all my friends who are committed to creating a brighter world at home and abroad."

—RANDY BOOTHE, BYU Young Ambassadors artistic
director and executive producer for BYU's College
of Fine Arts and Communications (retired),
Emeritus Faculty, BYU School of Music

For HKM.

Your influence has been felt at every step.

ISBN 13: 978-1-4621-4293-4

Published by CFI, an imprint of Cedar Fort, Inc.
2373 W. 700 S., Springville, UT 84663
Distributed by Cedar Fort, Inc., www.cedarfort.com

Library of Congress Control Number: 2022936759

Cover design by Shawnda T. Craig

Edited by Evelyn Nichols

Printed in the United States of America

10 9 8 7 6 5 4 3 2 1

Printed on acid-free paper

FOREWORD

Leading into my sophomore year in college, I was selected to be the managing editor of *The Scroll*—the weekly student newspaper at Ricks College (now BYU–Idaho). This assignment came with a full-ride scholarship, which was thrilling, but it was also overwhelming. Many of the writers, designers, and advertising team members I would be overseeing were returned missionaries and non-traditional students. My life experience seemed more akin to cocoon status, while my fellow students appeared to have butterfly lives of travel and full resumes. And what was more, my native personality is introverted and independent. I would need to be more decisive and outgoing than ever before.

In preparation for the fall semester when I would begin my journalistic leadership role, I felt prompted to put Nephi's admonition to the test. I would "liken the scriptures" and see what I could learn from them about how to lead. Naturally, I used a reporter's notebook (small flip notebook with tall vertical pages) to record my findings.

As my read-a-thon began, I watched Nephi show leadership by turning to his mentor (Lehi) when he encountered the unexpected situation of having a broken bow. I saw Esther ask others to join their faith and strength with hers when facing the complicated task of asking the king to free her people. I saw Jacob weepingly acknowledge the difficulties of those he served and then motivate them with love and care. I cheered for Abish when she prepared herself and then speedily took action when an opportunity presented itself with little warning. I saw mothers of the stripling warriors set the vision for their sons: By having faith in God, they could succeed against all logical odds. I saw Pahoran forgive and see the good in his colleague Moroni who wrote a message that I'm sure he wished he could "unsend" (the idea of a regrettable email is easily liken-able to myself).

I also saw examples of poor leadership. King Noah was a coward when his subordinates needed a leader. Chemish played small instead of stepping into his opportunities to become a legacy leader. The brother of the prodigal son struggled to have abundance when others were in the spotlight who were less deserving in his eyes.

After spending my summer "interviewing" leaders of the past, I approached my semester as the managing editor with more confidence. I watched myself grow—not only mentally, but also in stature as I began to stand with more confidence to lead the weekly staff meeting. A few months later, I was asked to stay in the head student position at the paper for a second semester—an unprecedented decision by the student newspaper advisor.

My "pinch me" double-semester opportunity propelled this quiet Idaho girl to future leadership positions in my own publishing business, as well as in academic, nonprofit, and political arenas. I've used scriptural lessons to help me as the chairwoman of Utah Philanthropy Day. I've leaned on verses to prepare me to be on Utah Valley University's Board of Trustees. And when I spent a decade as a ward and stake Young Women president, I looked to the scriptures to help me lead both young women and adult women in our organization.

When I learned of my friend Shawn Moon's important compilation of leadership lessons from the scriptures, I once again wanted to grab a reporter's notebook and scribble down takeaways. It's a pivotal time for me personally. I am seeking new and better ways to lead my family into chapters of young adulthood. My business has post-Covid growth to envision. And I'm leading Girls Camp again this summer in a new ward when my energy level might be more in line with that of a hymnbook coordinator.

Shawn is one of the leaders who has inspired me to be a better CEO. I watched him personally and generously solve a business challenge that was not of his own making. He led with empathy, and I observed him walking the talk in my conference room when a lesser leader would have shrugged his shoulders and said, "not my problem."

Truthfully, the world has myriad problems, all in need of solutions. "Learning Leadership From the Scriptures" is a giant step forward in developing leaders who can bring charity and an eternal perspective to each person within his or her sphere of influence. As the book opens with the story of Esther, I was immediately inspired with her willingness to accept the call to leadership, despite personal risk.

Are we not all born for such a time as this?

Learning Leadership from the Scriptures has quickly become my new lifeline as I am resetting leadership approaches in all parts of my life. As I turned each page, I found familiar quotes as well as new-to-me gems that surely must represent a lifetime of Shawn clipping quotes, data points and anecdotes. This book is Shawn's greatest work to date, and that is no small statement given his literary pedigree. It's clear Shawn feels an urgency to create more and better leaders so we can have stronger families, wards and communities. Leadership is one of the most significant solutions to the problems in this chapter of history, and my friend Shawn expertly describes scriptural-turned-modern-day leadership lessons and applies them to our personal lives, our families, and our callings.

This book answers my journalistic questions of the who, what, where, when, why and HOW of leadership. This is headline-worthy.

Read on, and lead on.

—Jeanette Bennett, founder and CEO, *Utah Valley Magazine*

CONTENTS

INTRODUCTION

But they that wait upon the Lord shall renew their strength; they shall mount up with wings as eagles; they shall run, and not be weary; and they shall walk, and not faint.

—Isaiah 40:31

Before you are a leader, success is all about growing yourself. When you become a leader, success is all about growing others.

—Jack Welch[1]

It was a dangerous and precarious time for ancient Israel, a time where "every man did what was right in his own eyes" (Judges 21:25). Without a central leader to unify their nation, the Israelites functioned in tribes, were often disjointed in their communication and collaboration, struggled to maintain their culture and identity, and too frequently succumbed to wickedness and idolatry. For far too many, what was considered "right" from their own perspective was "evil in the sight of the Lord" (Judges 6:1). It was a season of warfare and occupation, a time of chastening and self-inflicted impoverishment. But it was also a time when, because of these extremities, the Israelites would, when circumstance pressed upon them, turn to the Lord, plead for help, and mercifully obtain deliverance and redemption. Such was the case with Gideon and the Midianite occupation.

To facilitate the great lessons the Israelites needed to learn, the Lord called Gideon to lead them out of the oppressive grasp of the Midianite invaders. But Gideon was a somewhat reluctant leader. His task was daunting—perhaps too great. The sheer magnitude of the conquering Midianites seemed as "grasshoppers for the multitude" (Judges 6:5), so vast they couldn't be numbered. And like the invasive grasshoppers and the inevitable devastation they cause, the Midianite infestation had one objective: to destroy Israel.

This was the context of Gideon's call to leadership. His nation, his community and his family were under siege. His very way of life, his traditions, his culture, his beliefs—even life itself—were all at risk. With so much at stake, he asks the angel who was sent to call him, "Oh my Lord, wherewith shall I save Israel? Behold, my family is poor . . . and I am the least in my father's house" (Judges 6:15). One can feel Gideon's angst as he is called to lead in such a turbulent time.

Have you ever felt that way? Have you ever had a call come and the requirements of that call seem more than you can manage? Have you ever felt there is too much to lose or too much at stake? Have you ever been asked to lead and feel like you don't have the qualifications or experience? How do you manage these feelings of insecurity and inadequacy? Or maybe you've been called, and that call brings enthusiasm and excitement, but you don't know where to begin your work.

Like Gideon, we also live in precarious times, times when, as Isaiah prophesied over 2,600 years ago, evil would be called good and good would be called evil; times when fundamental rights and privileges are under attack; times when we see technological advancements and progress thought unimaginable even just a few years ago; times when communication and access to information is instant and constant and unlimited; times with unprecedented global growth in the Church that both inspires us and significantly challenges the status quo; times when, despite miraculous advances in modern health care, we face the challenge of global heath crises; times that both dazzle the imagination and threaten the foundations of our society. We live in times of war and pestilence; times of extreme poverty juxtaposed with unlimited abundance. We live in a time where so many are filled with goodness, light and virtue, while others are motivated by greed, darkness and debauchery. Even with the restored gospel on the earth, with living prophets and apostles who lead by inspiration, and with access to personal revelation, we still live in a time of significant confusion and "great uneasiness" (JSH 1:8). We live in a time where leadership is critical, and that leadership must come from each of us.

So much has been written on the topic of leadership. A quick perusal of available books on the subject reveals tens and tens of thousands of titles, with more being published every day. Why does the topic demand such attention?

Clearly, the need to develop leadership skills is a salient, pressing issue. Addressing leadership needs in the business community has spawned a global industry in excess of $366 billion in annual revenues at the time of this writing (this figure does not include revenue for individuals taking training courses for personal or non-work-related development, revenues of educational institutions, universities and for-profit educational companies, or revenues of community colleges from students paying tuition. It only represents dollars paid by corporations to educational institutions for corporate training initiative).[2]

Beyond our professional lives, leadership is demanded in nearly every aspect of our lives. We have all been inspired by athletic excellence that exceeds the individual talents of the team. How do great teams win, despite not always having the greatest athletes? There is clearly something about how these teams possess the leadership intangibles that propel their success. Great music, dance, theatre, community involvement, law enforcement, military endeavors, all require leadership. And what about our families? How important is leadership in the home?

Is leadership simply the domain of circumstances where people are working together in a supervisory or managerial environment or where synergy and collaboration are required? Or can (or must) I consider myself a leader in my personal life?

What about leadership in the Church? Where is it needed, and how can one develop both one's own skills and the skills of others to be better able to contribute in ways that would be pleasing to Heavenly Father, regardless of whatever calling we may have or not have?

These questions will be explored in the chapters to come. Leadership is a big and complicated topic, one with multiple layers and applications, one that doesn't have a simple definition.

I have spent over thirty years studying the topic of leadership. My professional experience has taken me across the world, working, teaching and consulting with leaders of every kind and at every level in organizations and agencies both large and small. I have seen a leadership culture transform schools, with children as young as five years old assuming leadership responsibilities in ways that CEOs would admire. I have seen the difference effective leadership has on corporate financial performance as well as military and governmental initiatives. I have seen organizations succeed despite critical and potentially crippling economic circumstances. I have seen people proactively respond to and thrive in the wake of devastating natural disasters because they exhibit leadership traits—whether they held a formal position or not. I have seen lives change for the better because of the guidance of a loving and wise leader. I have seen marriages improve, and relationships between parents and children flourish where they once floundered.

I have learned that leadership matters.

Where does one find adequate resources to assist in the development of leadership skills? While so much advice and direction exists from numerous sources (much of it is exceptional and some of it could be described as pablum and drivel), there is one source that is filled with remarkable examples of leadership: the scriptures. In the scriptures we learn of prophets, apostles, military leaders, kings, queens, humble missionaries, courageous women, fathers, mothers, children, and regular every-day people who provide sterling examples of leaders standing firm when needed, showing willingness to be vulnerable, working to achieve hard but important objectives in the face of extreme opposition. And of course, we have the perfect model of leadership in the form of the Savior, Jesus Christ, whose example of leadership demands from us a lifetime of study and careful and deliberate application.

Speaking to a group of business leaders on the topic of leadership, President Spencer W. Kimball declared:

> The scriptures contain many marvelous case studies of leaders. It would do us all much good if we were to read them and read them often. We forget that the scriptures present us with centuries of experience in leadership, and, even more importantly, the fixed

> principles upon which real leadership must operate if it is to succeed. The scriptures are the handbook of instructions for the would-be leader.[3]

This book is for anyone who has a leadership role of any kind. And since a key leadership responsibility for any and every person is the leadership of their own life, the leadership principles taught in the scriptures have general application—they provide leadership development lessons for everyone. My intent is to provide an organizational framework and insights on this most important topic based on guidance from this wonderfully rich and abundant source. Certainly, we have the life and mission of Jesus Christ. Volumes could (and should) be written about His leadership. There is no way to include every leadership lesson or example from the life of the Savior—the well we draw from as we examine His life is simply too vast and too deep. President Kimball noted this reality as he stated, "There are far more things to be said about the Lord Jesus Christ's remarkable leadership than any single article or book could possibly cover."[4]

The truth is, in addition to His unequaled and incalculable volume of examples, there are models of leadership found on nearly every page of the scriptures. So this book is not an exhaustive treatise on scriptural leadership lessons. I'm not sure it's possible to write one. What I have attempted to do is structure how one might organize one's thinking about leadership, share abundant examples and lessons from the scriptures, and then make applications from those examples to our lives and responsibilities today. Specifically, with the scriptures as the backdrop and guide, I'll address how we might define leadership, why leadership is important for our day, where, specifically it applies, and how we can develop it through twelve specific practices.

I love the concept of a "last lecture." This is where those teaching have an opportunity to share their final, most critical messages. There are examples of "last lectures" throughout the scriptures, and while all of what is contained in the scriptures is important, I always perk up when I get to these sections.

After recording his family's travels and travails in their journey from Jerusalem to the promised land, the establishment of new homes, their moves and re-establishment of new homes, their wars and contentions, their testimonies and admonitions, Nephi caps his personal record with critical council. One of his final lessons is a reminder of the importance of studying the word of God. He declares, "Feast upon the words of Christ; for behold, the words of Christ will tell you all things what ye should do" (2 Ne 32:3).

The Lord, through his written word, through angels, through the Holy Ghost, and through his leaders will teach us what to do—in all aspects of our lives, even in our roles as leaders.

Despite Gideon's insecurities and doubts about his abilities to effectively lead his people to deliverance, the Lord helps him understand a different view of himself. The angel says to Gideon, "The Lord is with thee, thou mighty man of valor." And, in his humility and with the Lord by his side, Gideon would go on to do remarkable things. But to do the great things the Lord had in store for him, he needed to convince an army. Thirty-two thousand men came to join him. But the Lord told him that was too many, "Lest Israel vaunt themselves against me, saying, Mine own hand hath saved me" (Judges 7:2). So, Gideon invites all who are fearful to return to their homes, and 22,000 accept his invitation. Gideon's force is now significantly depleted, with only 10,000 men to go against the Midianite army—an army so vast it could not be numbered. Imagine the conversation he had with his own army at this point! How does one motivate others to do something that, with every rational thought, seems un-doable?

But the Lord's leadership lessons for Gideon are not over, as He informs Gideon that his newly-reduced force is yet too large, and once again, establishes a plan to whittle his soldiers down—this time to a mere 300. If convincing his men that 10,000 was sufficient against such a vast foe was difficult, what was the conversation like with his lieutenants when he retained only 300? Somehow, Gideon, the once self-conscious and self-doubting leader, engages and inspires his intrepid soldiers with a compelling vision and bold plan that accomplishes the promised deliverance from the Midianites.

That is the power of inspired leadership. Gideon was called to do something seemingly impossible—something that no right-thinking person would conceive. But Gideon's heart, his goodness, and his leadership capabilities were known by the Lord. He was magnified in his efforts, he followed the inspired guidance he received with faith, he engaged others' hearts in his cause—as improbable as it seemed—and obtained the Lord's objective.

As a leader in the Lord's kingdom, you can expect His assistance, even (and especially) when you don't feel up to the task or when you feel the assignment is too much. He has declared, "For behold, this is my work and my glory—to bring to pass the immortality and eternal life of man" (Moses 1:39). This means that everything the Lord does has His purposes—this purpose—in mind: our immortality and eternal life, and the immortality and eternal life of all His children. He has called you to help in his great and grand plan. He will not leave you alone. He will not call you to lead—in whatever capacity—without also providing his divine guidance. He has promised each of us that He will, "Go before [our] face. [He] will be on [our] right hand and on [our] left, and [His] Spirit shall be in [our] hearts, and [his] angels round about [us], to bear [us] up" (D&C 84:88), and that the "Lord giveth no commandment unto the children of men, save he shall prepare a way for them that they may accomplish the thing which he commandeth them" (1 Nephi 3:7).

Speaking of the need for leaders to step up and step forward and embrace opportunity to engage, Elder Jeffrey R. Holland stated,

> The future of this world has long been declared; the final outcome between good and evil is already known. There is absolutely no question as to who wins because the victory has already been posted on the scoreboard. The only really strange thing in all of this is that we are still down here on the field trying to decide which team's jersey we want to wear![5]

The Lord needs leaders to accomplish His work. He needs Relief Society presidents and Primary teachers, He needs faithful ministers and young women's advisors, He needs deacon's quorum second counselors and young women's class presidents. He needs clerks and bishops and high counselors. He needs mothers and fathers, cousins, grandparents, daughters and sons. He needs individuals who have bone-deep conviction of the Lord's mission and plan for each of us, and who have developed a personal sense of purpose around that plan. He needs leaders who assume responsibility for their choices, who develop Christ-like attributes, who love and lift and build others.

He needs leaders who can create a compelling vision for their work and use that vision to inspire others to enlist their finest efforts. He needs leaders who can engage and motivate others, and who can help others see and understand their own significant worth and potential and ability to contribute. He needs leaders who can make a difference.

He has called you.

PART I
THE "WHAT, WHY, WHERE, AND HOW OF LEADERSHIP"

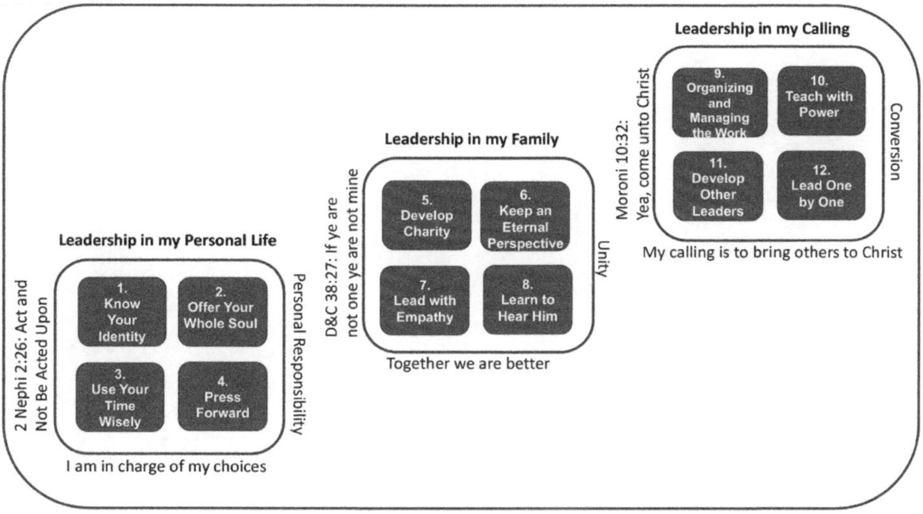

CHAPTER ONE
WHAT IS LEADERSHIP?

No power or influence can or ought to be maintained by virtue of the priesthood, only by persuasion, by long-suffering, by gentleness and meekness, and by love unfeigned; By kindness, and pure knowledge, which shall greatly enlarge the soul without hypocrisy, and without guile.

—D&C 121:41–42

A shepherd watches over sheep. In scriptural stories the sheep are in danger; they need protection and nourishment. The Savior warns us that we must watch the sheep as He does. He gave His life for them. They are his. We cannot approach His standard if, like a hired servant, we watch only when it is convenient and only for a reward . . .

The members of the Church are the sheep. They are His, and we are called by Him to watch over them. We are to do more than warn them against danger. We are to feed them.

—Henry B. Eyring[1]

In Persia, in or around 479 B.C., King Ahasuerus was in search of a wife. His eye fell on Esther, a courageous and beautiful Jewish maiden, and he selected her to become his queen. Esther's parents had died years before, and she had been raised by her older cousin, Mordecai, as his daughter. During this post-Babylonian exile period, many of the Jews who had lived in the area had returned to Jerusalem, but there remained a significant population scattered throughout Persia.

King Ahasuerus had promoted a certain man named Haman to serve in a position of authority "above all the princes." Haman was a powerful and prideful man who required strict reverence and homage from all the king's subjects, expecting them to bow down to him. Mordecai, despite forceful daily encouragement from the king's courts to do so, continuously refused the order. Word of Mordecai's refusals to bow down reached Haman, who quickly became enraged. In retaliation, Haman convinced the king that not only did Mordecai possess a rebellious spirit, but that all the Jews throughout his kingdom, with their diverse and peculiar laws and unfamiliar customs, presented a serious threat and should therefore be eliminated. The King agreed, issuing a decree to "destroy, to kill, and to cause to perish, all Jews, both young and old, little children and women" (Esther 3:13) on a certain day, and that those who carried out the killings would receive the spoils from the Jews as a reward, while Haman would enrich the king's treasury as an acknowledgement for issuing the order.

Great mourning naturally occurred throughout the Jewish community after the King's decree. Esther, now the queen, likewise was distraught. Mordecai asks her to plead the cause of the Jews to her husband, but Esther reminded Mordecai that the king has a law that if anyone enters the inner court of the king unbidden, he could put that person to death. Alternatively, the king can, under his own law, extend a golden scepter, granting that person reprieve, but the risk for Esther was great.

To this risk, Mordecai says to Esther, "Who knoweth whether thou are come to the kingdom for such a time as this?" (Ether 4:14)

Esther's response highlights her courageous resolve—her resolve to be a leader regardless of the difficulty or personal inconvenience—as she responds to her cousin, "Go, gather all the Jews that are present . . . and fast ye for me, and neither eat nor drink three days . . . and my maidens will fast likewise; and I will go in unto the king . . . and if I perish, I perish" (Ether 4:16).

Esther's faith and courage to extend herself, to rely on the blessings of heaven to do the difficult tasks appointed her, results in the reversal of the king's decree, the salvation of her people, and the demise of Haman (who was eventually hanged on the very gallows he had constructed for the destruction of the Jews).

Mordecai's charge to Esther is a call to lead, and Esther's remarkable willingness to rise to the challenge and accept that call—one that brought the greatest of personal risks—is a charge that can be extended to each of us as well, for "who knoweth [but that you and I] are come to the kingdom for such a time as this!" There are moments in history that require the best efforts a generation can give. We are in just such a moment.

Here are a few questions to consider about leadership: What does it really mean to be a leader? Are some born with leadership skills and therefore destined for greatness? And is leadership manifest only through specific positions or callings? Can leadership skills be developed? Where does one start? How do you have lasting influence with others? Leaders have followers, right? So how do you help others catch the appropriate vision of your initiatives in such a way that they are not only willing to get things done for you but perhaps even willing to sacrifice to accomplish your goals? In order to lead others, what groundwork or preparation do you need?

Often when you think of leaders, you may think of a "boss," and indeed a leader may be a "boss," but not necessarily. Leadership is essential for one who occupies a supervisory role, but it is also critical for one in the middle, and just as important for the one at the entry level of an organization or team.

Ask yourself: "Why would anyone follow me; of all the choices one could make, why would someone choose me to lead?" Compare and contrast different leaders in your life: What is it that makes you want to follow some and distrust others? What is it about Washington, or Mother Teresa, or Gandhi, or Martin Luther King that inspires you? What about Church leaders? Do you trust your relief society president or bishop or stake president or the prophet because they are in positions of authority, or is it something else? Would you trust them even if they didn't hold these positions? Here's a more important question: do others trust you?

I was intrigued and touched the day following the passing of President Gordon B. Hinckley. Many of the youth of the Church wore their Sunday best to school in his honor that day. The Washington Post noted this gesture:

> On Monday morning this week, 12 hours after the passing of the 97-year-old leader of The Church of Jesus Christ of Latter-day Saints, President Gordon B. Hinckley, an extraordinary and spontaneous thing happened. Young teenagers in Salt Lake City began showing up for school that day, dressed not in their usual jeans and winter clothing, but in their "Sunday best." Young men sat in classes in white shirts and ties, suits and coats. Thousands of them did this, with no prompting from parents or other adults and to the surprise of teachers. The idea, it seems, started with a few and then spread at unbelievable speed through text messaging, child to child. This was their way of showing respect to a man seven times their age and several generations their senior. Such was the power of this one extraordinary leader of The Church of Jesus Christ of Latter-day Saints to touch the lives of ordinary people.[2]

What was it that connected this ninety-seven-year-old man to teenagers across the world? Why did they feel so?

I had the opportunity to speak with a fifth-grade class (ten-year-olds) about the subject of "Leadership." These students considered three questions related to the topic: "A leader is someone who . . . ," "A leader in my life is. . . . ," and "I can be a leader by . . . " They shared some wonderful insights that are both simple and profound:

A leader is someone who . . .

- is kind and nice
- is trustworthy
- shows courage
- doesn't have to be rich or poor
- you can rely on
- you can respect
- leads people down the right track
- never gives up
- wants teamwork
- tells the truth
- is friendly

- is in charge when something goes wrong
- doesn't have to be the president or secretary. They don't even have to have a job!
- has to be brave and smart. A leader is someone who cares.
- has gratitude
- does the right thing
- is loyal
- takes responsibility
- doesn't have to have a special job like president, teacher, or principal
- takes a stand
- does what he believes in
- has courage to do scary things

A leader in my life is . . .

- me
- my parents
- my dad. He is my best friend.
- my teacher
- my mom. Sometimes I feel left out by others but my mom makes me feel better.
- my brother Eric
- my mom. Even though she can be mean sometimes, I still know she is my idol. When I grow up I want to be just like her.
- my uncle Chip. He is in the military and went to Iraq. He inspires me to be brave.

I can be a leader by . . .

- being loving
- helping other people
- not being a bully
- being a friend to those who need a friend

- being good to my little brother
- breaking up fights
- being courageous
- being trustworthy
- being daring and taking risks for others
- being nice to my siblings. Sometimes I'm a little bit cranky.
- stepping up at any moment of the day.
- being kinder and more confident in people
- never giving up
- facing my fears.

Remarkable insight for a group of youngsters!

Leadership is about influencing others, and in order to do this, you must first lead your own life. In other words, leadership and influence with others begins with leadership of self. It is what the U.S. Army calls "the great force multiplier." For the Army, great leadership can lift ten women or men to do what otherwise might require 100. Effective leadership brings out the best in yourself and others, allowing you to leverage your time, efforts and resources.

The great Archimedes (287–212 B.C.), one of the world's finest mathematicians, was a man before his time. Not only did he invent integral calculus and the field of hydrostatics, but his numerous contributions include a unique numbering system, the most accurate approximation of π (Pi) to date, a new way of approximating square roots, and an examination of the properties of levers and pulleys. On one occasion, his friend King Hiero had a ship mired in the harbor, and despite the efforts of many men, the ship would not budge. Archimedes declared to the king "Give me a place to stand on and I will move the earth." The king asked Archimedes to prove his statement by freeing the stuck ship. Using his knowledge of leverage, Archimedes built a machine that allowed him to single-handedly move the ship. By using levers and the appropriate positioning of the fulcrum, one man's efforts did what many men combined could not do.[3]

So it is with our efforts. Our contributions may seem small and insignificant at first, but the ultimate impact can have far-reaching impact. Like Archimedes' fulcrum and lever, leadership allows one to accomplish great things, even when faced with challenges that seem beyond normal abilities.

Leadership is the ability to influence yourself and others in achieving sustained results. As they achieve these results, leaders convey vision, develop trust, establish confidence, remove barriers, and inspire the best efforts and talents of others. In the process, they develop and mentor others to become leaders in the same way.

Let's look at some further definitions of leadership. There are thousands, and this is certainly not intended to be definitive, but you will see some common themes emerge.

> To be effective Church leaders, we must learn this critical lesson: leadership in the Church is not so much about directing others as it is about our willingness to be directed by God.
>
> —Elder Dieter F. Uchdorf[4]

> It is a curious thing, Harry, but perhaps those who are best suited to power are those who have never sought it. Those who, like you, have leadership thrust upon them, and take up the mantle because they must, and find to their own surprise that they wear it well.
>
> —J. K. Rowling[5]

> He who lives only unto himself withers and dies, while he who forgets himself in the service of other grows and blossoms in this life and in eternity.
>
> —President Gordon B. Hinckley[6]

> You were born to lead as mothers and fathers because nowhere is righteous leadership more crucial than in the family. You were born to lead as priesthood and auxiliary leaders, as heads of communities, companies, and even nations. You were born to lead as men and

women willing "to stand as witnesses of God at all times and in all things, and in all places" because that's what a true leader does.

—Sheri Dew[7]

To handle yourself, use your head; to handle others, use your heart.

—Eleanor Roosevelt[8]

If you do not magnify your callings, God will hold you responsible for those whom you might have saved had you done your duty.

—President John Taylor[9]

The greatest leader is not necessarily the one who does the greatest things. He is the one that gets the people to do the greatest things.

—Ronald Reagan[10]

You are not here merely to make a living. You are here in order to enable the world to live more amply, with greater vision, with a finer spirit of hope and achievement. You are here to enrich the world, and you impoverish yourself if you forget the errand.

—Woodrow Wilson[11]

Our chief want is someone who will inspire us to be what we know we could be.

—Ralph Waldo Emerson[12]

I alone cannot change the world, but I can cast a stone across the water to create many ripples.

—Mother Teresa[13]

Leadership is about taking responsibility, not making excuses.

—Mitt Romney[14]

Yet such is oft the course of deeds that move the wheels of the world: small hands do them because they must, while the eyes of the great are elsewhere.

—J.R.R. Tolkien[15]

My definition of a leader . . . [is the one] who can persuade people to do what they don't want to do, or do what they're too lazy to do, and like it.

—Harry S. Truman[16]

We humans have a lamentable tendency to spend more time theorizing reasons behind human suffering, than working to alleviate human suffering, and in imagining a heaven above, than creating a heaven in our homes and communities.

—Terryl & Fiona Givens[17]

The superior leader gets things done with very little motion. He imparts instruction not through many words but through a few deeds. He keeps informed about everything but interferes hardly at all. He is a catalyst, and though things would not get done well if he weren't there, when they succeed he takes no credit. And because he takes no credit, credit never leaves him.

—Lao Tse, Taoist Philosopher[18]

A manager takes people where they want to go. A great leader takes people where they don't necessarily want to go but ought to.

—Rosalyn Carter, Former First Lady[19]

If your actions inspire others to dream more, learn more, do more and become more, you are a leader.

—John Quincy Adams[20]

There is an urgent need for leaders of the Church at all levels to spiritualize their leadership more so that our overarching purposes are not lost in the mechanics of meetings, organizations.

—President Harold B. Lee[21]

If we desire to lengthen our stride in the management of the kingdom at all levels of its operation . . . we must be more willing to expend more of our time, talent, and means in providing leadership training.

—President Spencer W. Kimball[22]

Yours is a great responsibility in this day when the need for courageous leadership is so urgent. You can become those leaders. ... Our [people] need to develop qualities of leadership. They need to learn the value of staying power—stick-to-it-iveness. They need to learn devotion to duty—the devotion to duty that keeps a good doctor on the job right around the clock in an emergency; the devotion to duty that leads a scientist or a teacher to persevere in a low-paying position in public service because that is where his maximum contribution can be made.

—President Ezra Taft Benson[23]

The need for leadership through the wards and stakes of Zion [is increasing] dramatically. What is needed is not just people of training and skill, but rather we will need a generation of great faith, those who have learned discipline and discipleship. What will be needed is a generation who understand not only how to organize a ward but also how to build faith, how to sustain the weak and faltering, and how to defend the truth.

—President Howard W. Hunter[24]

You can be a leader. You must be a leader, as a member of this Church, in those causes for which this Church stands. Do not let fear overcome your efforts...Cast that fear aside and be valiant in the cause of truth and righteousness and faith. If you now decide that this will become the pattern of your life, you will not have to make that decision again. You will put on "the armor of God," and raise your voice in defense of truth, whatever the circumstances now and in all the years that lie ahead.

—President Gordon B. Hinckley[25]

The Church has no corps of professionals. It must depend upon leaders developed from within the membership as a whole ... the Church's need is greater than ever now, both in terms of numbers and a requirement for greater devotion and skill ... so must the need for more capable and responsible leadership multiply.

—Elder Neal A. Maxwell[26]

> I am looking for a lot of men who have an infinite capacity to not know what can't be done.
>
> —Henry Ford[27]

> Being a leader is like being a lady; if you have to go around telling people you are one, you aren't.
>
> —Margaret Thatcher[28]

The Academy Awards, known generally as "The Oscars," annually holds its celebration of its own greatness. Award nominations are extended to individuals across multiple roles associated with producing and performing great cinematic productions. Great pomp and circumstance always accompanies this event, as red carpet-lined sidewalks lead nominees and other attendees from their stretch limousines into the elaborately appointed theatre. Highlights of the nominated shows and politically themed speeches dominate the evening. Award-winners receive warm (and at times thunderous) ovations, acknowledging their hard work and finely honed talent. Similar award shows celebrate live theatre, the television industry, athletic excellence, and musical performance across multiple genres. And many others.

I don't begrudge the celebration of exceptional performance. The nominees and winners of these awards achieve their recognition as a result of great dedication and sacrifice. I admire the work and extreme effort so many exert in producing beautiful, moving and instructional art and exceptional athletic performance. We are better as a society when we have this contribution. But I'm often left wondering why we elevate to extreme levels of greatness—sometimes above everything else in our society—those who can deliver a line or throw a ball or sing a song. I love those things as much as anyone. I follow my teams, watch inspiring movies, and consider the theatre one of my family's cherished pastimes. But what about the every-day leaders—those who are not nor will ever likely be in the public eye—who get up, do their best, and sacrifice beyond measure to serve their customers, build a business, provide for their families, and serve in and strengthen their churches and communities? These people seldom get the "red-carpet" treatment, though they most certainly deserve it.

Who are the great leaders in your life? Why do you consider them great leaders? What did they do to inspire you? How would you differentiate them from all the other people with whom you have worked or associated? What sets great leaders apart from other leaders—regardless of calling or position or title or level?

Here are at least six ways extraordinary leaders (at every level) are differentiated between those who may have a responsibility, but don't stand out.

<table>
<tr><td rowspan="3">1.</td><td colspan="2">Matthew 18:12–13

How think ye? if a man have an hundred sheep, and one of them be gone astray, doth he not leave the ninety and nine, and goeth into the mountains, and seeketh that which is gone astray?

And if so be that he find it, verily I say unto you, he rejoiceth more of that sheep, than of the ninety and nine which went not astray.</td></tr>
<tr><td>What great leaders do . . .</td><td>What they don't do . . .</td></tr>
<tr><td>They make a difference. They achieve significant, long-lasting and meaningful results. Often their impact is evident in how a team or an organization performs, and certainly that's true. But, perhaps more importantly, great leaders make a lasting, positive difference on the individual lives of those those they serve and with whom they interact. They understand that the key to influencing the 99 is in meeting and addressing the needs of the one.</td><td>They don't simply put in their time or go through the motions of their stewardship. They don't accept a responsibility and then put forth token effort, knowing that effort was less than their finest, and leave those with whom they interact wanting for or needing more.</td></tr>
</table>

D&C 138:55–56

I observed that they were also among the noble and great ones who were chosen in the beginning to be rulers in the Church of God.

Even before they were born, they, with many others, received their first lessons in the world of spirits and were prepared to come forth in the due time of the Lord to labor in his vineyard for the salvation of the souls of men.

	What great leaders do . . .	What they don't do . . .
2.	They see others for who they really are—children of God, with profound potential. There are no "average" people. There are no "pawns." To them, everyone is a king or queen on the chessboard, a "noble and great one."	They don't expect mediocracy in and from others—they don't just see people merely for who they are today, or how they're behaving today.

	Matthew 22:37–38 Jesus said unto him, Thou shalt love the Lord thy God with all thy heart, and with all thy soul, and with all thy mind. This is the first and great commandment.	
3.	**What great leaders do . . .**	**What they don't do . . .**
	They possess pure motive, that is, to bless others' lives in every interaction because they understand the first great commandment—to love God with all their heart. Every action is influenced by that love.	They don't allow pride, ego and a desire for praise and admiration of others to be the motivating factor in their work.

	Matthew 22:39–40 And the second is like unto it, Thou shalt love thy neighbour as thyself. On these two commandments hang all the law and the prophets.	
4.	**What great leaders do . . .**	**What they don't do . . .**
	They emulate the Savior's love in daily actions and behaviors. They establish the goal that in every interaction, others will feel the Saviors love because of their efforts. They understand—at deep levels—the second great commandment—to love God's children—all of them.	They aren't apathetic toward those they serve, conveying a "take-it-or-leave it" sentiment. Nor do they share love conditionally or extend charity and good will to some but not to all.

	Alma 46:19–20 And when Moroni had said these words, he went forth among the people, waving the rent part of his garment in the air, that all might see the writing which he had written upon the rent part, and crying with a loud voice, saying: Behold, whosoever will maintain this title upon the land, let them come forth in the strength of the Lord, and enter into a covenant that they will maintain their rights, and their religion, that the Lord God may bless them.	
5.	**What great leaders do . . .**	**What they don't do . . .**
	They build people through involvement. They understand the best way to engage the hearts and minds of those they serve and with whom they serve is to engage them, to enlist them in the purpose and vision of the work.	They don't simply give tasks without providing context.

Moisah 18:8–10

And it came to pass that he said unto them: Behold, here are the waters of Mormon (for thus were they called) and now, as ye are desirous to come into the fold of God, and to be called his people, and are willing to bear one another's burdens, that they may be light;

Yea, and are willing to mourn with those that mourn; yea, and comfort those that stand in need of comfort, and to stand as witnesses of God at all times and in all things, and in all places that ye may be in, even until death, that ye may be redeemed of God, and be numbered with those of the first resurrection, that ye may have eternal life—

Now I say unto you, if this be the desire of your hearts, what have you against being baptized in the name of the Lord, as a witness before him that ye have entered into a covenant with him, that ye will serve him and keep his commandments, that he may pour out his Spirit more abundantly upon you?

6.	**What great leaders do . . .**	**What they don't do . . .**
	They possess a depth of character. They stand willingly as "witnesses of God at all times and in all places," in both word and action. They have deeply rooted integrity and personal purity, in every circumstance whether in public, with their families, or in their private lives, giving confidence and trust to all with whom they interact.	They don't demonstrate inconsistency in behavior—with "shallow roots," causing them to be vulnerable to opposition or misunderstanding or whims of circumstance.

As you examine the influential leaders in your life, do they map to these differentiators? President Spencer W. Kimball invites us to consider important leaders in our individual experience and the difference they have made: "If you were to select just two or three individuals in your life who have been most influential, what specifically did they do that was most helpful to you at a critical or important time in your life? On reflecting for a few moments, you are apt to conclude that such a person really cared for you, that he or she taught you something you needed to know. Reflect now upon your own performance."[29]

I love this definition of leadership: "Leadership is communicating another's worth and potential so clearly they begin to see it in themselves."[30] Let me add just one additional thought to that definition: "Leadership is *seeing* and communicating another's worth and potential so clearly they begin to see it in themselves." Think back on your life—on those influential people who made a difference for you. Who were they? How did they see you? What did they do to communicate your worth and potential in ways that allowed you to see it—perhaps in ways you didn't initially see or understand, but because they did, you began to believe it and live up to that potential? How did they challenge you? How are you different today because of that leader?

I was speaking once to large group of business leaders in Mexico City and posed these same questions. One gentleman shared an interaction he'd had with a leader thirty five years prior. It was a short interaction, and the leader who provided the direction probably wouldn't even remember what had occurred, or if he did, would not consider it a significant moment. But it had had an indelible impact on the gentleman with whom I was talking. I asked him what changed in his life as a result of his interaction with this leader. He responded, "Everything! The trajectory of my life is entirely different today as a result of this leader."

Who, within your area of stewardship, could benefit from your leadership? Are you seeing and communicating the worth and potential of others so clearly they begin to see that potential in themselves?

CHAPTER TWO
WHY DOES LEADERSHIP MATTER?

Ye are the light of the world. A city that is set on an hill cannot be hid. Neither do men light a candle, and put it under a bushel, but on a candlestick; and it giveth light unto all that are in the house. Let your light so shine before men, that they may see your good works, and glorify your Father which is in heaven.

—Matthew 5:14–16

Leadership is a choice, not a position.

—Stephen R. Covey[1]

After Father Lehi received the vision of the tree of life and shared it with his family, Nephi had a desire to know for himself the things his father had seen. With faith in the Lord and trust in his father, Nephi pondered his father's words and received his own magnificent manifestation. In this vision, Nephi described this tree as, "beyond, yea, exceeding of all beauty; and the whiteness thereof did exceed the whiteness of the driven snow" (1 Ne 11:8). Juxtaposed against this remarkable tree, a tree "precious above all," (v 9) Nephi beheld a large and spacious building, a building without moorings or foundation, tossed by the whims and popular sins of the world.

In a confusing and morally ambiguous world—a "dark and dreary waste"—a world where we are required to operate amid uncertainty and with loud voices attempting to pull us in any number of directions, Lehi's and Nephi's visions illustrate two significant extremes that are realities of our mortal journey and highlight the critical need for leadership.

First, despite the mists of darkness that encumber mortality, there are guides to lead us to the tree, which represents the love of God—a love so profound, so beautiful, so transcendent it exceeds the ability for one to fully describe it. On the other hand, not far from the tree, just across the path and river that flows alongside it, stands the building—a building so great and so vast and so impressive it appears nearly endless, extending "in the air, high above the earth." This building houses many powerful and influential figures—the wise and proud of the world—who are devoted to and focused on fighting against the Lord and His plan. These influential voices see the humble seekers of truth, those pressing forward the best they can, some holding tightly to the rod of iron and others "feeling their way," "wandering strange roads," groping through the darkness hoping to gain insight and direction as to their purpose in life. Those in the building use every means possible to influence these seekers toward the building. In their efforts to persuade and dissuade, no method is left unused, whether subtle or straightforward, no means too unsavory for their ends, or too far out of bounds. They mock, scorn, abuse, ridicule, tempt, belittle, argue, beguile, deceive, insult, beg, compensate, flatter, incent, cajole—all for the purpose of pulling God's children—us, our families, our friends, our communities, our nations—away from the love of God and the abundant blessings that naturally attend this love.

We all have a propensity to look for examples to follow. The mists of darkness are real. They're fraught with obstacles and uncertainty. And there are powerful leaders in the large and spacious building with loud and compelling voices who wield their influence and desperately seek followers.

What is our voice in all of this? What leadership role are we expected to assume? Are we willing to stand idly by as we watch this human drama unfold? Are we naïve in thinking the influences of the large and spacious building have no impact on us or our families? How can we take more control of our own lives and circumstances and draw our families, loved ones, friends, and others of God's children toward the tree so they can partake of its fruit? And how can we be the catalyst for others to do the same?

There is so much at stake. President Boyd K. Packer reminds us,

> In the Church we are not neutral. We are one-sided. There is a war going on, and we are engaged in it. It is the war between good and evil and we are belligerents defending the good. We are therefore obliged to give preference to and defend all that is represented in the Gospel of Jesus Christ, and we have made covenants to do it.[2]

One might ask, "Why me?" The lure of the building can be tempting. Those in it know our weak spots and cater to them. Wouldn't it be so much easier to let go of the rod and wander over for just a bit? It looks so fun! And why is my leadership important? Can't someone else carry the load?

Brad Wilcox answers those questions this way:

> Our mortal experience could be compared to God sending all of His children on a cruise ship from one shore to another. The journey is filled with opportunities to learn, grow, be happy, and progress, but it is also full of dangers. God loves all of His children and is concerned about their welfare. He does not want to lose any of them, so He selected some He could trust and made them members of His crew. That's us.
>
> So when we look around on this cruise ship called earth and see other people sitting in lounge chairs drinking, gambling in casinos, and partying late into the night and wonder why we can't, we must remember who we are. We are not ordinary passengers. We are members of the crew. And before we complain too long and too loudly about having crew member responsibilities [that the other] passengers don't have, we need to remember that crew members get something passengers don't get: a paycheck.
>
> There is nothing we could ever be asked to do in Christ's Church for which we have not already been paid—paid in advance and paid in full, for we have been given a birthright. Because God trusts us, He sent us to earth with an extra portion and charged us with the well-being and safe return of all His family. Think of it! Of all the people on the earth, God looks to us, the members of His Church, to save

> the world. No wonder President Brigham Young once said, "All the Angels in heaven are looking to this little handful of people."
>
> It is one thing to be loved and another to be trusted.[3]

According to the November 11, 2000 US News and World Report cover story, the population of the Church is predicted to grow to approximately 265 million members worldwide by 2080. This would put the Church "second only to Roman Catholics among Christian bodies. 'Mormonism,' says Rodney Stark, professor of sociology and religion at the University of Washington, 'stands on the threshold of becoming the first major faith to appear on Earth since the prophet Mohammed rode out of the desert.'"[4]

That is an incredibly bold estimate, and other more recent studies show the number substantially lower. Assuming it is only 10% accurate, and Church membership grows to between twenty five and thirty million members, just think of the substantial need for leaders in the Church! We will be the ones counted on to lead and will be expected to be ready to contribute. In a July 1996 press conference, President Gordon B. Hinckley was asked, "What do you see as the greatest challenge facing the Church as you enter the twenty-first century?" His answer was simple: "Growth." Regarding the growth of the Church and subsequent need for leadership, President Hinckley added, "All our local leaders are presided over by volunteer workers not compensated financially in any way. As we grow, it becomes necessary to train leaders, and that is a challenge. That is the same challenge Brigham Young faced. We have faced it all through the years and will continue to face it as the Church grows across the world."[5]

Indeed, the Church and the world need our leadership. And more importantly, our families need our leadership, as President Wilford Woodruff intimates:

> There never was a generation of the inhabitants of the earth in any age of the world who had greater events awaiting them than the present... And an age fraught with greater interest to the children of men than the one in which we live never dawned since the creation of the world.[6]

When discussing the nature of how and why we serve, I've occasionally reminded those with whom I serve that ours is a volunteer organization. My point with that statement is that we (I) need to accept and acknowledge whatever level of service others can give. I stand by that statement with one amendment. We all operate and serve in different times and seasons in our lives. Some have a house full of children, with all the demands that requires. Others have massive pressures at work, often requiring extreme hours or extended travel. Some deal with illness, while others deal with financial hardships. And some deal with all the above at the same time. We still volunteer our best and give generously with our time and resources. So yes, this is a volunteer church. But it is also a covenant church, wherein we have made sacred promises to build, to lift, and to bless. That requires our finest efforts—our "covenant" efforts.

Being a leader, regardless of circumstance or position, is a paradigm. As we have discussed, effective leadership is a requirement for any calling. Think about what it would mean if you saw yourself as a leader in your calling as a Primary teacher, versus simply putting in your time. How would you approach your weekly assignment? Would you prepare your lesson for the day's class during sacrament meeting, or would you be prayerful and thoughtful throughout the week and consider the needs of each of the children in your class? Would you know their concerns? Would they feel your love for them individually?

CHAPTER THREE
WHERE IS LEADERSHIP REQUIRED?

Behold, thou art my son . . . And I have a work for thee.

—Moses 1:4, 6

I am only one, but still, I am one. I cannot do everything, but still, I can do something. I will not refuse to do the something I can do.

—Helen Keller[1]

It was a time of seemingly endless warfare and unrelenting dissention, as the Nephite armies battled not only their enemies, the Lamanites, but also devastating political discord and sabotage from within their own ranks. After ten years of nearly constant war, every resource was needed to defend the Nephite's freedoms and way of life. Moroni, the chief commander of the Nephite armies, had rallied his people at the beginning of the conflict to enter a covenant to preserve their "rights, and their religion" (Alma 43:47), ensuring them that the Lord would protect and defend them if they promised to be faithful to His commandments. So great was the commitment of the people that they cast their garments at Moroni's feet as a show of their conviction and cried, "We covenant with our God, that we shall be destroyed . . . if we should fall into transgression; yea, he may cast us at the feet of our enemies, even as we cast our garments at thy feet to be trodden under foot, if we shall fall into transgression" (Alma 46:22).

Moroni traveled throughout all parts of the Nephite nation, rallying his people and building his army. Fathers and sons enlisted and marched forth with Moroni and his captains.

But the Lamanite foe was formidable and determined. They had wily and vengeful leaders with vast numbers and abundant resources, while the Nephites struggled at times to maintain their support of the cause. Forces within the Nephite government allied with the enemy, exacerbating the challenge for Moroni and his army, even attempting to overthrow the rightful leaders amid all that was occurring. In these trying times, leadership emerged from three unexpected areas: 1) Helaman the prophet, 2) the young, untested and untried sons of the people of Ammon, and 3) the courageous mothers of these young men.

Certainly, Helaman had seen battle. Such was the nature of his time—nearly every man would have. But his primary concern was in preaching the word of God and in leading the affairs of the church, not in leading thousands of youthful, inexperienced soldiers into battle against such an experienced and blood-thirsty foe as the Lamanites. Yet Helaman felt compelled by the need and buoyed by his love for the young men and their remarkable parents, and inspired by their undaunted faith, he moved forward with courage. He calls to the young men of the people of Ammon, "What say ye, my sons, will ye go against [this formidable foe] to battle?" (v.44).

The people of Ammon had once been Lamanites, fierce in their convictions and confident that they had been wronged by the Nephites. But they had experienced the mighty change of heart that occurs with conversion to Jesus Christ and His teachings and with that conversion, they gave up their lands, their homes, their traditions and their weapons. They transformed from a once ferocious and murderous people to a community so converted and so committed to the Lord and to loving their fellow men that the very thought of giving an offense to another, even to their enemies, was abhorrent. This change was so great and so profound they buried their weapons of war and made a sacred oath never to raise them again, willing to sacrifice their own lives to preserve that oath. Meanwhile, their new brothers and sisters within the Nephite nation were fighting and dying to protect those very rights. Motivated by their great love for their new community and unwilling to simply stand by and do nothing, the people of Ammon were prepared to deny their oath and take up their weapons once again to assist in their defense.

An oath was a powerful thing for these people. Once given, it was defended at all costs. That the people of Ammon would even consider taking up arms was a testament to the intensity of the times. The faithful Nephites, led by Helaman, were unwilling to allow the people of Ammon to go back on their word, despite the danger and perils they faced, and willingly defended Ammon's people.

Since the time of their oath, however, a new generation had arisen, one that was too young at the time to make the oath, but that now was mostly grown and therefore able to contribute in some way. They were the sons of the people of Ammon—young and inexperienced—certainly untested in battle (and considering they were to go up against the battle-hardened Lamanite army, this was not an insignificant fact). They were faithful, willing and eager to give their all—literally—to the Nephite cause. They were "all young men," but more than that, "they were exceedingly valiant for courage, and also for strength and activity." They were "men who were true at all times in whatsoever thing they were entrusted. Yea, they were men of truth and soberness, for they had been taught to keep the commandments of God and to walk uprightly before him" (Alma 53:20–21). Despite their youth and inexperience, they possessed the willing determination of leaders.

How did these very young men develop the fortitude to stand so courageously for righteousness? Was it simply a naïve, unbridled enthusiasm as they got swept up in the moment? They certainly didn't have formal military training. Given their parents' oath, they had been reared on the notion that raising arms against another of God's children was an ineffective way of resolving conflict. More compelling than that message, however, was their profound faith they learned from their faithful parents and were the blessed beneficiaries of the teaching and guidance of their mothers, specifically, who willingly consented to their enlistment. These young men knew that if they fought with pure motive and pure hearts, God would deliver them. They knew that with surety, because they knew their mothers knew that as well. And indeed, they fought with such ferocity, "mighty power" and "miraculous strength" they frightened the experienced Lamanite foes into surrender.

Helaman would later recount to Moroni the startling success these young men, buoyed and inspired by their prophet-turned military commander and the unwavering faith of their mothers, achieved:

> And now I say unto you, my beloved brother Moroni, that never had I seen so great courage, nay, not amongst all the Nephites.
>
> For as I had ever called them my sons (for they were all of them very young) even so they said unto me: Father, behold our God is with us, and he will not suffer that we should fall; then let us go forth; we would not slay our brethren if they would let us alone; therefore let us go, lest they should overpower the army of Antipus.
>
> Now they never had fought, yet they did not fear death; and they did think more upon the liberty of their fathers than they did upon their lives; yea, they had been taught by their mothers, that if they did not doubt, God would deliver them.
>
> And they rehearsed unto me the words of their mothers, saying: We do not doubt our mothers knew it. (Alma 53:45–48)

And the result? Helaman writes:

> But behold, to my great joy, there had not one soul of them fallen to the earth; yea, and they had fought as if with the strength of God; yea, never were men known to have fought with such miraculous strength; and with such mighty power did they fall upon the Lamanites, that they did frighten them; and for this cause did the Lamanites deliver themselves up as prisoners of war. (Alma 53:56)

War raged on for an additional two years, and throughout these two years, Helaman and his intrepid band of warriors continued to answer the call, willingly and with faith. The battles were fierce, and the foe remained bent on the total subjugation of the Nephites, and though as a result of several fierce battles the valiant sons of Helaman all sustained numerous injuries, all were preserved.

These examples of leadership lead us to ask this question: Where is leadership required for us today? The short answer: everywhere and all the time. It is necessary as we work diligently to navigate the complexities of our personal lives. Do we understand even to the smallest degree who we really are and what is expected of and available to us? Are we clear on our goals, and do we do the things every day to help us achieve them? Do we fortify ourselves against an intensely determined foe? Do we manage our lives in such a way that we are working toward our potential? Are we effective in our interactions with others? Do we build and lift others? Do we help others along this same path? Are we creating a home environment that is nurturing the right things? Are we extending unifying love to all our family, whether we're a parent, a child, a sibling, a cousin, an aunt or uncle, a grandparent? Do we serve in our callings in such a way that our efforts invite the Lord's Spirit to guide us and assist in the work? Do we diligently take advantage of every opportunity to bring people unto the Savior?

Three Levels of Leadership

To organize where leadership is required and how we might go about addressing the various leadership needs, I have provided a simple organizing model. This framework consists of three levels:

- Leadership in my personal life
- Leadership in my family
- Leadership in my calling

In the subsequent chapters, I examine each of these levels in detail, beginning with a foundational scripture, then evaluate that scripture through the lens of a governing principle (or natural law) and an over-arching mindset. I then provide four actionable leadership practices for each level, each supported with specific instruction from the scriptures that can help anyone focus on and improve their ability to lead their own lives and have effective influence with others.

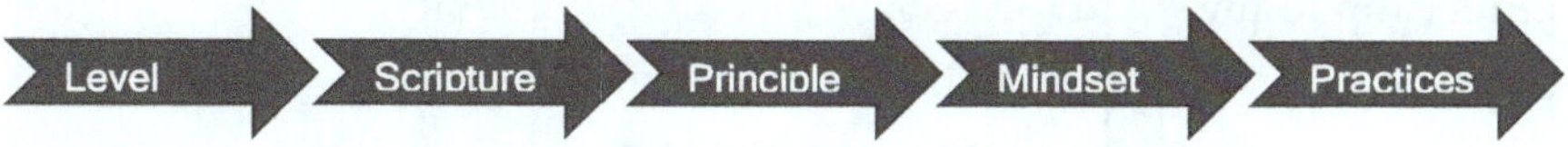

Principles/Natural Laws

In the physical world, principles—or natural laws—prevail. For example, gravity is defined by the *American Heritage Dictionary* as, "The natural force of attraction exerted by a celestial body, such as Earth, upon objects at or near its surface, tending to draw them toward the center of the body." The law of gravity is operational whether we acknowledge it or not. If we choose not to believe in it as a principle that applies to us, it does not invalidate its effect in my life. We might say, "This gravity business is ok for you, but I just don't buy into it." We will still fall if we step off a tall building. Natural laws are impartial. They don't favor one person over another. They're not up for debate, and they treat everyone equally. If you follow them, you'll succeed, but if you disregard them, you will fail.

Knowing how principles operate can empower you to great things. For example, a large aircraft weighs over 750,000 pounds. Yet an understanding of the law of gravity and other principles of flight, such as lift, thrust, and drag, allows us to get these large chunks of metal, filled with people, to fly through the air at amazing speeds, and with safety.

Society's natural laws are as timeless and universal as the physical laws and bring predictable results. If we ignore or violate them, we will fail. As noted filmmaker Cecil B. de Mille said, "It is impossible to break the law. We can only break ourselves against the law." The list of principles associated with leadership is endlessly long—each of which, if honored, guides leaders to greater effectiveness. For our discussion, I'll focus on these three critical leadership principles, each supported by a foundational scripture.

Leadership Level	Foundational Scripture	Governing Principle
Leadership in my personal life	2 Nephi 2:26: "To act for themselves and not to be acted upon."	Personal Responsibility
Leadership in my family	D&C 38:27: "I say unto you, be one; and if ye are not one ye are not mine."	Unity
Leadership in my calling	Moroni 10:32: "Yea, come unto Christ, and be perfect in him, and deny yourselves of all ungodliness."	Conversion

Leadership in my personal life: Personal Responsibility

Father Lehi taught his children: "And the Messiah cometh in the fulness of time, that he may redeem the children of men from the fall. And because that they are redeemed from the fall they have become free forever, knowing good from evil; *to act for themselves and not to be acted upon,* save it be by the punishment of the law at the great and last day, according to the commandments which God hath given" (2 Nephi 2:26, emphasis added). The principle of personal responsibility highlights the critical role choice plays in our mortal experience—to "act" and not simply be "acted upon." No one makes our choices for us—that remains our individual obligation and duty. Our parents can't make choices for us, our friends can't, nor can other leaders. Alma similarly instructed Corianton, "Therefore, O my son, whosoever will come may come and partake of the waters of life freely; and whosoever will not come the same is not compelled to come; but in the last day it shall be restored unto him according to his deeds" (Alma 42:27). We are responsible for the choices we make, and our effectiveness as a leader comes in direct proportion to how we use that choice.

Leadership in my family: Unity

The principle of unity stands as a prominent theme of Jesus' ministry. In His final meeting with his Apostles, knowing they would soon be sent to all the world, Jesus prays to His Father:

> As thou hast sent me into the world, even so have I also sent them into the world.
>
> And for their sakes I sanctify myself, that they also might be sanctified through the truth.
>
> Neither pray I for these alone, but for them also which shall believe on me through their word;
>
> That they all may be one; as thou, Father, art in me, and I in thee, that they also may be one in us: that the world may believe that thou hast sent me." (John 17:18–21)

Prophets throughout time have reminded and commanded us to reject contention and embrace that which brings us together. A leader's job is to unify—to bring people together in Christ. And nowhere is that more important than in the family. Every family has individuals who are in different places, with different levels of commitment to covenants and different challenges to address. Part of our role—whether we're the mother, father, sister, cousin, nephew or granddaughter—is to unite the family. President Henry B. Eyring has taught:

> The requirement that we be one is not for this life alone. It is to be without end. The first marriage was performed by God in the garden when Adam and Eve were immortal. He placed in men and women from the beginning a desire to be joined together as man and wife forever to dwell in families in a perfect, righteous union. He placed in His children a desire to live at peace with all those around them.
>
> But with the Fall it became clear that living in unity would not be easy. Tragedy struck early. Cain slew Abel, his brother. The children of Adam and Eve had become subject to the temptations of Satan. With skill, hatred, and cunning, Satan pursues his goal. It is the opposite of the purpose of our Heavenly Father and the Savior. They would give us perfect union and eternal happiness. Satan, their enemy and ours, has known the plan of salvation from before the Creation. He knows that only in eternal life can those sacred, joyful associations of families endure. Satan would tear us from loved ones and make us miserable. And it is he who plants the seeds of discord in human hearts in the hope that we might be divided and separate.
>
> The ministry of the apostles and prophets in [Jesus'] day, as it is today, was to bring the children of Adam and Eve to a unity of the faith in Jesus Christ. The ultimate purpose of what they taught, and of what we teach, is to unite families: husbands, wives, children, grandchildren, ancestors, and finally all of the family of Adam and Eve who will choose it.[2]

The Spirit of God never generates contention (see 3 Ne. 11:29). It never generates the feelings of distinctions between people which lead to strife.[3] It leads to personal peace and a feeling of union with others.

It unifies souls. A unified family, a unified Church, and a world at peace depend on unified souls.

The Lord phrases it directly and unequivocally: "I say unto you, be one; and if ye are not one ye are not mine" (D&C 38:27).

Leadership in my calling: Conversion

Whether we're serving as the bishop, stake president, assistant ward girl's camp director, or secretary of the Primary organization, we share the same overarching goal: to bring those within our stewardships unto Christ. There really is no other objective. Every prophet in every dispensation was charged with that imperative, and everything we do in our callings is a means to that end. In his final salvo to the ultimate readers of the Book of Mormon, Moroni, whose life was difficult from his first breath to the end of his solitary wanderings in the wilderness, offers a penetrating, last admonition, one that cuts through any clutter we may feel as a result of our busy lives—lives that have multiple competing priorities, duties, responsibilities, questions, and demands: "Yea come, unto Christ, and be perfected in him, and deny yourselves of all ungodliness; and if ye shall deny yourselves of all ungodliness, and love God with all your might, mind and strength, then is his grace sufficient for you, that by his grace ye may be perfect in Christ" (Moroni 10:32). That invitation should be the conclusive and decisive objective of our leadership.

Principles Govern

I'm sure you have met people who have obtained great success—as success is defined by the world. They may have gathered riches, or achieved a degree of notoriety or fame, and did so by stepping on others, seeking their own objective at the expense of everything else. Is it possible to get results by violating the so-called principles of human effectiveness? Well, the answer is both yes and no. It is certainly possible to achieve a short-term objective at the expense of others.

I once determined to win a game of Monopoly by bending the rules to meet my own selfish needs. As the banker, it was easy to slip a few extra bills under my section of the board with each transaction.

Ultimately, I won the game. In fact, it wasn't even close. And I celebrated in front of my family with great enthusiasm. But when my children learned the truth of how I won, they refused to play with me for a long time.

Think of your school experience. Have you ever "crammed" in school? Have you ever put off studying for an important test or project until the last minute? Cramming is a learned behavior with many—it certainly was with me. I developed quite an ability to get an acceptable grade by cramming in my studies. But what are the consequences? Can you get the right grade or test score? The answer is yes. I did. Do you remember—long term—what you studied? Not usually. So if the purpose of your scholastic experience is to "get the grade," short-term results (cramming) may work in a shoddy way. But if the purpose of your educational experience is to learn, to gather lasting knowledge and achieve a true education, there are better study methods to consider.

Does the practice of cramming work on the farm? In other words, can you put off planting all spring and summer, work hard and fast in September—plant quickly, water intensely—and expect a rich and robust harvest in October? Of course not. The principle of "you reap what you sow" is in effect. The same is true in our relationships and our leadership. You cannot ignore them and expect them to flourish. You cannot demonstrate a pattern of untrustworthy behavior and expect people to continue to trust you. Short-term gains might be possible, but long-term success will elude you.

Regarding natural laws, President Russell M. Nelson has taught:

> After graduating from medical school, I pursued advanced education in surgery. At that time there was no such thing as heart surgery. Then I teamed up with other researchers in the daunting task of making an artificial heart and lung machine. We knew that such an apparatus could possibly maintain the body's circulation while repairs might be made on the heart. But during that early era, there was much we did not know.
>
> Then one day, two truths articulated in the Doctrine and Covenants spoke to my inquiring mind. These truths were, first, that all blessings are predicated upon obedience to law and, second, that to every kingdom there is a law given.

Well, I reasoned that if every kingdom had a law, there must be laws that govern the beating heart. I was determined to discover those laws and obey them. By doing so, blessings would come and lives could be saved.

In medical school I had been taught that if one touched the beating heart, it would stop beating. However, one of the first laws we discovered in the lab was that we could touch the heart of an animal without losing its heartbeat. This finding opened the door later to uncovering another law that made more complex open-heart operations possible.

We learned that if we added potassium chloride to blood flowing into the coronary arteries, thereby altering the normal sodium/potassium ratio, the heart would stop beating instantly. Then, when we nourished the heart with blood that had a normal sodium/potassium ratio, the heart would spring back to its normal beating pattern. Literally we could turn the heart off long enough to repair it and then turn it back on again.

Decades later, when I explained this to a group of medical students, one prominent professor asked, "But what if it doesn't work?" My answer? It always works, because it is based on divine law.

Divine law is incontrovertible! The same can be said of the law of gravity and the laws of foil and lift that allow airplanes to fly. Each is an absolute truth. Doctors or pilots do not have the power to change those laws, but their understanding of them safeguards lives.

My dear brothers and sisters, divine laws are God's gifts to His children. Just as our family's rules kept our children safe as they grew to adulthood, just as divine laws governing the heart and the flight of airplanes keep you safe on an operating table or while traveling, abiding by God's laws will keep you safe as you progress toward eventual exaltation. Let me say it as succinctly as I can: As you abide by God's laws, you are progressing toward exaltation.

The Prophet Joseph Smith taught that God "institute[d] laws whereby [we] could have a privilege to advance like himself." God's greatest blessings are reserved for those who obey His laws, as He explained: "For all who will have a blessing at my hands shall abide the law which was appointed for that blessing." God's laws are motivated entirely by His infinite love for us and His desire for us to become all we can become.[4]

Addressing Jesus' leadership, President Spencer W. Kimball declared, "Jesus operated from a base of fixed principles or truths rather than making up the rules as he went along. Thus, his leadership style was not only correct, but also constant."[5]

Mindsets—How I Think

The Psalmist wrote, "For as he thinketh in his heart, so is he" (Proverbs 23). Certainly, how we think influences everything we do.

Joel Barker, author of *Future Edge*, tells a story of a man driving along a mountain road at night. As he was rounding a curve, a man on the side of the road shouted, "Pig!"

"Well!" thought the man. "That was about the rudest thing I have ever heard. I can't believe the gall of some people! I do not know that man and have done nothing to offend him. Why would he choose to call me a pig?" Just then, as the man turned the corner on the road, he saw a pig in the middle of the road, slammed on his brakes, and narrowly missed driving off the steep edge. The man hadn't been trying to insult the driver; he had known there were pigs in the road and he was trying to warn him.[6]

This little illustration highlights one of the foundational elements to effective leadership: the ability to examine, and when necessary, challenge your viewpoints. Our view of the world has a tremendous influence on what we, individually, are able to accomplish. Our mindsets drive our attitudes, affect our confidence, and influence our relationships. Each of us possesses unique mindsets that shape what we do every day. These mindsets represent how we view ourselves, how we see others, and our perspective of the world. It's like viewing the world through colored lenses. One of the key skills necessary for effective leadership is the ability to examine and challenge our own viewpoints and perspectives.

Consider your own views: What role do your mindsets play in the results you achieve? The view we hold of ourselves and others can either limit or liberate us. Sometimes our perspectives are simply wrong, and yet we still behave according to those perspectives. Frequently, we base our perspective of who we are, our capabilities, our talents and abilities to contribute on what we think others think of us. For example, if I believe others will hold the opinion that I am not capable of doing something, I could let that negatively impact what I do. Do you ever limit yourself based on faulty mindsets, or perceptions that are only partially correct? If you want to make minor, incremental improvement, focus on changing your behavior. But if you want to make quantum, geometric improvement, change your mindset.

For many years, my work has required extensive travel. Because of the amount of time I'm in airports and on airplanes, I have developed certain habits and routines. As I get to the airport and arrive at my gate, I tend to look around and notice my fellow passengers. I often wonder why they're going where they're going, what their lives and experiences are, what their conversations were like with their loved ones that very morning, etc. I'm curious, but not curious enough, usually, to engage them in any real or meaningful conversation. I'm comfortable in my little bubble, where I can be with my own thoughts. Business executive and speaker, Ric Elias, shares a similar approach to his travel. He recounts one particular cold, January travel day as he waited in the airport for his flight to board, he looked around at his fellow travelers and wondered what their mornings had been like. To that point, his hadn't gone well. He was rehearsing in his mind a challenging conflict he had at work and a tense conversation he had has with his wife. Add to that the other pressures and contentions he was feeling (and that we all carry with us far too often), and he was just eager to get on his flight and move forward with his agenda. As it turned out that day, Ric was upgraded to seat 1D, a bulkhead seat in first class. During the boarding process, he engaged in some light banter with the flight attendant. Because he was in the front row, Ric was able to continue the conversation with the flight attendant seated facing him in the galley area as the plane ascended. Ric recounts that three things happened in the next few moments that forever changed his life. First, just as the plane took off and gained its initial altitude, he heard horrific sounds emanating from what he thought was the plane's engine area. It was a loud, screeching sound, like metal grinding against metal. Obviously frightened, Ric looked at the flight attendant, who was immediately calming. "This kind of thing happens from time to time," she said. "There is no cause for concern . . . the pilot will just turn the plane around, land it, and have the grounds crew and mechanics lake a look at it." Ric was somewhat comforted.

The second thing that happened was more arresting: the screeching sounds went away. The problem was that all the sounds went away. The engines went completely silent. This time, the flight attendant looked as frightened as Ric felt.

Finally, the third thing occurred, and it forever altered how Ric (and everyone else on that plane) saw his life: at that point, Captain Chelsey "Sully" Sullenberger come over the plane's intercom and uttered three fateful words: "Brace for impact." The plane was going down. There was a total of ninety seconds from Captain Sully's announcement to when the plane hit the chilly waters of the Hudson River, just enough time for the passengers to examine all the things they would do differently in their lives if given the chance.

As US Airways flight 1549 took off from LaGuardia airport the morning of January 15, 2009, it hit a flock of migrating northern geese, who were sucked simultaneously into both engines, destroying both instantly. Thankfully (and heroically), Captain Sully, copilot Jeffrey Skiles and their crew had enough presence of mind to bank the plane around in such a way they avoided any physical structures in New York City, glided just over the George Washington Bridge, and carefully and skillfully land the plane on the ice-filled Hudson River. Apart from a few minor scrapes and bruises, no one was injured, and what could have been an utter catastrophe ended as a significant inspiration for so many (certainly for anyone who flies!).

The experience left an indelible mark on the passengers, the crew, and the rest of us. An inspired world watched the aftermath with gratitude and appreciation. The memory of all 158 passengers lining the partially submerged wings of the Airbus A320 as it floated temporarily on the surface of the Hudson River waiting for the harbor patrol boats to rescue them remains firmly etched in our collective minds.

For Ric (and the other passengers, I'm sure), it was a time of deep reflection. He remembered the feelings of frustration he'd had that morning—the conflict he had felt with his work circumstance, the unkind works he had expressed to his wife, and the other things that at the time seemed so important and pressing—and he realized that none of those negative feelings mattered. Not one of them. He had unnecessarily carried them with him that morning, neatly packed in his mind and heart like another piece of carry-on luggage, stowed with his other belongings. He had an instant and important shift in his thinking, and that shift led him to a change to his entire approach to life.[7]

How we think influences what we do every day. And what we do has a major impact on the result we achieve. Is our thinking in line with the principles—the natural laws—associated with effective leadership?

Don't underestimate the power of a mindset. One of the traits of great leaders is an ability to remain open, a realization that no one has all the information all the time. Be careful about judgments you make of others. Remember that your perspective is based on your experience, and that by its very nature it is incomplete. A friend of mine coined this profound statement: nobody knows everything about anything. Our perspectives are always limited, and sometimes, they are dead wrong. Honestly evaluate your heart: Do you ever judge others unfairly based on poor or limited information? Do you ever judge yourself the same way? Remember, you are capable of many things. Recognize that capability.

Sometimes we do things or behave simply out of habit. While preparing Sunday dinner for her husband, a new bride took a ham, cut off both ends, placed the ham in a roasting pan, and put it in the oven. The husband was perplexed, and asked, "Why did you cut the ends off the ham?" His wife thought a moment, and replied, "I don't know . . . that's how my mother always did it." So she called her mother and asked her the same question. "I don't know," the mother replied. "That is what my mother always did." She then called her grandmother: "Why did you always cut the ends off the ham before you baked it?" The grandmother replied, "Because my roasting pan was too small. That was the only way I could get it to fit."

Be open to new ways of seeing problems and situations. Don't get stuck in the rut of old thinking. Remember, how you see the world influences what you do, which drives the results you achieve. If you don't like the results you are getting, examine your mindsets. There is great power in thinking differently.

Your influence with others grows as you help them broaden their perspectives of their own capabilities. Early in my career, a colleague and I were asked to open our company's first field office, about two thousand miles away, and I was expected to represent my organization to the highest levels of government officials and corporate leaders. Grateful for the appointment and enthusiastic about the opportunity, I nevertheless could not quell all my youthful trepidations. A conversation with one of my leaders the day I left did much to reassure me. I told him of my excitement and assured him that I would generate significant client opportunities for the senior members of our firm to come and close. He stopped me in mid-sentence and in a very direct way, reminded me that I was a now senior member of the firm and didn't need to rely on anyone else. As simple as it was, that short conversation completely changed the way I viewed myself and my capabilities. I elevated the expectation I had of myself to match the expectations and trust this leader held for me. His view of me helped me shift my own thinking and became a catalyst for new and enhanced behaviors. It caused me to stretch and work in different and better ways.

Below is more detail on the leadership framework, including the governing principles and critical mindsets associated with the following principles:

Leadership Level	**Foundational Scripture**	**Governing Principle**	**How I Think**
Leadership in my personal life	2 Nephi 2:26: "To act for themselves and not to be acted upon."	Personal Responsibility	I am in charge of the choices I make—no one else can make them for me.
Leadership in my family	D&C 38:27: "I say unto you, be one; and if ye are not one ye are not mine."	Unity	Together, we are better. Regardless of where people are, my family is a place of learning, of building, of growth, and of love.
Leadership in my calling	Moroni 10:32: "Yea, come unto Christ, and be perfect in him, and deny yourselves of all ungodliness."	Conversion	In every action, in every word, and in every program, my job, regardless of a specific calling, is to help others come closer to the Savior and to make and keep sacred covenants. There is no other agenda.

It might be helpful to think about leadership in two ways: formal authority (influence as a result of a specific role, title or position), and moral authority (leadership associated with a way of being, the ability to persuade and influence even if no official role or title exists). In fact, as you think about your leaders, you may discover some of them had or have formal leadership positions, and you may have realized that some had tremendous influence without an official title. Sometimes it is the informal leaders that inspire the most and that make the greatest impact and that is because of their moral authority. Leadership is not just the domain of those in certain positions. It is everyone's responsibility. And everyone—those in positions and those not in positions—can benefit from a discussion about developing leadership skills.

There may be times in your life when you are asked to accept a responsibility for which you don't feel particularly prepared. Take comfort in President Monson's inspired statement: "Whom God calls, God qualifies."[8] As the Lord declared to Abraham, "Is anything too hard for the Lord?" (Genesis 18:14). That question extends from Abraham to you and me. Will the Lord sustain you in your leadership efforts, whether formal or otherwise? Can He inspire and direct you? Will He? Does He care enough about you and the work in which you are engaged? The apostle Paul, who, with the Lord's help, transformed his entire life as he assumed his apostolic duties, provides clarity to these questions: "I can do all things through Christ which strengtheneth me" (Philippians 4:13). And so can we.

You've probably heard the story about the elementary school teacher who, one snowy winter afternoon, as one of her young students was leaving school for home, stopped to help the boy put on his goulashes. They were clearly too small for his shoes, but after several minutes of tugging, twisting and struggling, she finally succeeded in pulling them on. The boy then replied, "These are not my goulashes." Exasperated, the teacher then spent the next several minutes going through the process of removing them, after which the boy replied, "These are not my goulashes. They're my sister's. But I couldn't find mine this morning and my mother made me wear hers." So once again, the teacher had to go through the process of putting them on his feet again.

Over the years—and perhaps sooner than you think—you will have opportunities to provide leadership in ways that don't exactly "fit" your talents. Keep "tugging, twisting and struggling" anyway. Make the conscious decision to be an active and willing participant in building the Lord's kingdom. I have heard so many former full-time missionaries declare with boldness how much they loved serving. Unfortunately, I have seen some of these same missionaries, when a few years or even just a few months elapse after their return home, lose their passion for the Lord's work.

Instead of viewing leadership and service as a privilege, some view it as a burden. Ministering becomes routine, just something that has to be done, if indeed it is done at all. Preparing a Sunday school lesson for a bunch of thirteen-year-olds who don't want to be there is hard, even more so when you don't want to be there. Service projects, family home evening, girl's camp and youth conference can either be a blessing or a curse, depending on your paradigm or your attitude. The critical leadership mindsets addressed above (I am responsible for the choices I make; together, we are better, regardless of where individual family members are, my family is a place of learning, of building, of growth, and of love; in every action, in every word, and in every program, my job, regardless of a specific calling, is to help others come closer to the Savior and to make and keep sacred covenants—there is no other agenda) are offset by "limiting" thinking like: I am a victim of my circumstance; I see my family as an obstacle or burden; I see callings that come my way as an obligation that I fulfill (or don't), but they don't bring me joy.

Look for and pray for opportunities to serve your family and in the kingdom, without respect to the so-called "importance" or visibility of the calling. Be willing to serve with diligence and enthusiasm in whatever callings you receive. "Every great and commanding movement in the annals of the world is the triumph of enthusiasm. Nothing great was ever achieved without it," observed Ralph Waldo Emerson.[9] Prepare now for whatever opportunities come your way.

CHAPTER FOUR

HOW DO I STRENGTHEN MY ABILITY TO LEAD EFFECTIVELY?

And when Enoch had heard these words, he bowed himself to the earth, before the Lord, and spake before the Lord, saying: Why is it that I have found favor in thy sight, and am but a lad, and all the people hate me; for I am slow of speech; wherefore am I thy servant?

And the Lord said unto Enoch: Go forth and do as I have commanded thee, and no man shall pierce thee. Open thy mouth, and it shall be filled, and I will give thee utterance, for all flesh is in my hands, and I will do as seemeth me good.

—Moses 6:32–33

To every man there comes in his lifetime that special moment when he is figuratively tapped on the shoulder and offered a chance to do a very special thing, unique to him and fitted to his talents. What a tragedy if that moment finds him unprepared or unqualified for the work which would be his finest hour.

—Winston Churchill[1]

The Book of Ether stands as a microcosm of the Book of Mormon—it is metatheatre within the broader tome. Like Mormon's comprehensive compilation from over 1,000 years of religious history, the Book of Ether tells of a people led by the Lord (and as an effort to remove themselves from the turmoil of Babel and the confounding of languages that resulted from the tower builders' pride) to a land of promise. Many generations—known to the reader as the Jaredites—lived in this promised land, some righteous and many not. When the Jaredite civilization eventually grew so wicked that the Spirit of the Lord ceased to remain with them to any degree, they became ripe for destruction.

But for several generations throughout their history, the Jaredites were a righteous and obedient people, let by prophets, and faithful to the foundation of faith they inherited from the forebearers. When they were righteous, they enjoyed the abundant blessings of the Lord. Chief among these faithful forebears was the brother of Jared, about whom the Lord declared, "Never has man come before me with such exceeding faith as thou hast" (Ether 3:9).

The Brother of Jared is given an assignment from the Lord. After some initial instruction, he loses sight of the need to call on the Lord regularly and receives a stern heavenly chastening for his inattentiveness. But he quickly and penitently responds with an open and honest heart, with both faith and diligence, and moves forward courageously with the Lord's instructions as he prepares his traveling company for their journey. Barges are built, flocks and fouls and even fishes and bees are gathered in preparation for their oceanic excursion into uncharted and unknown waters.

Several perplexing issues ensue in the process of their preparations. The need for the flow of breathable air in the airtight barges is addressed, as the Lord inspires the Brother of Jared to place holes in both the top and bottom of the boats to allow for the flow of oxygen. Other design instructions are given and acted upon that make the journey across the deep sea possible and settlement in the new world a reality.

One major problem remains, however. Faced with the quandary of providing light for their barges (as the boats were to be sealed "tight as a dish" and the travelers, understandably, have no interest in crossing the vast, unpredictable sea in total darkness) the Brother of Jared takes the initiative to molten sixteen stones out of rock as part of the plan he presents to the Lord. If the Lord would simply touch the stones, the Brother of Jared implores, "They shall shine forth unto us in the vessels which we have prepared, that we may have light while we shall cross the sea.

"Behold, O Lord, thou canst do this. We know that thou art able to show forth great power, which looks small unto the understanding of men" (Ether 3:4–5).

The Brother of Jared's faith combines with his diligence to create a solution for his people. He doesn't simply stand idle, hoping that the Lord will provide a solution to their lighting problem. He doesn't wait, wondering why, when he was called to do this difficult task (and is therefore on the Lord's errand) that answers aren't presented simply as blueprints to follow. He is proactive. He is resourceful. He takes initiative. He uses his best judgment to identify a solution. He puts in great effort—he doesn't simply gather sixteen random stones. He mines the elements from rock, uses intense heat to liquify them in order to make the pure and transparent stone, and then presents his very best solution to the Lord: "I know, O Lord, that thou hast all power, and can do whatsoever thou wilt for the benefit of man; therefore touch these stones, O Lord, with thy finger, and prepare them that they may shine forth in darkness; and they shall shine forth unto us in the vessels which we have prepared, that we may have light while we shall cross the sea" (Ether 3:4).

The Lord accepts the Brother of Jared's efforts: "And it came to pass that when the brother of Jared had said these words, behold, the Lord stretched forth his hand and touched the stones one by one with his finger. And the veil was taken from off the eyes of the brother of Jared, and he saw the finger of the Lord" (Ether 3:6).

The Brother of Jared combines faith with thought, creativity, initiative and action—and not only does the Lord approve of the Brother of Jared's solution, his eyes are opened, and he is brought back into the Lord's presence. And like the very sixteen stones he presents, the Brother of Jared is touched by the Lord's finger, allowing him to bring illumination and leadership to a dark and desperate world.

In the previous chapter I provided a framework for where leadership is required in our lives. Again, the simple answer to that question is: everywhere. Great bishops are required in the Church. So are primary teachers, mothers, fathers, cousins, friends, teachers, advisors, and siblings. To help us all develop greater leadership capabilities, I have identified four core practices associated with each of the levels (1. individual leadership, 2. leadership in my family, and 3. leadership in my callings). These practices, drawn directly from the scriptures, provide practical application on how to develop and enhance our abilities to lead. Note: These practices are not intended to represent a comprehensive list. The scriptures contain literally hundreds, if not thousands of leadership practices. These simply provide a place to start the conversation on how to improve our leadership effectiveness.

These practices are not intended to be sequential—one does not need to master one before moving on to the second. There is no magic in their positioning in the lineup. But they are cumulative. For example, while I have identified "using your time intentionally" as a practice for personal leadership, certainly the activities associated with doing so have relevance to leadership in our families and in our callings as well, and when combined with the other practices at each level, each strengthens and supports one another.

There is a synergistic nature to these practices, where the whole is far greater than the sum of the parts, where the simple mathematical equation of one plus one does not equal two.

Take a standard eight foot pine two-by-four, for example. On its own it can support about 607 pounds. But if you add a second two-by-four and fix them together with a small amount of glue and a couple of standard nails, it can hold up about 4878 pounds. Add a third two-by-four, again with a small amount of glue and a couple nails. Their capacity to bear a load improves to around 8,881! Why is this so? If you measure the individual parts' capacity to bear a load, they (the sum of the individual parts) don't get anywhere close to this level of strength. There is something about the combining of the two or more boards that brings more than just incremental improvement—it is exponential. Similarly, a natural synergy occurs when these practices are combined to improve our leadership. The same phenomenon also occurs when leaders effectively work with people. The outcome of that work is often far greater than what one individual can achieve in isolation, especially when the Lord is included in that partnership.

These practices are intended to build capability, one upon the other, across each of the three levels. And remember, these practices are not the only leadership practices identified in the scriptures—they're certainly not the only things we should do. But each of these practices, if applied, and then combined with other practices, can meaningfully and positively help each of us narrow our focus and improve our abilities to lead in all aspects of our life.

One does not need to delay developing a leadership skill identified in a practice for the "Leadership in my calling" level because you haven't checked all the boxes in the "Leadership in my personal life" section. Truthfully, there aren't boxes to check. Every practice is important and, frankly, necessary. And each individual circumstance leaders face is different. Some people have certain talents that bring effectiveness in certain areas, while others naturally shine in different areas. But as you are formulating a plan for your own development, it can be helpful to take a sequential approach as you develop a focus.

The following chart highlights the Levels, the Foundational Scripture associated with the level, the Governing Principle, and the corresponding Mindsets noted in the previous chapter. I have then summarized the four practices associated with each level, which will be explored in greater depth in subsequent chapters.

Leadership Level	Foundational Scripture	Governing Principle	How I Think	Practices
Leadership in my personal life	2 Nephi 2:26: "To act for themselves and not to be acted upon"	Personal Responsibility	I am in charge of the choices I make—no one else can make them for me.	**Practice 1:** Know Your Identity **Practice 2:** Offer Your Whole Soul **Practice 3:** Use Your Time Intentionally **Practice 4:** Press Forward
Leadership in my family	D&C 38:27: "I say unto you, be one; and if ye are not one ye are not mine."	Unity	Together, we are better. Regardless of where people are, my family is a place of learning, of building, of growth, and of love.	**Practice 5:** Develop Charity **Practice 6:** Keep an Eternal Perspective **Practice 7:** Lead with Empathy **Practice 8:** Learn to Hear Him

Leadership Level	Foundational Scripture	Governing Principle	How I Think	Practices
Leadership in my calling	Moroni 10:32: "Yea, come unto Christ, and be perfect in him, and deny yourselves of all ungodliness."	Conversion	In every action, in every word, and in every program, my job, regardless of a specific calling, is to help others come closer to the Savior and to make and keep sacred covenants. There is no other agenda.	**Practice 9:** Organizing and Managing the Work **Practice 10:** Teach with Power **Practice 11:** Develop Other Leaders **Practice 12:** Lead One by One

I invite you to spend time pondering what a particular practice could mean to you. Where are your strengths? What are some areas that might be improved upon? What feedback would others give you on certain leadership skill areas? How could you improve your skillset around that practice?

At the conclusion of each chapter, I've provided some suggestions on how to apply the practice. Prayerfully consider how the Lord might assist you and enlighten you as you strive for improvement in a particular area. Make Him your partner as you work to strengthen your leadership acumen. Work to apply the skillset (practice the practice!). In other words, remember the "Three P's": *ponder* your strengths and areas for improvement, *practice* to develop greater skills in desired focus areas, and *pray* for the Lord's guidance, insight and direction.

Now let's explore the practices, beginning with "Leadership in My Personal Life."

PART II

LEADERSHIP IN MY PERSONAL LIFE

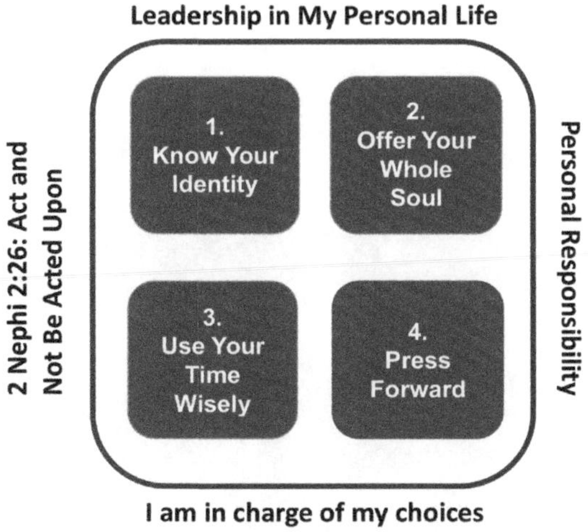

Leadership Level	Foundational Scripture	Governing Principle	How I Think	Practices
Leadership in my personal life	2 Nephi 2:26: "To act for themselves and not to be acted upon"	Personal Responsibility	I am in charge of the choices I make—no one else can make them for me.	**Practice 1:** Know Your Identity **Practice 2:** Experience Personal Conversion **Practice 3:** Use Your Time Intentionally **Practice 4:** Press Forward

CHAPTER FIVE
KNOW YOUR IDENTITY

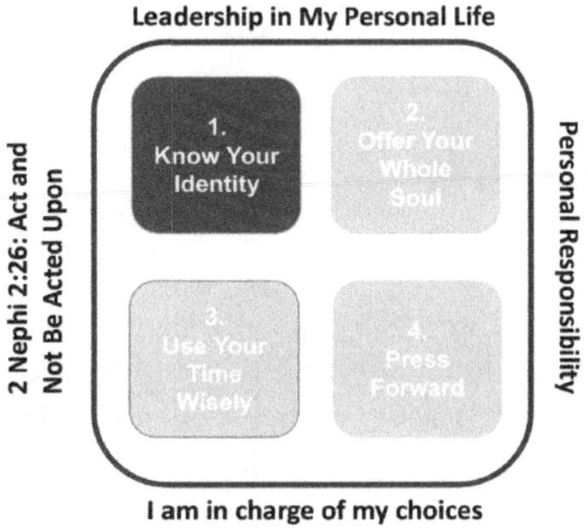

Now the Lord had shown unto me, Abraham, the intelligences that were organized before the world was; and among all these there were many of the noble and great ones;

And God saw these souls that they were good, and he stood in the midst of them, and he said: These I will make my rulers; for he stood among those that were spirits, and he saw that they were good; and he said unto me: Abraham, thou art one of them; thou wast chosen before thou wast born.

—Abraham 3:22–23

You are good. But it is not enough to be good. You must be good for something. You must contribute good to the world. The world must be a better place for your presence. And the good that is in you must be spread to others.

—Gordon B. Hinckley[1]

Who are you, really? The answer to that question is not a simple one. You might consider the answer to align with the various roles you play in life. For example, you might say you are a mother or father, a friend, an extended family member, an athlete, an academician, a professional, an attorney, a businesswoman, a musician, a disciple. But who are you really? What is your true identity? Certainly, an accurate answer is: "I am a child a God." But do we understand what that really means? Have we articulated it clearly such that it serves as a guide for our plans, choices and daily behaviors? Do we lead our individual lives with that identity in mind?

Consider the following groups of people—both Lamanites—described in these two scriptures:

Group One

Mosiah 10:11–12

> Now, the Lamanites knew nothing concerning the Lord, nor the strength of the Lord, therefore they depended upon their own strength. Yet they were a strong people, as to the strength of men.
>
> They were a wild, and ferocious, and a blood-thirsty people, believing in the tradition of their fathers, which is this—Believing that they were driven out of the land of Jerusalem because of the iniquities of their fathers, and that they were wronged in the wilderness by their brethren, and they were also wronged while crossing the sea.

Group Two

Alma 27:27–28

> And they were among the people of Nephi, and also numbered among the people who were of the church of God. And they were also distinguished for their zeal towards God, and also towards men; for they were perfectly honest and upright in all things; and they were firm in the faith of Christ, even unto the end.

> And they did look upon shedding the blood of their brethren with the greatest abhorrence; and they never could be prevailed upon to take up arms against their brethren; and they never did look upon death with any degree of terror, for their hope and views of Christ and the resurrection; therefore, death was swallowed up to them by the victory of Christ over it.

Mormon identifies the first group harshly—a wild, ferocious and blood-thirsty people. And while they were strong and capable, they didn't have a foundation of faith. They were steeped in a cultural tradition that their fathers had been wronged—cheated out of their inheritance and birthright. This resentment fueled a constant hatred toward the Nephites.

The second group might be described as equally strong but possessing a zeal driven by a love for their Lamanite brethren, despite the hatred they received in return. For them, malice toward the other Lamanites became repugnant, and though they were persecuted by them, their faith in Christ brought a strength and courage that both propelled them forward and became a catalyst for a significant change of heart from their brethren. Both groups were Lamanites. Both came from the same heritage where they have been taught that they had been wronged. But one had a deep understanding of their true identity, and it served as a guide to how they lived their lives. It provided courage, clarity, direction, and purpose, and proved a powerful influence for good on the lives of thousands of would-be enemies.

The process for clarifying and articulating our identity can be difficult and requires careful and deep introspection. Sometimes, the roles we play help provide insight and direction. For example, missionaries develop a strong identity for their missions, and that identity fuels them in their work.

In my mission—the great Pennsylvania Philadelphia Mission—we quoted D&C 4 out loud and in unison at the beginning of every meeting. Those inspired words became part of who we were and what we strived to become as the Lord's servants. Following recitation of D&C 4, we quoted the Prophet Joseph's bold declaration from the Wentworth letter:

> Our missionaries are going forth to different nations . . . the Standard of Truth has been erected; no unhallowed hand can stop the work from progressing; persecutions may rage, mobs may combine, armies may assemble, calumny may defame, but the truth of God will go forth boldly, nobly, and independent, till it has penetrated every continent, visited every climb, swept every country, and sounded in every ear; till the purposes of God shall be accomplished, and the Great Jehovah shall say the work is done.[2]

Now, thirty-five years later (at the time of this writing), those words still spark deep emotion and a sense of being part of something significant and larger than myself. It still informs who and what I strive to become, despite my abundant daily shortcomings.

My oldest son served in the great Washington Tacoma mission. He shares this about his experience:

> Everything I am today is influenced by my service as a missionary. Not only do I view the Church differently as a result of my mission, to this day it impacts my church service, my love for members of the Church as well as my love for nonmembers of the Church. All are heavily impacted by my time in Washington. It increased my empathy for others and my appreciation for the sacrifice Church leaders offer. It changed the way I appreciate the scriptures and how I rely on prayer. And even though I feel I am very far from my missionary ideal—every day—I have a better understanding for how the Savior sees each of us.

We, too, would recite Section 4 and the Standard of Truth. After that, we all, with one voice, declared:

> We are revelatory missionaries; we are atonement-centered and baptism-focused. We bring people unto Christ by inviting them to accept his message and be baptized. We see the guidance of the Spirit in all we do. Faith is the power, baptism is the way, and obedience is the price.

This was the articulation of our identity.

So what is your identity? What do you stand for? If someone were to describe you to another person, what would they say? What's important to you? Do your words and actions reflect those priorities?

Each of us has three lives—our family life, our public/professional life, and our secret life—what we do and how we think when no one else is present. Is who we really are reflected in each? Is there cohesion and consistency in all areas of our lives? Do we exhibit integrity in every circumstance? Is that part of our identity?

It can be helpful to examine our lives—our identity—by racing to the end and looking back. In other words, fast forward in your mind to the end of your long and fruitful life. When all is said and done, what do you want to have done? And more importantly, what do you want to have become? Have you clarified that concept? Are you living consistent with it today?

This kind of self-evaluation and discovery can be difficult, and one might ask, "Why go through this process?" The answer to the question is simple: we become what we think about. Or as it says in Proverbs, "For as he thinketh in his heart, so is he" (Proverbs 23:7). If one has a desire to make a meaningful difference, it is far less likely that desire will be realized if these contributions are not articulated—if our "identity" is not given careful consideration and effort.

Who are we? Taking thoughtful time to clarify this answer helps bring your desired contributions into focus. Consider capturing your thoughts in a personal manifesto or mission statement—a written record of your identity. Just as the United States Constitution has directed the very structure and operations of our government and is the basis for day-to-day life in this country, this process can serve as an important guide for what you do and for what you will become. It can be a difficult but illuminating experience. It will help you narrow your focus and tighten your commitment. W. H. Murray, organizer of the 1951 Scottish Himalayan Expedition, writes,

> Until one is committed, there is hesitancy, the chance to draw back, always ineffectiveness concerning all acts of initiative and creation. There is one elementary truth, the ignorance of which kills countless ideas and splendid plans; that the moment one definitely commits oneself, then Providence moves too.

> All sorts of things occur to help one that would never otherwise have occurred. A whole stream of events issues from the decision raising in one's favor all manner of unforeseen events, meetings and material assistance which no one could have dreamed would have come their way.
>
> I have learned a deep respect for one of Goethe's couplets: "Whatever you can do or dream you can, begin it. Boldness has genius, power and magic in it. Begin it now!"[3]

It's amazing what happens when one makes a commitment to a clearly defined identity. When combined with determined action, you create a sense of momentum that is hard to stop. This is what it means to live by design rather than by default.

I was never passionate about scouting as a young man. I don't confess it proudly, but honesty demands it. With all the wit and wisdom and judgment of my thirteen years, I resisted scouting, and at times, even fought to avoid participation. I had a long-suffering scoutmaster and deacon's quorum advisor who demonstrated tremendous patience with me, and always went the second mile to ensure I was doing what I needed to do, pulling my weight and contributing my part. I know I gave him grief, caused him to raise his voice a few times in exasperation, but I also knew he loved me. He had a certain exuberance for the Lord's work that was hard to resist. I remember him taking a week off work to take us to scout camp. His singing "Oh what a beautiful morning" at the top of his lungs early each morning still echoes hauntingly in my head. I also remember the testimony he shared regularly over campfires, and his excitement for the progress we made in our lives.

As I got just a bit older, this scout master became my bishop. He saw me through my high school years, guided our family and others through trials and tragedy, prepared me for my mission, and was there to preside over my homecoming. I remember distinctly the advice and counsel he gave me as I was dating my wife, and his encouragement and support as Michele and I prepared to marry. My wedding reception is mostly a blur—there was so much going on that I actually remember very little. But I do remember that just as it ended, Bishop Harding and his wife joined Michele and me for a few quiet moments to express their congratulations. Given my experience with this man over the years, it was one of the highlights of the entire evening.

Just a few weeks later, I received word that this good man, who had served for over seven years as our family's bishop, was killed in a tragic accident in Spanish Fork Canyon, leaving behind his wife and ten children, a struggling business, and a deeply affected ward. From the world's perspective, this man did not achieve great success. He was not rich, lived in a small house, did not receive any national acclaim. All he did was change lives, and his impact will be felt for generations and, I believe, throughout eternity. His identity has shaped my life in meaningful and significant ways.

Think about your own contribution in life. What do you want to be remembered for? What will be your lasting legacy? Have you created a plan to achieve it? Consider the process of building a house. What would happen if the construction commenced without a detailed blueprint? It is almost ludicrous to imagine. Yet many live their lives in exactly that fashion. Indeed, some spend more time planning a two-week vacation than in planning the rest of their lives.

A choice movie, *Dead Poet's Society*, features a private school for boys in the northeastern United States. During their initial day at school, the wide-eyed and anxious boys proceed from one class to another, receiving the standard initiation speeches from each of their teachers. You watch their progression from class to class—first chemistry, then Latin, then trigonometry. Finally, they meet their new English teacher, Mr. Keating, played by Robin Williams. They discover that he is quite different from the other teachers, with a more unique and creative teaching style, as he pushes the boys to extend beyond their comfort zones to reach unexpected levels of understanding and appreciation. During their second day of class when they receive their textbook, Mr. Keating has one young man read the introductory essay to the literature text, which discusses a scientific and formulaic way of rating and understanding poetry. As the boy begins to read, it becomes clear to the class that Mr. Keating doesn't like the essay. He then stops the young reader and asks him to rip the introductory essay completely out of the textbook. It takes a minute for the boys to follow this advice, but soon pages are being torn from the book with enthusiasm. It's as if the essay's very presence alongside the works of Keats and Blake and Wordsworth and Shakespeare threatens the enjoyment and meaning and value the literature represents. As Mr. Keating says to his students, "In my class, you will learn to think for yourselves. . . . you will learn to savor words and language. No matter what anybody tells you, words and ideas can change the world." Mr. Keating then gathers his class together, and in hushed, dramatic tones, declares, "We don't read and write poetry because it is cute. We read and write poetry because we are members of the human race. And the human race is filled with passion. Medicine, law, business, engineering . . . these are noble pursuits, and necessary to sustain human life. But poetry, beauty, romance, love . . . these are what we stay alive for!" His final admonition is this: "The powerful play goes on and you may contribute a verse. What will your verse be?"[4]

What a wonderful and appropriate question for each of us to consider! What will our individual "verses" be; how will we make our contributions to the world?

Creating—or better said, discovering—your identity is a difficult but very powerful process. It will help bring clarity to the things you value and will help define how you spend your time and the contributions you will make. It will bring a greater sense of meaning to your work. I once read a statement that shocked me: "95% of Americans have never taken the time to think about goals or mission." In other words, we don't fully understand and carefully articulate our identity. Is this true for you? My guess is it is not. Hopefully you have spent a great deal of time thinking about goals and your ultimate contributions to the world. In either case, however, it is worth an investment of your time.

Take a minute and think about the following questions first posed by Charles Schultz, the creator of the Peanuts comic strip, and see what recollections it brings to you.

1. Name the five wealthiest people in the world.
2. Name the last five Heisman trophy winners.
3. Name the last five winners of the Miss America Pageant.
4. Name ten people who have won the Nobel or Pulitzer Prize.

5. Name the last half dozen Academy Award winners for best actor and actress.
6. Name the last decade's list of World Series winners.

How did you do?

The point is, none of us remember the headliners of yesterday. These are no second-rate achievers. They are the best in their fields. But the applause dies. Awards tarnish. Achievements are forgotten. Accolades and certificates are buried with their owners.

Here's another quiz. See how you do on this one:

1. List a few teachers who aided your journey through school.
2. Name three friends who have helped you through a difficult time.
3. Name five people who have taught you something worthwhile.
4. Think of a few people who have made you feel appreciated and special.
5. Think of five people you enjoy spending time with.

Easier?

Here's the lesson: The people who make a difference in your life are not the ones with the most credentials, the most money, or the most awards. They are the ones that care.[5]

Think about those who have made a difference to you. Was there a leader that helped change the trajectory of your life or the lives of others? Perhaps it was an influential teacher—someone who caused you to stretch your skills and think beyond your current mindset to future possibilities. Perhaps it was a friend or a coach or a church leader, a young men's or young women's leader, a bishop or mission president. It may have been a boss or colleague at work; maybe a parent, grandparent, aunt or uncle. Think about their leadership. What was it that was most meaningful? What did they do that caused you to want to follow them or take their advice? How would you describe their identity?

These leaders serve as terrific models to follow. Through them you have first-hand knowledge about what is effective and what is not. As they create this list, most people discover that those who have the greatest impact convey an almost tangible sense of love and concern and demonstrate an ability to paint a vision for you above what you can see yourself. Albert Schweitzer describes these people this way:

> In everyone's life, at some point, our inner fire goes out. It is then burst into flame by an encounter with another human being. We should all be thankful for those people who rekindle the inner spirit.[6]

When he was President of Brigham Young University, Elder Jeffrey R. Holland related an experience about a former colleague.

> For more than twenty-five years Ben E. Lewis was the executive vice-president of Brigham Young University. He is now retired. I recently asked him to do something very important for the university for which I wanted to give him a token of modest compensation. He refused the money. I argued with him and told him I was the president and he had to do what I said. He said he was retired and that he didn't have to do anything I said. I shoved the money at him and he shoved it back at me. We argued and then he told me this story.
>
> He said that following his undergraduate years at BYU (where he was a student body president, by the way) he had received an Alfred P. Sloan fellowship for graduate work at the University of Denver. As part of the Sloan fellowship, he and a handful of other students were regularly taken out into the Colorado business community to meet leaders and executives, and enjoy rather high-level exchange with them. One particular professor always took the group, and they spent many hours together.
>
> After each day's work with these business leaders, the professor would always stop somewhere for a beer with the students. Brother Lewis always ordered a soft drink. That led to a lot of conversation over many weeks, and the professor came to introduce

Ben everywhere they went—at every business, at every school, to every leader, and to every executive—this way: "This is Ben Lewis," he would say. "He's a Mormon and he doesn't drink beer." Everywhere and with everyone it was always the same— "This is Ben Lewis. He's a Mormon and he doesn't drink beer." Over the course of many months that phrase was repeated dozens and dozens and dozens of times. "This is Ben Lewis. He's a Mormon and he doesn't drink beer."

One day after a field trip to Fort Collins, the professor wheeled the group, up to a pit stop of some kind where, of course, he and the others ordered their beer. Except this time the professor ordered two beers. Ben asked him why. He said, "Because it's my birthday and you are going to have a beer with me." "No," Ben said, "I can't have a beer with you, but I do wish you a happy birthday."

"You will have a beer with me," his teacher said. "At least you must have one sip. It is very important to me, and I ask it of you this one time." And he put a dollar bill on the table. "Drink one sip of beer and that dollar is yours." Brother Lewis said he didn't want to give offense but, no, he would not be able to drink the beer, even for the dollar.

That conversation, with some increasing tension, escalated until the man had placed $50 on the counter. He was obviously intent on having Ben participate in this unusual birthday party, and he was in a position to do a student considerable academic harm if he were so inclined.

Brother Lewis wondered what to do. He did not want to offend a man who had been particularly kind to him. It was now a very awkward situation, and virtually everyone in the restaurant was aware of some difficulty over at their corner table. One sip would soothe the situation. Surely the Lord would know the integrity of his heart in this matter. Certainly, no permanent damage would be done. Furthermore, $50 in 1941 meant a lot to a working student who wasn't at all sure where his next meal was coming from.

> There, a long way from home, as he mulled over this difficult situation and wondered how to handle the problem, words so clear and loud spoken directly to his brain nearly startled him from the table. As audibly as I speak to you, Brother Lewis said he heard the words from an unseen source. "This is Ben Lewis. He's a Mormon, and he drinks beer."
>
> Then he said there in my office, "I didn't drink the beer, and I can't take the money. I'm a Mormon. This is Brigham Young University. I love it with all my heart. I have given my life to it. I want to give more. I can't take the money."[7]

This story isn't about BYU or drinking beer or the fact that he didn't take the money. The point of the story is that your decisions, your behaviors matter. They will one day determine what is written about your identity, and who—and what—you are known to be.

No one's life is perfectly aligned to their ideal. We all fall short every day in both our understanding of and actions toward our desired identity. In the process of understanding and clarifying who we are, how does one make necessary changes?

Jacob, Nephi's valiant and ever-faithful brother, had grown up in the midst of affliction. Little in his life seems to have been easy—he was born in the wilderness while his parents and siblings were fleeing from the comforts of their Jerusalem home. He never knew those comforts. Jacob was on the run from his first days. Whether it was sleeping in tents, hunting daily for food, witnessing the contention and near constant conflict in his family, Jacob's life was filled with hardship. Upon his arrival in the promised land, Jacob helped his aging father and mother establish a new civilization, only to see his oldest brothers plot and scheme against his parents and other family members. After establishing their first home in the new world, they had to uproot yet again, embark on a new journey to a new place, and start all over. After decades of hard labor, some warfare, and undoubtedly tireless and unrelenting efforts, the Nephites begin to establish roots, and, with the Lord's blessings, to grow and prosper.

Jacob labored diligently throughout his life to fulfill the expectations of his father and brother. He was a man of revelation, a man of action, and a man who felt his duty keenly. For him, a calling wasn't just something he had been assigned haphazardly. Rather, it was "an errand from the Lord," and anything short of fully magnifying that calling would bring the responsibility of his people's sins upon his own head. There was no equivocation about where Jacob stood. He was "all in," fully and completely, and this devotion defined his identity. (Jacob 1:19).

Enos, Jacob's son, didn't have the same experience as his father. He undoubtedly had his own hardships to address but had the benefit of his grandparent's (Sariah and Lehi), his parent's, and his aunts' and uncles' examples of goodness juxtaposed against Laman's and Lemuel's approach. One could assume, just based on his heritage, that Enos had very significant expectations placed on his shoulders. He needed to know who he was and where he stood. But he didn't. He had, however, been taught and nurtured by his father, learning of the Lord's admonitions to repent and be clean. And while he didn't initially have his father's surety of testimony, his desire to know and his sincere faith burned within him. Enos' hunting excursion soon turned into a day of deep supplication. Answers to his fervent prayers didn't come immediately or with simply a token effort. It took hours. And when these hours stretched past daylight, that day of prayer turned into a night of crying unto the Lord for repentance, a prayer that was answered in remarkable fashion and his sins were forgiven.

We admire Enos for his intentional efforts to know of God's love, to know through his own experience with the Lord the power of the atonement. We love the fact that Jacob, his father, would teach Enos so well and so thoroughly, Enos would know how to approach the Lord. We admire the price Enos was willing to pay to learn and establish his own testimony and sense of identity. After his sins are forgiven, he asks the Lord a most poignant question: "Lord, how is it done?" (v.7)

What a powerful question! How does the miracle of repentance and forgiveness occur? How does one receive assurances from the Lord about where we stand with him and how we can come unto him, about who we really are and of the Lord's intentions for us? The Lord's response to Enos' question is intended for each of us as well: "Because of thy faith in Christ, whom thou hast never before heard nor seen" (Enos 1:8).

The lessons from Enos' yearning for more—his desire to understand his place and standing with God and his desperate, prolonged prayer—affirm there is a way prepared for each of us to grow, to develop, to become clean, and to lead, even if we haven't yet seen Him or heard His voice. He is there, and we must seek him earnestly. With him and through him, we learn our true identity and clarify our purpose.

King Benjamin reinforces this important concept. He calls his people together for a coronation event. He is anointing his son, Mosiah, as the new king—a process that will provide Mosiah with a new name—a new identity. And just as Mosiah receives a crown and new identity, King Benjamin provides the path for us, too, to receive a crown and new identity as Mosiah's coronation event becomes our own coronation event, outlining a covenant path—as daughters and sons of loving Heavenly parents—to becoming heirs and joint heirs with Christ (see Romans 8:16–17). King Benjamin declares:

> And now, because of the covenant which ye have made ye shall be called the children of Christ, his sons, and his daughters; for behold, this day he hath spiritually begotten you; for ye say that your hearts are changed through faith on his name; therefore, ye are born of him and have become his sons and his daughters.
>
> And I would that ye should remember also, that this is the name that I said I should give unto you that never should be blotted out, except it be through transgression; therefore, take heed that ye do not transgress, that the name be not blotted out of your hearts.
>
> I say unto you, I would that ye should remember to retain the name written always in your hearts, that ye are not found on the left hand of God, but that ye hear and know the voice by which ye shall be called, and also, the name by which he shall call you. (Mosiah 5:7, 11–12)

As part of our true identities, we covenant to follow Him, to love and serve as He does, and to make His name our name, in both word and action—a covenant we renew each week. Through His grace and love, we become His. That is who we really are. That is our identity.

Some things to consider doing:

1. Jot down some ideas regarding these questions:
   - What do I want to have in this life (physical possessions)?
   - What do I want to do (accomplishments, travel, etc.)?
   - What do I want to be (attributes of character)?

2. Choose a scripture, quote or story that represents what you'd like your identity to be.

3. Discuss with a loved one—if someone was writing a book of scripture about you, what would the description of your life be?

4. In what ways are you falling short today?

5. How does your weekly experience with the sacrament, with a renewed commitment to take upon you Christ's name, influence what you do each week? What steps might you consider taking to better represent the identity you are striving for?

6. Summarize your thoughts in a written personal constitution or personal mission statement.

CHAPTER SIX

OFFER YOUR WHOLE SOUL

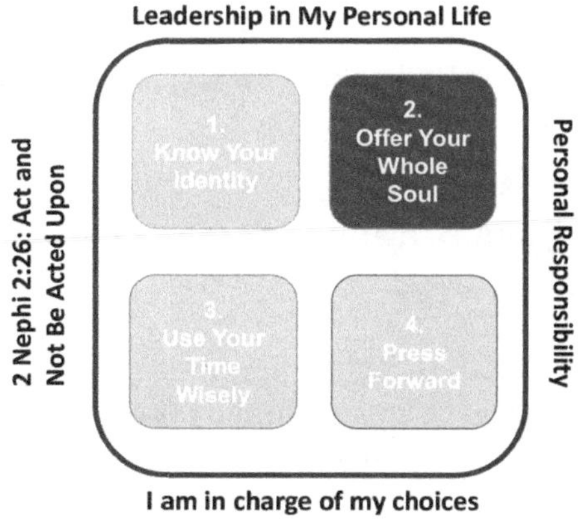

And now behold, I say unto you, my brethren, if ye have experienced a change of heart, and if ye have felt to sing the song of redeeming love, I would ask, can ye feel so now?

—Alma 5:26

I believe in Christianity as I believe that the Sun has risen, not only because I see it but because by it, I see everything else.

—C. S. Lewis[1]

Reformation of the world begins with reformation of self. We cannot hope to influence others in the direction of moral virtue unless we live lives of virtue. The example of our virtuous living will carry a greater influence than will all the preaching, postulating, and theorizing in which we might indulge. We cannot expect to lift others unless we are standing on higher ground.

—Gordon B. Hinkley[2]

Readers of the Book of Mormon gain a deep appreciation for Lehi, Sariah, Nephi, Sam, Jacob, and their families. Nephi's record, which he wrote under commandment from the Lord (2 Nephi 5:30) and which Mormon included as part of his compilation of a thousand years of religious history because they, the records, were "choice unto" him, and for a "wise purpose" known to the Lord (Words of Mormon 1:6–7), provides detail about their journeying and arrival in the promised land, their preaching and admonitions. Though shorter in length, the words of the Nephite prophets following Lehi's, Nephi's and Jacob's inspired council are also included in Mormon's record and contain important and "choice" leadership instruction as the baton of leadership is passed from leader to leader for nearly 290 years, including guidance from Jarom, Omni, Amaron, Chemish, Abinadon, Amaleki, and Benjamin. Here's a highlight of their leadership instruction:

- Leaders are mighty in their faith in the Lord, leading to the safety and protection of their people (Jarom 1:7).

- Leaders labor tirelessly, Jarom writes, exhorting with all long-suffering the people to diligence (Jarom 1:11).

- Leaders teach and persuade their people to look to the Messiah (Jarom 1:11).

- Leaders, as Amaleki taught, harken to the voice of the Lord (Omni 1:12).

- Leaders admonish continuously, leading their people through uncertain times (Omni 1:13).

- Leaders possess unique gifts and use their gifts to bless their people (Omni 1:18–20).

- Leaders are just and encourage others to believe in that which is good (Omni 1:25).

- Leaders fight (work) alongside their people, engaged shoulder to shoulder in the work (Words of Mormon 1:13).

- Leaders invite others to come unto Christ. In doing so, they offer their whole souls as an offering to Christ and encourage others to do the same (Omni 1:26). They are fully engaged, give their best, and don't hold anything back.

- Leaders labor with all the might of their whole soul (Words of Mormon 1:18).

- Leaders establish peace (Words of Mormon 1:18).

- Leaders allow the Lord to work His will through them (Words of Mormon 1:7).

Two hundred and seventy years of leadership condenses down to these important and impactful lessons: Leaders are mighty in their faith, they labor diligently, exhort their people with long-suffering and patience, and invite and admonish their people continuously to harken to the voice of the Lord. They use their gifts to lift and teach. They provide constant encouragement and engage synergistically with their people. Their focus is on what the Lord wants—it is His will, not theirs, that drives their efforts. These leaders maintain a focus on Christ and teach the importance of His central prominence in our lives.

One leadership attribute stands out as a critical and salient lesson for today's leaders: in the midst of all our competing priorities and modern challenges, leaders today—you and I—are invited to offer our whole souls to the Lord. The Lord asks us to give our finest efforts, to become fully consecrated, regardless of what role we play or position we hold. We are asked to be willing to set aside individual agendas and to embrace the Lord's love and expectation. We are asked to make His work our work—with all we have, regardless of our title or position.

Think about what this means for you—to let the Lord do His work through you as you serve Him with your whole soul.

One of the covenants we make each week is simple to say and so difficult to achieve. It is to be willing to "take upon them the name of thy Son" (Moroni 4:3, D&C 20:77). That's a steep climb, an effort not for the faint of heart. When we take upon ourselves the name of Jesus Christ, it means that what we do and what we say is in accordance with what He would do and what He would say. It means, in part, that we offer our whole souls to Him. It means we become His disciples.

As we are out and about in society, going to work, to the store, traveling, engaging in business, teaching and working with our families, are we modeling the behavior of a disciple of Jesus Christ? Would others view what we do and hear what we say and immediately come to the easy conclusion that, "That person must have taken upon themselves the name of Jesus Christ, because their conduct models His." Or would they say something different?

At a Brigham Young University commencement address in April 2019, Arthur C. Brooks, best-selling author, social scientist, and president of the American Enterprise Institute, shared that while lecturing at BYU several years earlier, he received a briefcase as a gift from university administrators. This was a special briefcase with the BYU logo prominently displayed on its front. Dr. Brooks, though appreciative of the gift, remarked that he felt a little "weird" walking around carrying it. He said, "I am not a member of the faculty at BYU, nor am I a member of The Church of Jesus Christ of Latter-day Saints. I am a Catholic. It felt like false advertising." He shared his feeling with his wife, Esther, who replied, "That is ridiculous. Use the briefcase. It is beautiful."

Dr. Brooks then related the following:

> So I loaded it up and took it out on the road. I travel all the time. I am in airports constantly. And here is the thing. I noticed that people would look at my briefcase and then look up at me. I found that it was changing my behavior. I was acting with greater love and kindness than I ordinarily would. People would look at my briefcase, and I would want to help with their luggage. I would want to give up my place in line. That sort of thing. Why? Because I was unconsciously trying to live up to the high standards of

> kindness of your church and your university. At the very least, I was trying not to hurt your well-earned reputation.
>
> You know what else? I even stopped carrying cups of coffee. Look, I love coffee, but I didn't want people to think that a member of your church is a hypocrite! I had this paranoid fantasy of some guy telling his wife, "I saw this Mormon guy in O'Hare airport ordering a venti latte at Starbucks. I knew they were hypocrites." I didn't want that.
>
> And you know what? That briefcase made me a happier person, a more loving person. I was like the person I wanted to be. Why? Because I was trying to be like you. So what is the lesson here? It is not that your BYU briefcases have magic properties. It is that your greatest witness to the world as members of this community is the conduct of your lives. Our nation and world need this. They need you, more than ever today.[3]

Indeed, the world needs disciples of Jesus Christ—men and women, mothers and fathers, children, grandchildren, nieces, nephews, ministers, relief society presidents and the newest members of the teachers quorum—who choose to follow the Savior, who choose to lead with their whole souls—at all times and in all places, and who carry His name in all circumstances and in any condition. The world needs those who are willing to mourn with those who mourn, who will provide comfort to those in need of comfort, those who courageously stand as a witness of God—in word, in thought, and in action (see Mosiah 18: 8–9).

In 1838, while serving as the president of the Quorum of the Twelve Apostles, Thomas B. Marsh lived in Far West, Missouri with his wife Elizabeth.

Sister Marsh and her neighbor, Sister Lucinda Harris, the wife of George W. Harris, decided to exchange milk so they could each make a larger cheese than they otherwise could on their own. They agreed to send each other both the milk and the cream from their cows. But Sister Marsh saved a pint of cream from each cow and sent Sister Harris the milk without the cream. A quarrel arose, and the matter was referred first to the teachers quorum, then to the bishop. When he determined that Sister Marsh had violated her agreement, she and her husband were upset and appealed the matter to the high council and then finally to the First Presidency. Each council approved the original decision that Sister Marsh had been in error.

Thomas B. Marsh declared that he would sustain the character of his wife. Soon afterward, he turned against the Church and went before a government official to declare that the Latter-day Saints were hostile toward the state of Missouri.[4]

President Gordon B. Hinckley said of this incident: "What a very small and trivial thing—a little cream over which two women quarreled. But it led to, or at least was a factor in, Governor Boggs' cruel exterminating order which drove the Saints from the state of Missouri, with all of the terrible suffering and consequent death that followed. The man who should have settled this little quarrel, but who, rather, pursued it, . . . lost his standing in the Church. He lost his testimony of the gospel."[5]

After nineteen years of darkness and bitterness, Thomas B. Marsh painfully made his way to the Salt Lake Valley and asked Brigham Young to forgive him and permit his rebaptism into the Church. He wrote to Heber C. Kimball, First Counselor in the First Presidency: "I began to awake to a sense of my situation . . . I know that I have sinned against Heaven and in thy sight." He then described the lesson he had learned: "The Lord could get along very well without me and He has lost nothing by my falling out of the ranks; But O what have I lost?! Riches, greater riches than all this world or many planets like this could afford."[6]

I have a tender spot in my heart for Thomas B. Marsh. I was not there to appreciate the full context of his disaffection from the Church, and it's easy to judge another with the benefit of a broader perspective. One can easily isolate a single action and boil it down to a simple morality tale. Reality is generally more complicated than just one incident. Proximity to and between leaders at the time was difficult. Resentment and frustration understandably grew when communication became difficult, with face-to-face reconciliation nearly impossible. The tragic and sudden loss of his fourteen-year-old son dealt a painful blow. Thomas B. Marsh loved his wife, and the issue with the milk and cream was only one of the challenges with which he dealt. He had given much to the Church, felt misunderstood, and allowed these feelings to fester into actions that caused great pain to others—actions he deeply regretted later.

Nevertheless, the consequences of his resentment were far reaching, severely impacting the lives of the Saints in Missouri and, ultimately, his and his family's standing in the Church.

Elder Jeffrey R. Holland has declared, "It is easy to be righteous when things are calm, and life is good, and everything is smooth. The test is when there is real trial or temptation, when there is pressure and fatigue, anger and fear, or the possibility of real transgression. Can we be faithful then? Such integrity is, of course, the majesty of 'Father, forgive them, for they know not what they do,' right when forgiving and understanding and being generous about your crucifiers is the last thing that anyone less perfect than the Savior of the world would want to do. But we have to try. We have to wish to be strong, whatever the situation or the provocation or the problem, no true disciple of Christ can check his religion at the door."[7]

Several years ago, my wife, two small children and I were living in the Washington D.C. area. The first summer we lived there we were privileged to experience the hottest summer on record for the area. Ninety percent humidity combined with day after day of triple-digit heat was nearly unbearable, and, in fact, hundreds of people died. That summer was followed by what was called the storm of the century. We woke up one morning to two feet of snow. The next day, it snowed another two feet. The snow stopped everything in its tracks, both literally and figuratively. It was so deep people couldn't get out of their driveways. Roads remained clogged with the accumulated snow for days. Emergency vehicles were not able to function, and there was a statewide call for four-wheel drives to assist the hospitals. Trucking and distribution companies were among those services affected, as they were not able to re-supply grocery stores, even if people were able to get to the stores.

We had two small boys at the time who needed milk. Fathers and mothers are supposed to take care of their children, and we had not fully prepared to have what we needed at home. That brought an interesting and unsettling feeling for me. Needing to take care of my kids, I pulled on my boots and slogged my way, on foot, to the grocery store, but, alas, the shelves were completely bare. At that time, the Southern states did not have the infrastructure or equipment to deal with even small amounts of snow, so at the first hint of bad winter weather, people rushed to the grocery store and decimated the supplies of milk, bread, and toilet paper. By the time I arrived at the store there was nothing left to purchase. Literally, it looked like a war zone, with empty shelves and evidence of mass panic. A little despondent, I made the snowy trek—on foot again—back to our home empty-handed, worried about what we were going to do for our small children.

Later that evening, about 10:30 p.m., we received an unexpected knock on our door. It was Shandra Hervey from our ward. She lived several miles away, but there she stood, with three-quarters of a gallon of milk. Shandra and her husband had several children, and he was out of work. But there she was, on that cold, dark, snowy night, with a smile on her face and a nearly full jug of milk in her hand. She said she felt impressed that we could probably use the milk, so she had braved the treacherous weather and had taken from her own supplies to serve us.

She was not in a formal leadership role in our ward. Nor was she my wife's visiting teacher, and her husband was not our home teacher. In fact, we hadn't really gotten to know her very well. She did it because she was open to the promptings of the Spirit, because she lived her life in a way that made her eligible for and open to inspiration, and because she had developed as part of her nature the desire and habit of serving others. In other words, she was filled with His love, offered her whole soul to the Lord, and lived and served accordingly.

Everything in the gospel can be considered in three phases: do we know it, do we do it, and has it become part of our character. That, I believe, is how Jesus is telling us to lead, regardless of who we are or where we serve. That is what it means to offer your whole soul to the Lord as an offering.

Some things to consider:

1. Trust in the commandments and follow them with a loving heart.

2. Participate fully in the organization of the Church. Develop a love for your ward community. Make that a priority.

3. Pray daily for inspiration on who could benefit from your service. Then act on the promptings you receive, no matter how subtle these prompting feel.

4. See others around you as children of God and treat them accordingly.

CHAPTER SEVEN
USE YOUR TIME INTENTIONALLY

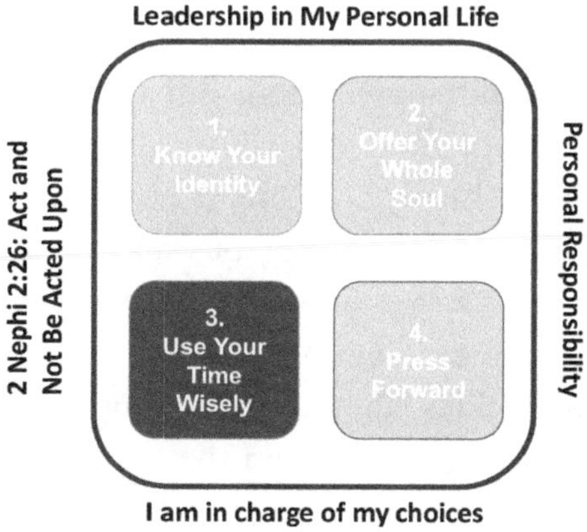

Commit thy works unto the Lord, and thy thoughts shall be established.

—Proverbs 16:3

Everyone who has taken a shower has an idea. It's the person who gets out of the shower, dries off, and does something about it who makes a difference.

—Nolan Bushnell[1]

The Israelites began their Egyptian occupation with Pharaoh's blessings and support. After Joseph's inspired interpretation of Pharaoh's dream, he was appointed by Pharaoh to be in a position of authority in Egypt, second only to Pharaoh himself. Joseph then embarked on a seven-year preparation for the devastating famine envisioned in Pharaoh's dream. At thirty years old, Joseph travelled throughout the land preparing, organizing and gathering food for their coming times of destitution. After seven years of Joseph's leadership on this assignment, Egypt was so prepared, their abundant resources were described as vast as the "sand of sea" and "without number" (Genesis 41:49) and became the catalyst for saving not just Egypt, but surrounding nations as well.

Pharaoh, obviously, was vindicated in his choice of the young Joseph to be second in command of all of Egypt. He loved Joseph and was pleased when Joseph's family came to dwell there. At Pharaoh's invitation and welcoming, Joseph's family was invited to receive all of Egypt's bounty and to "eat of the fat of the land" (Genesis 45:18).

Thus began a new era for the Israelite nation in Egypt, one that initiated in goodwill and appreciation. But that goodwill was not to last. Joseph's Pharaoh died, as did those who followed. Eventually, there arose one who "knew not Joseph" (Exodus 1:8) and as the Israelites became increasingly prosperous and productive, they also came to be perceived as a significant threat to the Egyptians. So, the painful era of Egyptian bondage and slavery followed. For over four hundred years the Israelites labored under whip and lash, waiting for a promised deliverer to free them from their yoke of bondage.

Eventually Moses was called to be that deliverer. Having been miraculously preserved by the Lord to be raised in the hearth of Pharaoh, Moses' firsthand witness of the Egyptian's oppression of the Israelites prompted him to action. And though initially reluctant, as it seems many of God's prophets were as they began their ministry, with Aaron by his side, Moses assumed the mantel and got to work.

Consider for a moment all that Moses had to do. He had traded a life of leisure and prominence with Pharaoh for a life of desert-dwelling and wandering. His work was not easy. Resentment and extreme resistance on the part of the Egyptians and the hardness of their hearts was to be expected. The back and forth with the plagues would have been exhausting—frogs, lice, flies, boils, hail and fire, the death of cattle, locusts, darkness, and eventually the loss of their first-born sons. There certainly were endless tasks on Moses' and Aaron's to-do lists in order to go through all that was required to deliver an estimated 2.4 million Israelites from bondage. But as daunting as that was, the constant and seemingly unrelenting murmuring by the Israelites throughout their forty years of wandering must have been more than anyone could have anticipated. One wonders if Moses, in a quiet moment of reflection, might have uttered some discouraging words at least once about how he had found himself in this predicament.

Imagine you were called to lead so many people into an uncertain destination. Exodus provides a count of "about six hundred thousand men on foot," then includes this phrase: "besides women and children." The 600 hundred thousand would have represented the able-bodied military-aged men and doesn't provide a count as to the total population. The numbers were large, and the task represented a massive undertaking (Exodus 12:37). Shortly after you escape the boundaries of Goshen, the heart of Pharaoh hardens once again and he marshals an army, filled with horses and chariots, to pursue and overtake you. That is the predicament the Israelites faced, who cried to Moses, "It would have been better for us to serve the Egyptians, than that we should die in the wilderness" (Exodus 14:12).

Sometimes as leaders we feel we have done everything we have been asked to do. We have responded to the call, we have sacrificed personal time and luxuries, we've worked diligently to manage our time (as best we can) and have placed the priorities of those we serve over our own. We have participated in meetings where we planned every detail. We have prayed and fasted and prayed again that we would be successful in our endeavors, with the firm faith that these endeavors are in accordance with what the Lord would have us do. We have a schedule with demands on our time that seems impossible to accomplish. There is only so much one person can do. And then, with our backs to the proverbial Red Sea, we look back and see Pharaoh and his armies bearing down on us with intent to destroy everything we have done or stand for. Success is out of our hands, and failure, despite everything we have done or planned for, is eminent. We simply cannot do all that is asked of us with the time we have.

Except that the Lord is in change. "Be still, and know that I am God," he commands (Psalms 46:10), and later comforts us, "Be thou humble, and the Lord thy God shall lead thee by the hand, and give thee answers to thy prayers" (D&C 112:10). God knows the pressures we face, the constraints we feel regarding our time and talents, and when we feel our backs are against the "Red Sea," with everything we've worked toward crumbling before our eyes, He will deliver, and the sea will part.

For much of my career I have studied and taught principles of time management. There are many wonderful models and approaches—some more theoretical and others very tactical. All of them, however, can benefit from an overarching mindset, that of focusing on the things that really matter. As German writer and statesman Johann Wolfgang von Goethe famously said, "Things which matter most must never be at the mercy of things which matter least."[2]

In an address given at BYU Women's Conference in May 2018, Michelle Craig shared this family vignette:

> It was a great day.
>
> You know, the first time you feel confident enough to leave home without hiring a babysitter, certain that your oldest child can hold down the fort? It was such a day for my brother and his wife. As the kids were soundly sleeping in their beds, the happy parents couldn't pass up this rare opportunity for a date night out. After writing detailed instructions, they went to a nearby movie theater, leaving 11-year-old McKay in charge.
>
> Imagine their panic when they returned home a few hours later and saw and smelled the smoke of an electrical fire. They panicked, raced around the house checking on all the sleeping children, and then confronted McKay, who, unalarmed, was reading on the couch.
>
> "Hey!" my brother yelled, "What's going on? Don't you smell that?"
>
> "Sure," McKay casually replied, "I do. I looked around and didn't see anything. And you know, it was kind of irritating at first, but you get used to it."
>
> In things that really matter, McKay was right. We can become casual in our response to warning signs. In addition, if we don't spend time doing what it takes to work on things of eternal consequence, we can get used to running around in a panic, putting out one fire after another, and the result can be devastating.[3]

Why is it that some seem to accomplish so much more than others? Do they have more time? Actually, each of us has exactly the same amount of time every week—168 hours, no more, and no less. It comes down to how we spend that time that makes all the difference. C. S. Lewis wrote: "The future is something which everyone reaches at the rate of sixty minutes an hour, whatever he does, whoever he is."[4] As you consider how you focus your time, ask yourself these questions:

1. What is one activity that, if done extremely well, would have a significant, positive impact on your professional, school life or in your calling?

2. What is one activity that if done with excellence would have a significant, positive impact for good on a key relationship with a friend or family member?

3. What is one thing, that if done superbly well would make a profound difference for good in your personal life?

Think deeply about those questions. Likely you will find that the answers are not complicated—in fact, you'll probably find the answers are rather simple. They represent the truly important things that should and could be done. With those questions in mind, here's one follow-up question that might be a bit uncomfortable for some (it is for me): If these things have such importance, why are we not doing them regularly and routinely?

Too often the answer to that question is: we're busy. We've got so much always going on, we get overloaded and focus only on what's in front of us instead of what really matters. Or we're so completely exhausted that we sit and vegetate on our favorite streaming service for hours because we don't have the strength or energy to do anything else.

Here's another quote from Goethe: "Plunge boldly into the thick of life, and seize it where you will."[5] I love the notion of "the thick of life." For me, that is what it means to live intentionally, to live by the principle of prioritization—that your ultimate success depends on your ability to align your behaviors with your highest values. It is the habit of "organizing ourselves and preparing every needful thing" (D&C 88:119), then "going and doing" those needful things (1 Nephi 3:7).

So much of my thinking on this subject has been influenced by remarkable thought leaders like Stephen R. Covey, Hyrum W. Smith and A. Roger Merrill, with whom I worked for many years. If you've been involved in any corporate training on the topic of time management or organization, you've likely been exposed to some of the ideas and tactics addressed here. Regardless, I recommend a thorough study of the following helpful resources: *The 7 Habits of Highly Effective People, First Things First, What Matters Most,* and *5 Choices to Extraordinary Productivity.* This chapter doesn't capture the detail of these books, but the fundamental paradigm for each is represented in the following example:

A consultant, standing before a group of corporate leaders, took from a box under the podium several large rocks, each between the size of a baseball and a softball. Each rock represented a key activity or priority in the lives of the executives. For example, one rock was labeled "important project." Another was "key relationship," and another was "preparation for an important meeting." There were seven or eight rocks in all. The consultant then put these large rocks into a glass jar. She said, "This jar represents all the time you have in one week." The executives were impressed with how much she was able to fit into the jar. The consultant then asked, "Is the jar full?" They replied that it was. The consultant then took out two large handfuls of pea-gravel. Surprisingly, after shifting the jar just a bit, all the pea-gravel fit into the jar with all the large rocks. She asked the group again, "Is the jar full?" The class replied: yes; in fact, now the jar was full. The consultant then took out two large scoops of sand and poured them into the jar. Again, after just a bit of sifting, all the sand fit among the rocks and gravel. At this point, the participants were not surprised when the consultant took a picture of water and poured two cups into the jar. "Now the jar is full," she said. Then she asked this key question: "If I had started with the gravel, sand, and water, how many of the big rocks would I have been able to put into the jar?" The answer: very few.

Our lives are a lot like that jar. If we can identify our priorities and first plan the "large rocks" of our lives, we will be amazed at what we can accomplish. But if we go about our lives with a "whatever happens" attitude, very little of what is truly important will happen. The minutiae of our daily activities (the water, sand, and gravel) will consume us. One young woman from Fiji wrote me, "I am involved in so many activities I have trouble balancing all the different aspects of my life." Perhaps you have felt that same way.

All of us have activities that require immediate attention—the legitimate emergencies and urgencies of life. For example, you might have a test tomorrow, or a friend or family member is injured. You might have a health issue that requires you to address it now. Perhaps there is a project due at work. These are the activities that clearly need to be done, and immediately. Their accomplishment is crucial to you personally.

At the same time, each of us have activities that don't have a burning fuse, but nevertheless are important. These could include relationship building, planning, preparation, completing school and other assignments on time, quiet time, exercising, and relaxing and recharging our personal batteries. These are the activities that provide renewal and, if left undone will create more emergencies in our lives. For example, if you never take the time to service your car, you will eventually find yourself in a crisis. Flossing your teeth is seldom a pressing issue, but failure over the long run to adequately care for your teeth will result in an unpleasant situation in a dentist's chair. Relationships are the same way. They are usually not urgent, but if constantly neglected, they will ultimately manifest themselves in pressing ways. Alexander Graham Bell put it this way: "Before anything else, preparation is the key to success."[6]

Then we have activities that press upon us but, on close inspection, are just not important. In fact, I suspect we all have a lot of these. They may be important to others but have little to no significance to us personally. Yet we often find ourselves submerged in these activities. They are right before us and are generally popular in nature. These activities masquerade as important because they are pressing, not because they are really essential, and can include things such as interruptions, some phone calls, constant social media (all the notifications we simply must respond or react to immediately), other people's priorities, and peer pressure. These activities are the real time bandits—they steal our focus and energy away from that which really does matter.

It is possible to take relaxation and play too far, and when we do, we are deep in slacker mode—too much binging on our favorite streaming service, too many hours playing video games, mindlessly surfing the internet, endless social media and other timewasters. And some day, we'll be asked to account for our use of this time.

Regarding these various activities, a friend shared this same point, using slightly different language:

> To prioritize and make the time for all my varied goals, I feel it is important to mentally categorize things into "essential," "important," "good," and "worthless" categories. Never fail to accomplish the "essentials" first, and only then move onto "important" then "good," then make sure I don't even bother with the "worthless."

So how can I become more deliberate in how I manage my time? In my experience, the key to effective time management comes down to this easy to say and difficult to do practice: say "no" to those things in your life that are of no consequence, no matter how unpopular it may feel at the time. Some things may drop. Some details may go overlooked. But if they are of no consequence, does it matter?

Here are three simple steps to living more purposely and deliberately:

1. Set aside time once a week to review what you have identified in Chapter 5: Discovering your identity. Give thoughtful time each week pondering and reflecting on who you are, what roles you are playing, and the important people in your life. Consider your family, key relationships, your callings, and other priorities. Sunday is a great time to do this. I recommend taking no less than twenty minutes—but twenty minutes one time each week is a very small price to pay for what will result.

2. Identify one or two priorities with important people and/or critical activities that align with your priorities from step one and include them in your plan for the week. Do this before

you allow all the regular minutiae to overwhelm your schedule and you will be surprised at how focused on important matters you'll become. These represent the "big rocks" in our lives.

3. Then plug everything else into your week. This will be all the to-do's, meetings, appointments, etc. that are part of living and managing your life.

4. Take five minutes at the end of each day to review what you have accomplished and review the next day's activities, based on priority.

That's it. There are lots of other things one can do to organize their time, but this provides the foundation to effectively leading your life. It doesn't take much time to execute this, but it does take some thought and a little discipline. You will find your effectiveness greatly enhanced if you use a formal planning system. Don't just try to remember everything—invest in a planner or PDA and use it. If you are inclined toward technology, great. If not, find system where you can write down your commitments. You will find exponential improvements in effectiveness if you write your plan down in one place, not scattered over a hundred different "post-it" notes or other various scraps of paper.

Again, this planning process will take about twenty minutes each week, and then another five minutes each day. But you will quickly realize the leveraged nature of this time. It will literally pull you out of activities that have little to no significance and will focus your efforts on the things that really matter. Your fulfillment in life will increase, the nature of your work will improve, and your relationships will be richer. It really is amazing what this simple planning process will do.

I work hard to follow this process in my own life. And I am far from perfect. I have found, however, that when I miss this planning activity, my life seems jumbled. I feel out of focus and out of touch. My stress and anxiety levels increase while my physical and mental energy wanes. And my relationships suffer. Conversely, when I invest just a little time and deliberate thought about who I am (a child of God), about what He wants me to accomplish, about my goals, about the important people in my life and how I might be able to bless or assist them, and then organize my time accordingly, I feel a greater sense of clarity and confidence, and my relationships with others (and especially with my Heavenly Father) feel more connected and vibrant.

A few years ago, as I was engaged in this process, I was thinking about my relationship with my youngest son, Matthew, who was thirteen-year-old at the time. Our relationship was good, but I was a busy dad and he was thirteen (truthfully, I was not much more than a nuisance to him and to me, he was someone who didn't want to clean his room). I had an upcoming business trip to New York City about three weeks in the future, so in consideration of where we were in our relationship and in an attempt to improve upon it, I asked if he wanted to accompany me—hit the Big Apple—just the two of us. It was in the fall and school was in session, so I wasn't sure if it would work with his schedule, but when he learned he could skip a couple of class days, he enthusiastically agreed to come, even if it meant hanging out with his dad. For three weeks we reviewed and planned different activities to do together. I let him finalize the details, with only one requirement: we were going to see a Broadway musical. For most, that would be considered a highlight of the trip, but he was a thirteen-year-old boy, and his interests were definitely elsewhere. Still, I persevered, but committed to him, "You get to pick the show."

We had a great time. We did all the things a thirteen-year-old might like—top of the Rockefeller Center, the Empire State Building, Times Square, great food, etc. But we still had to see the required play. Reluctantly, he accompanied me to the ticket booth. There were many good options—and I would have been excited to see any of them except one: the musical version of Rocky. And of course, that was the only one he would consider. I tried to dissuade him, to which he replied, "Dad, you promised me I would get to pick." Ugh. "How was it even possible that Rocky was an option?" I thought to myself. "When did they create a musical of that?" But he was right—I had promised that he could select the show. Now I was the reluctant one, but a deal was a deal, and I purchased the tickets.

It turns out the play was pretty fantastic. All the expected characters were there—Rocky, Mick, Apollo, Adrian. Rocky drank five raw eggs right in front of us. It was awesome. Our seats were in the right-side orchestra section, and for the final fight scene, they invited all those sitting in the center section to go on stage and sit on prepared risers while a full-sized boxing ring descended from the ceiling to the middle section. Matt and I found ourselves with ring-side seats. The final scene had Rocky and Apollo singing while swinging punches, fake blood was flying everywhere, and at the final bell with Rocky still standing against the undefeated and heretofore unchallenged heavyweight champion of the world, all of us in the theater—with Matt and I leading the way—stood on our feet and cheered.

We've done a lot of things together over the years, but that evening remains one of our most cherished moments. And I have thought often at how easy it would have been for that to not have happened. Life is busy. There is always so much to do. The demands on our time are often extreme and feel overwhelming. And if we're not careful, we'll miss something very important.

Matt has grown up since then. He's married to a wonderful girl and they are starting their lives together. Some day in the not-too-distant future, he'll have his own thirteen-year-old son or daughter, and he'll have this memory to draw upon.

President Thomas S. Monson taught: "We become so caught up in the busyness of our lives. Were we to step back, however, and take a good look at what we're doing, we may find that we have immersed ourselves in the 'thick of thin things.' In other words, too often we spend most of our time taking care of the things which do not really matter much at all in the grand scheme of things, neglecting those more important causes."[7]

One final thought on this subject: As Lehi, Sariah and their party were traveling in the wilderness, they awoke one morning to see a "ball of curious workmanship" outside their tent (1 Nephi 16:10). It was a compass, which, when they were faithful, guided them in "a straight course to the promised land" (Alma 37:44). Interestingly, they didn't receive a divinely crafted watch that told precise time, ensuring they accomplished everything exactly at the right moment. Instead, it provided the directional course they were intended to follow. So it is with us. As Alma taught his son, "For just as surely as this director did bring our fathers, by following its course, to the promised land, shall the words of Christ, if we follow their course, carry us beyond this vale of sorrow into a far better land of promise" (Alma 37:45). Sometimes time management is more about direction than a minute-by-minute schedule.

Remember, the Lord has a plan for you. You need to understand His will and be in concert with that. But how do you do it when you have so much to do and competing priorities—a daughter in need, work pressures and deadlines, financial challenges, and demands in your calling? When you turn your life over the to the Lord, you need to understand that He understands your needs and your priorities and issues—in all areas of your life. When you have absolute needs in multiple areas, appeal to the Lord. He knows what lies ahead and will direct your efforts and use of time.

When we feel the weight of the world pressing upon us, and we don't know how we'll get it all done, we have to do as the pioneers taught us: get up in the morning, load our handcarts, and head to Zion. We start with what we can do—what's most important. Then do the next thing, and then the next. And as long as we're heading in the right direction, at some point, the Lord parts the Red Sea. Sometimes managing all we have to do as leaders, with the limited time we have and mounting pressures to succeed, requires faith that, regardless of the unknown, despite the barriers, despite the unrelenting demands we feel on our lives every day, we will be delivered.

Some things to consider doing:

1. Carve out twenty minutes at the beginning of this coming week. Carefully and prayerfully ponder your identity, your goals, your patriarchal blessing.

2. Identify a few key activities you want to do this coming week. This will likely tie to some longer-term goals. These activities might help you complete a goal, or they might simply move you toward the goal's completion.

3. Plan those activities into your schedule—first, before anything else gets in the way.

4. Plan the remainder of your week.

5. Take a few minutes at the end of each day to review your success and set the coming day's schedule and priorities.

6. Rinse and repeat.

CHAPTER EIGHT
PRESS FORWARD

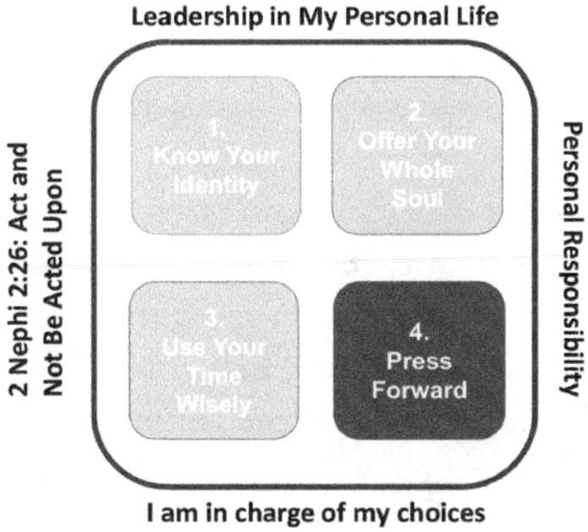

This one thing I do, forgetting those things which are behind, and reaching forth unto those things which are before. I press toward the mark for the prize of the high calling of God in Christ Jesus.

—Philippians 3:13–14

God doesn't care nearly as much about where you have been as he does about where you are and, with His help, where you are willing to go.

—Elder Jeffrey R. Holland[1]

We will not be asked to "run faster than we have strength" (Mosiah 4:27), but in our leadership responsibilities (at all levels), we will be asked to run, and we will be pushed to the limit in doing so. I take great comfort in Peter's example, when, as the Lord's disciples were on the Sea of Galilee one tempestuous evening, they witnessed Jesus walking on water toward their boat. Some of the disciples were fearful and wondered aloud if they were witnessing a spirit.

Peter, however, recognized the Savior, and fueled by his growing faith in the Lord, requested permission to join Jesus and walk on water. His initial effort was successful. But then the boisterous wind incited doubt and insecurity within him, and with fear overtaking him, he began to sink.

We might be tempted to criticize Peter for his lack of faith. The Master was right there, and Peter had permission to participate in this remarkable miracle. But just as he got started, his doubts overcame him, and he failed. Or so we might think.

For me, however, there is something remarkable about this vignette. Other disciples were in the boat with Peter, but only he had the faith and courage to make the attempt. The storm was raging, waves were hitting the boat, which was tossing and bouncing at the mercy of the elements. It was the fourth watch (between three a.m. and six a.m.) and the disciples had been fighting the weather most of the night. They were frightened and exhausted. With this backdrop, imagine what was going through Peter's mind as he approached the side of the boat! Peter somehow summons the faith and courage to step over and into the water. And then, in the midst of the tempest, he takes a step. And then another. I give Peter great credit for this heroic expression of faith.

But really, that's what we're required to do every day as the storms around us seem to increase in fury and velocity. We take a step. Then another. And then the tempest seems to overtake us, and we feel ourselves sinking in our trials and sorrows, sins and disappointments. We feel there is no way out. Our feelings might be captured in the words of the beloved hymn:

> Master, the tempest is raging!
> The billows are tossing high!
> The sky is o'ershadowed with blackness.
> No shelter or help is nigh.
> Carest thou not that we perish?
> How canst thou lie asleep
> When each moment so madly is threat'ning
> A grave in the angry deep?[2]

Peter, as he is sinking in the dark and indifferent sea cries out, "Lord, save me!" We should never forget Jesus' reaction, because it has application to each of us in our individual situations: "And immediately Jesus stretched forth his hand and caught him." (Matthew 14:30–31, emphasis added) And so He will for us. We must keep reaching, keep walking, keep working. We must remember that,

> The winds and the waves shall obey thy will:
> Peace, be still.
> Whether the wrath of the storm-tossed sea
> Or demons or men or whatever it be,
> No waters can swallow the ship where lies
> The Master of ocean and earth and skies.
> They all shall sweetly obey thy will:
> Peace, be still; peace, be still.
> They all shall sweetly obey thy will:
> Peace, peace, be still.[3]

Like Peter, we may find ourselves in situations where we are asked to do hard things, otherwise known as opportunities for personal growth and development. These experiences are part of the plan and will test our mettle. But we won't be left alone. And we won't be asked to endure that which is beyond our ability to endure.

We may face seemingly impossible tasks. God knows what this mortal experience entails, and failure is allowed, but should teach rather than defeat. Our agency includes our response to failure as well as triumph. Many of God's children, in far-flung places and abject poverty, have limited choices. Only their response to their limitations defines them.

Peter's leadership was being shaped and honed and carefully crafted. He was faithful, but his faith occasionally failed him. He was bold and courageous, but his courage sometimes faltered. But in each case, he reaches for the Master's hand, embraces it, and with His assistance, gets up and keeps moving. He presses forward.

Barriers to our goals and objectives occur every day, and the leader is unrelentingly required to see through them and address them. At times, it can feel like the walls are closing in. Don't be afraid of failure. If you don't fail miserably at some point in life, you are not trying hard enough. Sometimes these experiences are necessary because they teach us things we need to learn. And they are often the catalyst to move us towards what the Lord really wants us to do. French statesman, Charles Alexandre de Calonne, said it succinctly, "The difficult we do immediately, the impossible takes a little longer."[4]

Certainly, we're faced with daily challenges. Ancient Greek and Roman mythology introduced us to the Lernaean Hydra—the ferocious serpentine water-monster with multiple heads. These heads, like the challenges we face, are bent on our destruction (or failure). When one head is lopped off, two more grow in its place. And so, it seems, do our problems.

If you have ever felt this way, know you are in good company.

John Wooden is largely regarded as college basketball's most successful coach. Over a twelve-year span, his UCLA teams won ten NCAA championships, and at one point they had an eighty-eight game winning streak. What most fail to remember, however, is that his teams toiled in relative obscurity for thirteen years before they won their first National Championship, achieving a won-loss percentage of just over 57%. Year after year coach Wooden developed the underlying foundations, philosophies, and systems that ultimately led to his success. But it took time. In today's impatient culture, Wooden may have been terminated well before his system of success finally took hold. And what a tragedy if that had happened.

Similarly, Sam Walton, founder of Walmart, struggled for years to gain a foothold with a single dime store. It took him seven years to open his second store and twenty-five years to open his thirty eighth store. Eventually, after a lot of slogging through trial and error and an abundance of blood, sweat, and tears, his work began to pay off. Between 1970 and 2000, Walmart built over 3,000 stores and achieved more than $150 billion in annual revenues. "People have the impression that Walmart was just this great idea that turned into an overnight success," Walton observed. "But it was an outgrowth of everything we did from 1945 . . . and like most overnight successes, it was about twenty years in the making."[5]

Nothing that has lasting value is created overnight. All businesses have periods of significant challenge and uncertainty. So do the rest of our lives. Stay focused on your ultimate objectives. Develop a clear vision for what you're building. With that vision squarely in mind, identify the battles that must be won today. And then tomorrow do the same.

Toward the end of his remarkable record, Nephi discusses the importance of entering into the covenant path, beginning with our willingness to exercise faith in Jesus Christ. That faith leads us to repent and to our first essential ordinance, baptism, wherein we covenant to take His—Jesus'—name upon us. We then carry that name forward in all we do and for all to witness. We are blessed not only by the baptism of water, but also the gift of the Holy Ghost, which teaches truth, comforts our souls, and provides critical guidance and peace. Nephi then asks: "And now . . . after ye have gotten into this strait and narrow path, I would ask if all is done?" In fact, Nephi reminds us, we're just beginning. "Behold, I say unto you, Nay; for ye have not come thus far save it were by the word of Christ with unshaken faith in him, relying wholly upon the merits of him who is mighty to save" (2 Nephi 31:19).

"So," one might ask, "What's next? What do we need to do? How do we obtain eternal life? What's required of us?"

Nephi's answer is brilliant. In two sentences he sums up the purpose and objective of life in profound simplicity:

> Wherefore, ye must press forward with a steadfastness in Christ, having a perfect brightness of hope, and a love of God and of all men. Wherefore, if ye shall press forward, feasting upon the word of Christ, and endure to the end, behold, thus saith the Father: Ye shall have eternal life. (2 Nephi 31:20)

It sounds so simple!

The great Oliver Wendell Holmes, who served as a United States Supreme Court justice for thirty years, once said, "I would not give a fig for the simplicity on this side of complexity, but I would give my life for the simplicity on the other side of complexity."[6] That's an interesting statement—one that might cause the reader to pause for a moment in an attempt to comprehend what Mr. Holmes is teaching. However, I believe this statement captures much of our mortal experience.

Have you ever encountered a concept or idea which, at first glance, seems simple and intuitive? Maybe even simplistic and childlike? Take, for instance, the doctrine of Christ. We're taught the essence of what we're to learn and do in mortality is to have faith in Jesus Christ, repent of our sins, be baptized, receive the gift of the Holy Ghost, and then endure to the end. "Ok . . . got it," we might say. Then, the complexities of life seem to overtake us, nearly swallowing us in the volume of details, deadlines, pressures, and trials we encounter every day. We work our way through these complexities, hopefully holding with our might to the things that truly matter despite the raging tempests, gaining strength and understanding through obedience to a prophet's counsel, direction from the scriptures, and insights from personal revelation. At every phase of our lives, we have setbacks, commit sin, and encounter barriers to our success, sometimes self-imposed and other times imposed upon us. But we persevere and have occasion to review where we've been and what we've learned, and we realize that what we really need to do (have faith in Jesus Christ, repent of our sins, be baptized, receive the gift of the Holy Ghost, and then endure to the end) really is that simple. But because of the complexities we've just waded through, our understanding of the beauty and simplicity of the doctrine of Christ is far deeper and immanently more profound. We appreciate it at significantly different levels. This understanding and depth come as we do as Nephi counsels: we press forward with a steadfastness in Christ. Though we're not perfect, we do our best every day to maintain a brightness of hope, believing in good things to come because we've seen evidence of these good things in the past. We strive to love God and to place His priorities first in our lives. We serve others and pray to be filled with charity—to love the way Christ loves us. We gain strength and perspective from immersing ourselves in the word of God—both through the written word and the words of our inspired leaders. We make mistakes every day. We fall short of our expectations. We occasionally let others down. But we don't relent in our attempts. We repent. We grow. We strive to get better. We endeavor to hear Him regularly. We reach out to the Savior and find that He "reaches our reaching"[7] and pulls us up from the ominous and occasionally enticing deep. "Wherefore, be not weary in well-doing," the Lord pleads with us, "for ye are laying the foundation of a great work. And out of small things proceedeth that which is great. Behold, the Lord requireth the heart and a willing mind; and the willing and obedient shall eat the good of the land of Zion in these last days" (D&C 64: 33–34). Elder Jeffrey R. Holland implores us thus:

> I am asking you not to give up "for ye are laying the foundation of a great work." That "great work" is you—your life, your future, the very fulfillment of your dreams. That "great work" is what, with effort and patience and God's help, you can become. When days are difficult or problems seem unending, I plead with you to stay in the harness and keep pulling. You are entitled to "eat the good of the land of Zion in these last days," but it will require your heart and a willing mind. It will require that you stay at your post and keep trying.[8]

Ultimately, we need to have the faith that the Lord knows us and knows what is best for us. He expects all of us to do our best, to make an honest effort in all we do. There is no substitute for hard work, and we should pray as we work. In fact, Amulek reminds us that it is not only appropriate, but also imperative that we, "Cry unto him." "Cry unto him when ye are in your fields, yea, over all your flocks . . . cry over the crops of your fields, that ye may prosper in them. Cry over the flocks of your fields, that they may increase." (Alma 34:20, 24–25)

Mortality is filled with challenges for everyone. We all get our turn, and no one is immune. It is not unusual to lose a sense of perspective of that fact when we see how others live—or we think we see how they live through well-intended posts on social media, which reflect only the best and most carefully orchestrated events in their lives. But we compare these pristine moments against our own worst moments and conclude that everyone has his or her act together but us. We fall victim to the menacing and metastasizing cancers of comparison, competing, contending, criticizing, complaining, and living with constant cynicism. We succumb to four traps that can derail us in our attempts to press forward and endure to the end as Nephi counsels: 1) we fixate with regret on past failures or fear the prospect of future failures, 2) we feel overwhelmed with the trials we face,

3) we forget the overwhelming evidence of God's goodness and grace in our lives, 4) we fail to hold fast to what we know.

Past failures and fear of future failures

All of us have failures in our past, whether they're in our relationships or our professional endeavors or in unmet expectations. Perhaps most insidious is our tendency to dwell on past transgressions, though, through the miracle of repentance and forgiveness, those transgressions have long been forgotten by the One who matters. The Lord has been very clear on how He sees that circumstance: "Though your sins be as scarlet," Isaiah taught, "they shall be as white as snow; though they be red like crimson, they shall be as wool" (Isaiah 1:18). Through the Prophet Joseph, the Lord declared definitively, "Behold, he who has repented of his sins, the same is forgiven, and I, the Lord, remember them no more" (D&C 58:42).

As we consider our lives and our standing before God, we might occasionally ask questions like the following: What behavioral standard does the Lord expect of me? What do I need to do in order to qualify to return to His presence? In answer to those questions, in Matthew, and again in 3 Nephi, the Savior issues this imperative: "Be ye therefore perfect, even as your Father which is in heaven is perfect." It is not a suggestion, nor does he say, "Try really hard." He says, "Be perfect." It is a commandment.

It took me a while to understand His message, and perhaps it did for others as well. I am certainly not sinless. In fact, I make mistakes every single day. Does that disqualify me from the blessings of heaven? Have I failed even before I begin?

John S. Robertson gave a wonderful speech at Brigham Young University where he adds some clarity to the Savior's injunction. He taught,

> Let me be clear that today perfect means something much more specific than it did 400 years ago. Originally, when borrowed from French, it meant 'finished, complete, excellent." It came to French from Latin per-, "completely," and -facere, "to do" (see American Heritage Dictionary, s.v. "perfect"). In modern English, however, perfect always raises in our minds a much more specific

> idea of "flawless, without defect." We hear, for example, "he pitched a perfect game," or "she got a perfect score on the exam," and so on. But the idea of "flawless" as the principal meaning of perfect is new to the English language.[9]

The temple experience brings added perspective to this. In the temple, we learn that our Father did not intend us to live a sinless life. We have been given the remarkable gift of agency, and in the exercise of that agency, all of us will stumble and fall from time to time. Or every day. Thankfully, our Father's plan includes a Savior, through whom we can, indeed, become perfect, "completed," or made whole. Sinlessness has never been His standard for our mortal existence; allowing the Savior to complete us, to fill in the gaps, to make us whole, to help us overcome our transgressions and shortcomings, our temptations and pains, our afflictions and infirmities is His standard. (Alma 7:11, 12)

While sinlessness is not His expectation for us, perfection through Christ's grace is (see Moroni 10:32–25). And one measuring stick for our progress is our ability to qualify to enter the temple. Elder Bruce R. McConkie taught this wonderful truth:

> You don't need to get a complex or get a feeling that you have to be perfect to be saved. You don't. There's only been one perfect person, and that's the Lord Jesus, but in order to be saved in the Kingdom of God and in order to pass the test of mortality, what you have to do is get on the straight and narrow path—thus charting a course leading to eternal life—and then, being on that path, pass out of this life in full fellowship. I'm not saying that you don't have to keep the commandments. I'm saying you don't have to be perfect to be saved. If you did, no one would be saved. The way it operates is this: you get on the path that's named the "straight and narrow." You do it by entering the gate of repentance and baptism. The straight and narrow path leads from the gate of repentance and baptism, a very great distance, to a reward that's called eternal life. If you're on that path and pressing forward, and you die, you'll never get off the path. There is no such thing as falling off the straight and narrow path in the life to come, and the reason is that this life is the time that is given to men to prepare for eternity. Now

> is the time and the day of your salvation. You don't have to do what Jacob said, "Go beyond the mark." You don't have to live a life that's truer than true. You don't have to have an excessive zeal that becomes fanatical and becomes unbalancing. What you have to do is stay in the mainstream of the Church, loving the Lord, staying on the straight and narrow path. If you're on that path when death comes—because this is the time and day appointed, this is the probationary estate—you'll never fall from it, and for all practical purposes, your calling and election is made sure. Now, that isn't the definition of that term, but the end result will be the same.
>
> There's great, great hope for Latter-day Saints. There's great hope for anyone who will repent, believe, obey, strive, struggle and seek to work out his salvation.[10]

Again, living a sinless life is not the expectation; staying on the straight and narrow path—or working to getting back on the straight and narrow path through God's infinite grace—as manifest by our ability to enter the temple, is the expectation. There is an entire canon of literature and divinely inspired direction, both modern and ancient, to help us live lives that qualify us to enter the temples. And we should devote our lives to achieving and maintaining that standard of living.

In addition to acknowledging that we don't need to live sinless lives, we must be willing and eager to extend the same standard to others. Allow others to grow by forgiving them of their mistakes. Be willing to see others for who they really are. Love others as Christ loves them, despite whatever short-sighted and short-term attitudes and behaviors you might have witnessed. We've all fallen into the "short-term" hole from time to time. Elder Holland pleads with us:

> . . . not to dwell on days now gone nor to yearn vainly for yesterdays, however good those yesterdays may have been. The past is to be learned from but not lived in. We look back to claim the embers from glowing experiences but not the ashes. And when we have learned what we need to learn and have brought with us the best that we have experienced, then we look ahead and remember that faith is always pointed toward the future. Faith always has to do with blessings and truths and events that will yet be efficacious in our lives.[11]

Trials

Why does the Lord allow good people to go through hard things? I'm sure we've all asked ourselves this question many times. It's perhaps easier to answer when it's other people experiencing the trials. Trails make us stronger, of course. Muscle is never built without first being torn. It's the process of rebuilding and repairing the muscle fibers that brings strength. Trials instruct us. They refine us. In his moving poem, *Good Timber*, Douglas Malloch teaches:

> Good timber does not grow with ease,
> The stronger wind, the stronger trees.
> The further sky, the greater length.
> The more the storm, the more the strength.
> By sun and cold, by rain and snow,
> In trees and men good timbers grow.[12]

However, when we're the ones mired in the depth of adversity—when we feel the buffeting of the strong wind and the raging storms—it can be more difficult to maintain that perspective.

One evening, when our first child, Cameron, was eight months old, I was home watching him. He was in his highchair eating as I ran upstairs to grab something. While I was upstairs, I heard a crash and then screaming. I ran downstairs as fast as I could and found my baby on the floor in a pool of blood. Cam had pushed on the tray of his highchair, broken it, and had fallen onto the broken part of his tray, slicing his mouth terribly, requiring urgent medical attention. I grabbed him and rushed him to the emergency room where the doctor determined he needed an oral surgeon to sew him up. Cam was in a lot of pain, and it took a while for the doctor to get there, so by the time he finally arrived, my baby was frantic (as were his parents). He wouldn't hold still long enough to let the doctor work on his mouth, no matter how tightly I tried to hold him. So, the doctor eventually had to strap him onto a board and restrain his head. I will never forget the look of panic and fear in his eyes as we did this. He was little, but he had learned to trust his dad, and here I was letting him get strapped onto a cold, indifferent board. Though he couldn't say it, he looked at me accusingly as if I had betrayed his deepest beliefs and trust. Why did he have to go through this pain? Why was his father letting this happen? Of course, we know that for him to grow and heal and develop as he needed, I had to allow the doctor to do what he did. Anything less than that would have been contrary to what a loving father would do. He had to endure the fear and uncertainty and hardship of that experience to heal and grow.

Life gives us similar experiences. We question at times why a loving Heavenly Father would allow us to suffer and feel pain or loneliness. But our growth and healing and progression require it, and we emerge from these situations stronger and better. I love the scripture, "Be still and know that I am God" (D&C 101:16). And to Moses, after he had led the children of Israel out of Egypt and they are panicking as the Egyptians are bearing down on them with their backs against the Red Sea, the Lord declares to Moses: "Fear ye not, stand still, and see the salvation of the Lord, which he will shew to you today: for the Egyptians whom ye have seen today, ye shall see them again no more forever. The Lord shall fight for you, and ye shall hold your peace" (Exodus 14:13–14).

And of course, He delivered them. We all have moments where we face fear or are required to go through hard things. But the Lord will fight for us, is fighting for us, and we will be victorious (even when we feel like we won't be).

This life presents so much about which we are concerned, making the process of "pressing forward" continually challenging. Family concerns, job pressures, faith crises, turbulent health, relationship challenges, social issues, national and geopolitical turmoil. It's a long and growing list. But concerns and uncertainties are all part of our journey, and our job is to claim our faith in the One who knows the beginning from the end, to cry out to Him as often as we need, and to know His arm will be extended toward us to lift us up. The poet, Mary Oliver, captures our experience her poem, *I worried.*

I worried a lot.
Will the garden grow, will the rivers flow in the right direction,

> Will the earth turn as it was taught, and if not how shall I
> correct it?
> Was I right, was I wrong, will I be forgiven, can I do better?
> Will I ever be able to sing, even the sparrows can do it and I am,
> well, hopeless?
> Is my eyesight fading or am I just imagining it,
> Am I going to get rheumatism, lockjaw, dementia?
> Finally, I saw that worrying had come to nothing.
> And gave it up. And took my old body and went out into the
> morning, and sang.[13]

In the October 2006 session of general conference, Elder Joseph B. Wirthlin offered a magnificent address entitled "Sunday Will Come," wherein he discusses the devastating impact of that fateful Friday when the Lord was crucified, leaving his disciples lost and wondering where to turn. But then, that following Sunday morning, the Savior's long-awaited and long-prophesied triumph over death occurred. That Sunday marks the most significant event in the history of God's children—our victory over death and sin. The pain and sorrow and uncertainty that led to that moment were washed away, bringing hope and joy and purpose to a grateful and desperate world. The Father's plan was fulfilled. A way back was established. Elder Wirthlin testified:

> Each of us will have our own Fridays—those days when the universe itself seems shattered and the shards of our world lie littered about us in pieces. We all will experience those broken times when it seems we can never be put together again. We will all have our Fridays.
>
> But I testify to you in the name of the One who conquered death—Sunday will come. In the darkness of our sorrow, Sunday will come.
>
> No matter our desperation, no matter our grief, Sunday will come. In this life or the next, Sunday will come.[14]

Perspective gained over time and experience is a wonderful thing. When we're in the middle of our trials, we can lose this perspective. Our job, difficult as it feels in the moment, is to hold on, have patience, and press forward. What today seems overwhelming, will tomorrow be another valuable lesson in God's love. As the brilliant cartoonist, Bill Waterson, articulates through his beloved and universally relatable Calvin: "Isn't it funny how day by day nothing changes, but when you look back, everything is different . . . ?"[15]

Remember

A testimony sufficient to give us strength to persevere and press forward in and through difficult times—to hold on with a steadfastness in Christ regardless of what barriers and obstacles we encounter—comes and is reinforced by remembering God's tender mercies in our life. We are admonished to remember over and over, again and again. While all volumes in our scriptural canon reinforce this need, the Book of Mormon's emphasis is particularly powerful. Nephi begins his record with this invitation, speaking specifically about God's tender mercies in our lives:

> But behold, I, Nephi, will show unto you that the tender mercies of the Lord are over all those whom he hath chosen, because of their faith, to make them mighty even unto the power of deliverance. (1 Nephi 1:20)

The Book of Mormon ends with Moroni reinforcing this same message, reminding readers that the process for gaining a witness of the truth of the Book of Mormon includes these steps: we must 1) read, 2) ponder, and 3) pray. But we sometimes fail to include one additional essential step: to remember. Moroni writes:

> Behold, I would exhort you that when ye shall read these things, if it be wisdom in God that ye should read them, that ye would *remember* how merciful the Lord hath been unto the children of men, from the creation of Adam even down until the time that ye shall receive these things, and ponder *it* in your hearts. (Moroni 10:4, emphasis added).

What, specifically are we to remember and ponder, according to Moroni? His invitation is to remember "how merciful the Lord hath been unto the children of men, from the creation of Adam even down until the time that ye shall receive these things" (Moroni 10:4).

Certainly, to gain a testimony that will allow us to press forward with enduring faith and requisite strength we must read the Book of Mormon (and other scripture). We must consider what we read and pray about it. But a central message throughout that wonderful record is how God continually and endlessly extends His mercy and goodness in our lives. We must remember that.

How often do we feel the grace and goodness of God in our lives? How often do we receive direction from the Spirit, reminding us that we are known by Heavenly Parents who love us? Sometimes this direction is subtle, soft, and almost imperceptible. It requires that we listen carefully. Other times it is obvious, poignant and penetrating. But in all cases, it serves to reinforce the truth that we are not left alone. If you were to document every thought, every prompting, every feeling you get when you pray or read the scriptures, how long would that list become?

Think of the experience of buying a car—you do your research, you go on your test drive, you make the financial arrangements, and finally drive away in your new vehicle. You're excited. But as you drive down the road, you notice, for the first time perhaps, how many other cars are just like yours—the same make and model—and you never noticed it before. Are they there for the first time? Of course not. You're seeing them because you're now looking for them. Do we look for and see the influence of our Heavenly Father's love in our lives? Do we expect revelation? Do we cultivate a relationship with the Spirit, such that we regularly hear its sweet communication? Now, here's a most important question: do we remember these experiences?

How many times during a normal week do we feel the influence of the Spirit? How many times do we receive revelation or feel the blessings of a tender Heavenly Parent? When we're reading scriptures, do we have thoughts and feelings that come to our minds? When we're praying, how often do we have similar feelings? What about the impressions that come as we listen to talks at church or general conference? How about the insights we gain as we listen to or participate in uplifting music, or when we're involved in giving meaningful service? Have you ever given or received a blessing that has been instructive? Have you read your patriarchal blessing and had a confirmation that its words and promises are in accordance with the Lord's will for you as a unique individual? Have you ever been in discussions with friends and family and gained insight or felt prompted in any way? Have you been uplifted by temple service and felt of the Lord's love and direction when you enter that sacred building and participate in sacred ordinances?

If you can answer yes to any of these, you have received revelation; you have received confirmation that the Lord, indeed, knows and loves you, that He is watching over you and has not nor never will abandon you. An honest assessment of one's life, if an individual is doing anything to invite the presence of the Spirit, will expose that the Lord reveals His divine love for us multiple times each week—or likely more accurately, several times each day. Whether it is a thought or a feeling or a voice or in some other way, He is there.

If that's true, and we've received promptings and tender mercies—large and small—each week throughout our life, do a simple calculation about how often you can point to the Lord's influence and direction and love. If you are forty years old, you have been accountable for your choices for at least thirty two years (assuming accountability comes at age eight). If you have felt or received only two promptings a week (likely a grossly underestimated number), you have received confirmation of His love for you and for the truthfulness of His eternal plan at least 1,664 times. And it's likely far more than that. But because we "see through a glass darkly" (1 Cor 13), we far too often fail to recognize or remember His influence in our lives. We forget what has so generously been extended to us so frequently. That is why the Lord commands us to remember—an admonishment given more frequently than any other commandment in all of scripture—by my calculation and including derivatives, 631 times! Look for yourself. You'll probably find more!

And if we remember the overwhelming evidence of God's love, that love will lead us to deliverance. In whatever circumstance we experience, He is there. He is watching. He is guiding. He is leading. He is in the details of our lives. He is keenly aware of our current circumstances and of those we love and serve. And He brings to those circumstances an eternal perspective. He knows who we were before we came to our mortal experience—our character, our strengths, our talents, our choices, our faith, our valiance (see Alma 13:3; D&C

138:56; Jeremiah 1:5; Abraham 3:22–23; Ephesians 1:3–4). He brings that full perspective of our true selves to our current situations. He has not placed us here in a random or haphazard manner. He knows of our joys, our pains, our worries, our capabilities, our mortal weaknesses, our promise and potential. As Paul wrote to the Galatians, "It pleased God, who separated me from my mother's womb, and called me by his grace, to reveal his Son in me" (Galatians 1:15–16). Our Heavenly Parents knew when it was our time to come and the work we would need to do as His leaders—at this time in the history of the human family and in this current circumstance. We are here to do a mighty work—a work that has potential to impact for good our individual lives, our family's lives, and of the lives of those around us. We will not be left alone in this effort. Our perspective is, by design, limited. We see so little of the eternal view. Our task is hold fast to what we do know—to "doubt our doubts" as President Dieter F. Uchtdorf taught,[16] to press forward—and to remember what we have already learned, to build on the foundation that has been established. And our Heavenly Father has a clear view of who we will and must become. He knows of our ultimate eternal destiny and is guiding us along our unique and individual paths with that end in mind.

Elder Dale G. Renland reinforces the commandment to remember and the strength that comes when we do:

> I invite you to remember each day the greatness of Heavenly Father and Jesus Christ and what They have done for you. Let your consideration of Their goodness more firmly bind your wandering heart to Them. Ponder Their compassion, and you will be blessed with added spiritual sensitivity and become more Christlike. Contemplating Their empathy will help you "hold out faithful to the end," until you "are received into heaven" to "dwell with God in a state of never-ending happiness."[17]

Prior to meeting the Prophet Joseph, twenty-two-year-old Oliver Cowdery, a schoolteacher at the time, boarded with Joseph Smith Sr. and family during the school year. While living there, Oliver heard bits of the story about Joseph Smith's first vision, his obtaining the plates, and other background information relative to that revelatory period. Though they were initially reluctant to say too much, the Smiths eventually acquiesced to Oliver's prodding and shared the story of these events in detail. Oliver became eager to know for himself if what he was being told was true. To his prayerful questions, the Lord provided a sweet and poignant answer that, in fact, the stories and the work associated with them were true. Oliver then travelled to Harmony, Pennsylvania to meet Joseph in person and assist him in the work. While acting as a scribe for the translation of the Book of Mormon, Oliver continued to pray for guidance and confirmation and received this revelation in response to his pleadings:

> Verily, verily, I say unto you, if you desire a further witness, cast your mind upon the night that you cried unto me in your heart, that you might know concerning the truth of these things.
>
> Did I not speak peace to your mind concerning the matter? What greater witness can you have than from God? (D&C 6:22–23)

If we want strength to press forward, we must remember when we have cried unto the Lord and on the hundreds of times—if not thousands—He has spoken peace to our souls. "What greater witness can [we] have than from God?"

Hold Fast to What We Know

I love how Nephi describes in his father's dream how some "feel" their way to the tree of life by "clinging to the iron rod" and others "feel" their way to the large and spacious building. Notice the language Nephi uses:

> And it came to pass that I beheld others pressing forward, and they came forth and caught hold of the end of the rod of iron; and they did press forward through the mist of darkness, clinging to the rod of iron, even until they did come forth and partake of the fruit of the tree.
>
> And he also saw other multitudes feeling their way towards that great and spacious building. (1 Nephi 8:24,32)

Each of us has our own unique mists of darkness. Each of us has questions and distractions and competing priorities that can pull us off course. Some moments are clear, with obvious "rights" and "wrongs." But other moments will not be so clear, where the mists are so thick, we can't see the next step. The job for all of us is to keep holding on, to keep pressing ahead, for as long as it takes. Eventually, we will find ourselves at the tree where we'll fall to our knees in overwhelming gratitude as we experience the full love of God in all its splendor and glory: "He saw other multitudes pressing forward; and they came and caught hold of the end of the rod of iron; and they did press their way forward, continually holding fast to the rod of iron, until they came forth and fell down and partook of the fruit of the tree." (1 Nephi 8:30)

Novelist and poet, Emma Lou Thayne, shared the following from her book, *A Place of Knowing:*

> Many years into my adulthood, when asked by a Jewish poet friend why I stay in my Mormonism, I explained it with a story, the details recounted by my mother. It is my mother's story transposed into an allegory about my believing.
>
> When I was a little girl, my father took me to hear Helen Keller in the Tabernacle. I must have been about eight or nine and I'd read about Helen Keller in school, and my mother had told me her story.
>
> I remember sitting in the balcony at the back of that huge domed building that was supposed to have the best acoustics in the world. Helen—everybody called her that—walked in from behind a curtain under the choir seats with her teacher, Annie Sullivan. Helen spoke at the pulpit—without a microphone—but we could hear perfectly, her guttural, slow, heavily pronounced speech. She spoke about her life and her beliefs. Her eyes were closed and when it came time for questions from the audience, she put her fingers on her teacher's lips and then repeated for us what the question had been. She answered questions about being deaf and blind and learning to read and to type and, of course, to talk. Hearing that voice making words was like hearing words for the first time, as if language had only come into being—into my being at least—that moment. Someone asked her, "Do you feel colors?"

I'll never forget her answer, the exact sound of it—"Some-times . . . I feel . . . blue." Her voice went up slightly at the end, which meant she was smiling. The audience didn't know whether to laugh or cry.

After quite a lot of questions, she said, "I would . . . like to ask . . . a favor of you." Of course, the audience was all alert. "Is your Mormon prophet here?" she asked. There was a flurry of getting up from the front row, and President Grant walked up the stairs to the stand. She reached out her hand and he took it. All I could think was, "Oh, I wish I were taking pictures of that."

"I . . . would like . . . ," she said, "to hear your organ . . . play . . . your fa-mous song—about your pio-neers. I . . . would like . . . to re-mem-ber hear-ing it here." All the time she was speaking she was holding his hand he had given her to shake. I liked them together, very much. I remember thinking, "I am only a little girl (probably others know) but how in the world will she hear the organ?" But she turned toward President Grant and he motioned to Alexander Schreiner, the Tabernacle organist who was sitting near the loft. At the same time, President Grant led her up a few steps to the back of the enormous organ—with its five manuals and eight thousand pipes. We were all spellbound. He placed her hand on the grained oak of the console, and she stood all alone facing us in her long, black velvet dress with her right arm extended, leaning slightly forward and touching the organ, with her head bowed.

Brother Schreiner played "Come, Come, Ye Saints," each verse a different arrangement, the organ pealing and throbbing—the bass pedals like foghorns—as only he could make happen. Helen Keller stood there—hearing through her hand and sobbing.

Probably a lot more than just me—probably lots of us in the audience were mouthing the words to ourselves— "Gird up your loins; fresh courage take. / Our God will never us forsake; / And soon we'll have this tale to tell— / All is well! / All is well!"

I could see my great-grandparents, converts from England, Wales, France, and Denmark, in that circle of their covered wagons, singing over their fires in the cold nights crossing the plains. Three of them had babies die; my great-grandmother was buried in Wyoming. "And should we die before our journey's through, / Happy day! / All is well! / We then are free from toil and sorrow, too; / With the just we shall dwell! / But if our lives are spared again / To see the Saints their rest obtain, / Oh, how we'll make this chorus swell— / All is well! / All is well!"

So then—that tabernacle, that singing, my ancestors welling in me, my father beside me, that magnificent woman, all combined with the organ and the man who played it and the man who had led her to it—whatever passed between the organ and her passed on to me.

I believed. I believed it all—the seeing without seeing, the hearing without hearing, the going by feel toward something holy, something that could make her cry, something that could move me, alter me, something as unexplainable as a vision or a mystic connection, something entering the pulse of a little girl, something that no matter what would never go away. What it had to do with Joseph Smith or his vision or his gospel I never would really understand—all I know to this day is that I believe.[18]

I began this chapter with Peter. Here's one concluding thought from him. Peter proclaims his testimony of the greatness of Jesus, of His power, and of His mission: "For we have not followed cunningly devised fables, when we made known unto you the power and coming of our Lord Jesus Christ, but were eyewitnesses of his majesty" (2 Peter 1:16). I love his boldness in stating, in no uncertain terms, we are not deceived in our convictions. Peter firmly declares to his detractors, who question his experience and subsequent testimony, in words to this effect: "I was there when He invited me to walk on water. I was there on the Mount of Transfiguration. I was in the upper room when He washed and anointed our feet. I was there when He was taken by the high priest's servant. I cut off the ear of the servant, then watched in amazement as He healed His captor. I denied Him three times as He was put to trial, then witnessed as He was brutally crucified. I helped seal His body in the tomb and was there when He appeared as a resurrected being. I was in the room when He visited and taught us. I was fishing on the Sea of Galilee when He instructed us, after a long and fruitless night of fishing, to cast our nets on the other side of the boat, and we hauled in so many fish our nets would barely hold them all. I was there when He commanded us to feed His sheep, then later when He charged us to go into the world and preach His gospel. And I witnessed, firsthand, as He ascended into heaven. I am not following 'cunningly devised fables.' I have seen his majesty."

And so have we, in the varied and abundant ways He has extended His tender mercies to us and to our families. Now, we need to remember, to hold on, and to press forward. We "did not come this far only to come this far!"[19]

Some things to consider doing:

1. Begin and maintain a "Tender Mercies Journal" where you can record when you feel God's love and experience His sweet assurance that you are known and numbered by Him or when you feel His spirit in your life or when you have any revelatory experience. Refer back to what you have written often to help you remember these moments and experiences.

2. Reread and pray about your patriarchal blessing often.

3. Identify someone in your life for whom you may have a lingering resentment or frustration. Look past what you perceive as his or her shortcomings. Pray for this person and seek ways to rebuild and restore the relationship. Focus on his or her strengths and make this person's weaknesses irrelevant. Forgive him or her where necessary and seek their forgiveness where necessary. Create an opportunity to reconcile, one-on-one, with this person.

PART III
LEADERSHIP IN MY FAMILY

Leadership Level	**Foundational Scripture**	**Governing Principle**	**How I Think**	**Practices**
Leadership in my family	D&C 38:27: "I say unto you, be one; and if ye are not one ye are not mine."	Unity	Together, we are better. Regardless of where people are, my family is a place of learning, of building, of growth, and of love.	**Practice 5:** Develop Charity **Practice 6:** Keep an Eternal Perspective **Practice 7:** Lead with Empathy **Practice 8:** Learn to Hear Him

CHAPTER NINE
DEVELOP CHARITY

Let thy bowels also be full of charity towards all men, and to the household of faith, and let virtue garnish thy thoughts unceasingly; then shall thy confidence wax strong in the presence of God; and the doctrine of the priesthood shall distil upon thy soul as the dews from heaven.

The Holy Ghost shall be thy constant companion, and thy scepter an unchanging scepter of righteousness and truth; and thy dominion shall be an everlasting dominion, and without compulsory means it shall flow unto thee forever and ever.

—D&C 121:45–46

Above all the attributes of godliness and perfection, charity is the one most devoutly to be desired. Charity is more than love, far more; it is everlasting love, perfect love, the pure love of Christ which endureth forever. It is love so centered in righteousness that the possessor has no aim or desire except for the eternal welfare of his own soul and for the souls of those around him.

—Bruce R. McConkie[1]

King Solomon reigned for forty years during a period considered as Israel's "Golden Age." Throughout his reign, he established deep ties with many nations, opened trade routes, built a temple to house the Ark of the Covenant, and maintained a strong military presence that ensured Israel's security and prosperity. He was a king who "made silver and gold at Jerusalem as plenteous as stones, and cedar trees made he as the sycamore trees that are in the vale for abundance" (1 Chronicles 1:15). At his death, his son Rehoboam inherited his throne, who, upon his time of coronation, consulted some of his father's advisors in preparation to reign: "And they spake unto him, saying, If thou wilt be a servant unto this people this day, and wilt serve them, and answer them, and speak good words to them, then they will be thy servants for ever" (1 Kings 12:7). Their advice was both profound and simple: serve your people. Love them. Demonstrate kindness. Lighten the loads they carry. If you do this, they will love you in return and you will forever enjoy their loyalty. However, Rehoboam did not heed their counsel, instead followed the advice of his friends who had grown up with him amidst the privileges associated with his position. Their counsel? Reign with a heavy hand. Exact greater requirements than Solomon. Say to the people, "My little finger shall be thicker than my father's loins. And now whereas my father did lade you with a heavy yoke, I will add to your yoke: my father hath chastised you with whips, but I will chastise you with scorpions" (1 Kings 12: 10–11). And so the people revolted, causing a division among all of Israel and leading to the formation of two divided kingdoms instead of one united, mighty kingdom. Rehoboam neglected the wisdom of his elders and their counsel to lead with love and it forever altered the unity of Israel. He failed to grasp that a leader's job is to love and to serve.

One of the ways I study the scriptures is to envision myself in the time and context for when a particular sermon or parable or teaching was originally given. I try to feel what those who were there might have felt. What was happening around them? What was generally understood at the time and what new paradigms might I have obtained as a result of my experience? Jesus' teachings during his remarkable final week provide such moments of serious reflection for me. What would it have been like to have been there? What must His disciples have felt? Certainly, they didn't have a full understanding of the significance of that moment in human history. But as tensions mounted between Jesus and the elders, chief priests and scribes, and with Jesus' continued allusions to his death, that week was undoubtedly filled with penetrating poignancy (see Matthew 16:21–23, Matthew 17:22–23, Luke 18:31–34).

The chapters leading up to Matthew 24 show Jesus debating with the Pharisees, Herodians and Sadducees at the Temple. He then leaves the Temple for the final time, foretelling the destruction of the grand, sprawling edifice, where "there shall not be left here one stone upon another, that shall not be hewn down" (Matthew 24: 2), and proceeds to the Mount of Olives, which overlooks the Temple Mount. There He teaches his disciples the signs that will precede His second coming in dramatic and arresting imagery. I try to imagine how I would have responded to this. With, perhaps, a sense of impending gloom, I can imagine asking the Master how one can prepare for all that is to come. In Matthew 25, Jesus gives His answer in three crowning parables—His last lecture—where He offers a final, parting doctrinal gift. Of course, every parable has profound depth, with layers of meaning and offers multiple interpretations. But for my simple mind, Jesus captures the essence of his entire mission in these three parables: The parable of the ten virgins, the parable of the talents, and the parable of the sheep and the goats. These parables represent an urgent plea for discipleship and strike at the heart and soul of His life and mission. His message is not just for the here and now but for all of humanity with an arc that spans all time and eternity. After all that has occurred throughout the Savior's ministry—the transcendent teachings, the counter cultural messages, the metaphysical miracles, Jesus provides one last reminder for how we are to live as disciples and lead as leaders, a synthesis of all the critical messages He has taught to this point.

His first parable in Matthew 25 is of the ten virgins, five of whom were wise and five who were foolish. In anticipation of the bridegroom, who, they all knew, would eventually come, though they did not know exactly when, the five wise virgins carried "oil in their vessels with their lamps" (Matt 25:4). The five foolish virgins did not.

And eventually, just as they knew would happen, the bridegroom came. Those who carried oil were prepared.

Lesson one: among the many messages one can draw from this parable is this—*we must live our lives in such a way that we always have oils for our lamps.* Always. Are our spiritual reservoirs filled to such an extent that we stand prepared for whatever might come our way?

The second parable concerns a certain man who, in preparation for an extended journey into a far country, gave his servants care of his goods in the form of talents. To one he gave five talents, to another two, and to a third, one talent. Upon the man's return, his servants account for their use of the talents they received. The one who received five skillfully traded and transacted business in such a way that he now had ten to present to his master. Similarly, the servant who received two had gained an additional two to present his master. To each, the master responded, "Well done, thou good and faithful servant; thou hast been faithful over a few things, I will make thee ruler over many things; enter thou into the joy of the Lord" (Matt 25:21, 23). But the third servant, whether as a result of fear or slothfulness or some combination of the two, "went and hid [his] talent in the earth" (Matt 25:25) and therefore only had his original sum to present back to his master. The master's response to this servant is pointed:

> Thou wicked and slothful servant . . .
>
> Thou oughtest therefore to have put my money to the exchangers, and then at my coming I should have received mine own with usury.
>
> Take therefore the talent from him, and give it unto him which hath ten talents.
>
> For unto every one that hath shall be given, and he shall have abundance: but from him that hath not shall be taken away even that which he hath.
>
> And cast ye the unprofitable servant into outer darkness: there shall be weeping and gnashing of teeth. (Matt 25:26–30)

Lesson two: among the messages one can draw from this parable is this—*the invitation to live in such a way that we magnify all that we have been given to the building of the Lord's kingdom.* We've all been given gifts—different from one another and unique to us. As Moroni reminds us, "All these gifts come by the Spirit of Christ; and they come unto every man severally, according to his will" (Moroni 10:17). We cannot squander or hide or bury what we have received. We must develop our gifts, grow them, share them, lift others through and with them. We have been given them so that we can use them for good purposes. Our efforts to lead will be enhanced by our cultivation of the gifts we have received. And we will be magnified as we seek to expand them. As Ralph Waldo Emerson taught, "That which we persist in doing becomes easier to do, not that the nature of the thing has changed but that our power to do has increased."[2] Our very work in developing our gifts invites divine assistance to expand our ability to lead and have meaningful influence and impact. But if we seek to hide them, we run the very serious risk of losing everything.

The third and final parable presented by the Savior concerns the moment when the "Son of man shall come in his glory" (Matt 25:31). All the nations of the world shall be gathered for judgment—separated as a "shepherd divideth his sheep from the goats" (Matthew 25:32). The master sets the sheep on His right hand and the goats at His left, and to those on his right hand He declares, "Come, ye blessed of my Father, inherit the kingdom prepared for you from the foundation of the world."

So how does one find oneself on the right hand of God, ready to inherit what has been prepared from the foundation of the world?

Lesson three: *When all is said and done, demonstrating charity in our interactions with all of God's children is the quintessential lesson we are to learn in mortality.*

"For I was an hungered," the Savior taught, "and ye gave me meat: I was thirsty, and ye gave me drink: I was a stranger, and ye took me in: Naked, and ye clothed me: I was sick, and ye visited me: I was in prison, and ye came unto me."

We might ask, as the righteous individual asked the King:

> When saw we thee an hungred, and fed thee? or thirsty, and gave thee drink?
>
> When saw we thee a stranger, and took thee in? or naked, and clothed thee?
>
> Or when saw we thee sick, or in prison, and came unto thee?
>
> And the King shall answer and say unto them, Verily I say unto you, Inasmuch as ye have done it unto one of the least of these my brethren, ye have done it unto me. (Matthew 25:35–40)

Mormon and Paul both rank the characteristics we are to seek in mortality. While these characteristics are applicable to all, they certainly inform how we are to lead. Paul taught: "And now abideth faith, hope, charity, these three; but the greatest of these is charity" (1 Cor 13:13).

Mormon provides this reinforcement:

> Wherefore, my beloved brethren, if ye have not charity, ye are nothing, for charity never faileth. Wherefore, cleave unto charity, which is the greatest of all, for all things must fail—
>
> But charity is the pure love of Christ, and it endureth forever; and whoso is found possessed of it at the last day, it shall be well with him. (Moroni 7:46–47).

Under the Father's direction, Jesus created the earth. In doing so, He had divine understanding of all that was required for such work, including the principles undergirding the disciplines of cosmology, paleontology, molecular biology, astronomy, astrophysics, nuclear physics, geology, geochemistry, and geophysics. And more. To Moses, the Lord declared:

> Behold, I reveal unto you concerning this heaven, and this earth; write the words which I speak. I am the Beginning and the End, the Almighty God; by mine Only Begotten I created these things; yea, in the beginning I created the heaven, and the earth upon which thou standest.

> And the earth was without form, and void; and I caused darkness to come up upon the face of the deep; and my Spirit moved upon the face of the water; for I am God. (Moses 2:1–2)

Then, throughout His mortal mission, Jesus' faith-fueled power and His understanding of these principles is on further display as He commands the elements, and they obey Him. He alters the physical construct of the particles of the earth at His command. He walks on water. He turns water into wine. He heals physical bodies that had been damaged since birth. He has power over death. Imagine the body of knowledge He had and could have shared that might have advanced our understanding of science, technology, physics or medicine! Yet of all the concepts Jesus could have taught His disciples at that moment, He chose to highlight the single most critical lesson for anyone of us in mortality, and certainly an essential leadership characteristic for any leader at any level: to possess charity. As Mormon taught,

> Wherefore . . . pray unto the Father with all the energy of heart, that ye may be filled with this love, which he hath bestowed upon all who are true followers of his Son, Jesus Christ; that ye may become the sons of God; that when he shall appear we shall be like him, for we shall see him as he is; that we may have this hope; that we may be purified even as he is pure. (Moroni 7:48)

The fact that Mormon's pleading come at a time when everything he has worked to protect is under attack by vicious and unforgiving enemies bent on the destruction and annihilation of Mormon's entire civilization dramatically underscores the importance of his counsel: we must love as God loves and seek the ability to do so with everything we have and are. That is how we are expected to lead.

Charity is a gift of the Spirit, one that is "bestowed" if we diligently, purposefully and prayerfully seek it. Where enmity exists, love can prevail; where resentment has eroded previously cherished relationships, the pure love of Christ can soften hearts and offer healing; where disenfranchisement or distance has alienated one from the bonds of fellowship, kindness and humility can unite us; where doubt and uncertainty corrode a once confident testimony, loving service can rekindle the spark that previously burned brightly. Charity is a fruit of service and represents a virtuous cycle that moves us ever upward—as we serve others, we feel the Spirit guiding us. As we act on what the Spirit prompts us to do, we begin to love those we serve. And as we begin to love them, we desire to serve them even more. And so it continues.

Several years ago, I was conducting a missionary preparation class for high school seniors during the period when my son, Ryan, had received his call to serve in the Alpine German Speaking Mission but before he was to depart on his service. His mission spanned three countries—all of Austria, Southern Germany, and a significant portion of Switzerland. Ryan was eager to serve and had planned to do so his entire life, but like many whose departure is immanent, he had some growing reservations. For one, he spoke very little German. He knew the German dialect spoken in Austria differs significantly from the German spoken in Germany, and the German spoken in Switzerland is different than both the other two countries' language. So what limited German he did know would probably do him little good. The prospect of understanding the language's nuances and the need to eventually master them felt daunting—even overwhelming. Other uncertainties increasingly nagged at him. He wasn't sure what to expect as he envisioned finding people to teach. Would he knock doors? Would he contact people on the street? Would people care? How would he be received? How would he handle the relentless rejection he was certain was to come? He wasn't sure about the food and if he'd be able to adapt to a new diet. He wasn't sure about spending every waking moment with an assigned companion. He had many questions and unknowns and his comfort level with these ambiguities weighed on his heart. I invited Ryan to join me for our class, and as we began, I asked him to share his testimony of the gospel and his experience in receiving a call to serve from the Lord's prophet. As he began to share his thoughts and feelings, something changed for him. It caught him by surprise. It was as if a warm blanket suddenly enveloped him as a profound love for the people he was about to serve and with whom he was about to serve overtook his heart. Through nearly uncontrollable tears, he shared with our class his eagerness to experience the challenges of his new language and circumstance, and how—at that moment—he felt overwhelming love for all the people of his mission, his companions, and the new cultures he was to experience, even though he didn't fully understand these cultures. Of course, there was so much he didn't know. But there were two things he knew for certain—he loved those people, and he knew his Savior loved them. That was when his mission really started. It became the catalyst for a remarkable two years. Now that his full-time missionary service is several years in the rearview mirror, that same love abides and burns deep within his soul.

So many of Jesus' miracles were tactical in nature. Before he taught spiritual truths, he attended to the physical needs of His people. When the wine ran out at the wedding in Cana, He provided more. When 5,000 came to hear Him teach, he fed them. Again with the 4,000. When Peter, James and John had been fishing all night, Jesus built a fire and warmed them. And then fed them. His charge to Peter to "Feed my sheep" comes on the heels of Jesus literally feeding Peter. His leadership meets people where they are, helps address their immediate temporal and spiritual needs, and then elevates them to heights they theretofore would not have contemplated. His effectiveness of a leader is built on the foundation of His love for those he leads. And as a result, the hearts of those he leads and loves are changed, who then offer their very finest efforts for the remainder of their lives and eventually give their lives for the cause He established.

To His disciples—those whom He has chosen to be His leaders to carry on His work—Jesus gives this charge:

> Ye have not chosen me, but I have chosen you, and ordained you, that ye should go and bring forth fruit, and that your fruit should remain . . . These things I command you, that ye love one another. (John 15:16–17)

Elder Jeffrey R. Holland shared this insight on how the Savior prioritized the need for those He has chosen to carry the torch of leadership after His mortal mission was completed. He taught:

> I have often thought of the concern Jesus must have felt as He knew that His mortal ministry was coming to an end and that the daily, ongoing operation of His very young Church would fall

on the shoulders of a dozen very ordinary men who had been in the Church barely 36 months at best. Did they know enough? Had they understood any part of what He had tried so hard to teach them? Could they carry off this tremendous responsibility successfully? Furthermore, it can't have been too reassuring for Him to realize that one of the original Twelve would betray Him for a handful of silver coins, that three of them would sleep through His greatest hour of need, and that His chief Apostle would deny Him three times in almost a matter of minutes. Indeed, at one point "all the disciples forsook him, and fled," Matthew records in his gospel account.

So what could He say in those final hours that would offset these kinds of human frailties? What final lesson could He teach that would carry them through His physical absence? With a plea, indeed a commandment, that should pierce us today as much as it did then, the living Son of God summarized His entire ministry and their ultimate, ongoing responsibility in one concept—one grand, eternal principle:

"A new commandment I give unto you, That ye love one another; as I have loved you, that ye also love one another.

"By this shall all men know that ye are my disciples, if ye have love one to another."

This ultimate Christian commandment to love sounds so simple. Of course, it isn't simple or more people would demonstrate it. But it is not complicated. It consists of a handful of short words. We realize that over those three years of their service, Jesus's disciples had probably been given far more instruction than they could comprehend. In addition, the change from the complex law of Moses to the elevated gospel of Jesus Christ wasn't going to be easy for anyone coming out of the Israelite tradition. So Jesus consciously chose one principle, one measuring rod for success that is very easily grasped, if not necessarily so easily lived. He says to them in effect, "If you will remember this one commandment, you will have understood me and you will have understood my gospel. By keeping this declaration uppermost in your life, other people will immediately recognize that you are, in fact, my disciples—so, please, love one another."[3]

So how can we lead with love as the Savior requires? The Apostle Paul provides a powerful reminder and self-assessment as we strive to develop this essential leadership attribute. Despite whatever mighty works we achieve, admirable though they may seem to others, if we don't have charity, we are nothing. Paul teaches:

> Though I speak with the tongues of men and of angels, and have no charity, I am become as sounding brass, or a tinkling cymbal.
>
> And though I have the gift of prophecy, and understand all mysteries, and all knowledge; and though I have all faith, so that I could remove mountains, and have not charity, I am nothing.
>
> And though I bestow all my goods to feed the poor, and though I give my body to be burned, and have not charity, it profiteth me nothing. (I Cor 13:1–3)

Paul (and later reinforced by Moroni) then presents fifteen characteristics of charity against which we can evaluate our own leadership effectiveness. These are:

> Charity suffereth long, and is kind; charity envieth not; charity vaunteth not itself, is not puffed up,
>
> Doth not behave itself unseemly, seeketh not her own, is not easily provoked, thinketh no evil;
>
> Rejoiceth not in iniquity, but rejoiceth in the truth;
>
> Beareth all things, believeth all things, hopeth all things, endureth all things. (1 Cor 13:4–7)

Too many of us are well-practiced at talking about Jesus and His characteristics but may not be as practiced emulating them; we're skilled at discussing charity but aren't always charitable. The following self-assessment provides an opportunity to evaluate how we're doing against Paul's counsel. It includes fifteen statements, each aligned with one of Paul's characteristics and is based on a five-point scale, with five being "I nearly always do this" and zero or one meaning "I seldom model this behavior." You'll note two associated descriptions for each statement representing two extremes of the continuum to assist in your evaluation. The point of this assessment is not to definitively interpret each of Paul's statements. There is a depth associated with each of these that won't be captured in a simple one-liner. Instead, it's intended to provide a glimpse at how we're doing and offer some insight on what we can do to be more charitable leaders.

Charity Self-Assessment

1. I expect blessings according to my timetable and am frustrated when I don't get them just as I want them.

Charity suffereth long

I am patient with my circumstances during difficult times.

0 — 1 — 2 — 3 — 4 — 5

2. I am kind to those from whom I stand to gain.

Charity is kind

I am kind to others, regardless of their position, title, or possessions.

0 — 1 — 2 — 3 — 4 — 5

3. I feel threatened and insecure when others succeed.

Charity vaunteth not itself

I celebrate others' successes.

0 — 1 — 2 — 3 — 4 — 5

4. I tend to manipulate the impression others have of me to my benefit.

Charity envieth not

I look for opportunities to acknowledge the efforts and achievements of others.

0 — 1 — 2 — 3 — 4 — 5

Charity Self-Assessment

5. **Charity is not puffed up**

I am frustrated when others don't acknowledge my accomplishments. | I acknowledge divine guidance and assistance in what I'm able to achieve.

0 — 1 — 2 — 3 — 4 — 5

6. **Charity does not behave unseemingly**

My behavior in my private life differs in my public behavior. | I strive to model Christian discipleship in my public and private life.

0 — 1 — 2 — 3 — 4 — 5

7. **Charity seeketh not her own**

I am willing to undermine others for personal gain. | I look for opportunities to help others succeed.

0 — 1 — 2 — 3 — 4 — 5

8. **Charity is not easily provoked**

I am perpetually aggravated by the weaknesses I perceive in others. | I give others the benefit of the doubt on their weaknesses. I view others as more than one mistake, one behavior, or one disagreement I may have with them.

0 — 1 — 2 — 3 — 4 — 5

Charity Self-Assessment

9. **Charity thinketh no evil**

I approach others with skepticism and mistrust. — I seek the good in others and in my circumstances.

0 — 1 — 2 — 3 — 4 — 5

10. **Charity rejoiceth not in iniquity**

I participate in immoral thoughts and actions. — I consistently seek the virtues described in the 13th article of faith: We believe in being honest, true, chaste, benevolent virtuous, and in doing good to all men.

0 — 1 — 2 — 3 — 4 — 5

11. **Charity rejoiceth in truth**

I peddle in heresay, conspiracy, and rumor. — I boldly testify of and defend eternal truths.

0 — 1 — 2 — 3 — 4 — 5

12. **Charity beareth all things**

I skirt or avoid difficult assignments. — I go and do hard things with faith.

0 — 1 — 2 — 3 — 4 — 5

Charity Self-Assessment

13. **Charity believeth all things**

I am constantly cynical—even unwilling—to exercise faith.

0 — 1 — 2 — 3 — 4 — 5

I have a confidence born faith and practice.

14. **Charity hopeth all things**

I am perpetually overwhelmed by the negative things I experience today.

0 — 1 — 2 — 3 — 4 — 5

I have confidence in blessings that have not come yet.

15. **Charity endureth all things**

I give up easily when difficulties arise.

0 — 1 — 2 — 3 — 4 — 5

I have faith that regardless of the trial, God will prevail in my life.

After you have completed the assessment, tally your scores. Of course, no one is expected to score fives on every statement. A perfect score isn't the goal. There is nothing really scientific about the difference between an overall score of forty one and thirty seven, so don't worry about analyzing your results in that detail. But there are patterns that you might discover that can help you create more deliberate actions. What gaps have you identified? Where can you make a more concerted effort to invite the Lord's love to become more of a part of how you live and how you lead? Are there unique individuals that come to mind as you look at the different questions? If so, what specific ways might you serve and lift them? Are there relationships that need mending? Are there those you need to forgive? Are there areas where you need to repent? Are there some in your circle—or outside your circle—who feel alienated or alone and who could benefit from your connection? Where does the Lord need you to serve? How does He need you to serve? How does He need you to improve your ability to lead with love?

Brent L. Top, professor of Church history and doctrine and former dean of Religious Education at Brigham Young University, shared the following:

> While presiding over the Illinois Peoria Mission, my wife and I had the privilege of taking every group of departing missionaries on their last day in the mission field to the Nauvoo Temple for an endowment session. It became my practice to greet each elder and sister as they entered the celestial room with a big hug and a whispered expression of my love and appreciation for their service and commitment. I had been the beneficiary of just such a hug and tender expressions by Elder Dieter F. Uchtdorf, then a member of the Quorum of the Twelve Apostles, at an area mission presidents' seminar at the first of our mission. It was a critical turning point of our mission—a time when I felt totally overwhelmed and inadequate. Elder Uchtdorf's expression of love at that moment was a monumentally transforming event for me, and I wanted my missionaries to feel something akin to what I felt from him. I must admit, however, that it was easier to express those sentiments to some missionaries than it was to others. (Perhaps Elder Uchtdorf had the same feelings about me!)

> One elder in particular had given me more than his share of grief. In fact, many of the gray hairs that came after I was called as mission president can be attributed to him. He seemed to be in trouble all the time. On more than one occasion, I told him that I was going to send him home. Yet he would always promise me that he would try harder. His renewed commitment seldom lasted very long, however. And the cycle of rebuke, repentance, recommitment, and relapse would start all over again. Perhaps it would have been easier to have just sent him home. Yet I could see some of me in him, and I wanted him to succeed. I wanted him to return with honor. He wasn't an all-star, but now he had made it. He completed his mission and accompanied us to the temple before he flew home.
>
> As he came into the celestial room, I greeted him with the customary "I love you." Tears streamed down his face. "Thank you for extending me mercy," he whispered as his whole body shook with weeping. It was a tender moment, and both of us shed many tears of gratitude. Almost as if the veil parted, I sensed a coming day when I would embrace the Savior and with tears of thanksgiving and love say, "Thank you for extending me mercy."[4]

Jesus provides the model for how we are to lead. His charge to us is to follow that model by loving others how He loves them.

Some things to consider:

1. Using the Charity Self-Assessment, identify one area to focus on each week. Consider both areas of particular strength as well as areas where a gap exists between your current behavior and what you'd like it to be.

2. Cross reference your identified focus area and the corresponding statement from Paul with other scriptures. What insights do you gain?

3. Invite the Lord's help as you work to strengthen your chosen focus area. Remember: "With all the energy of heart" (Moroni 7:48).

CHAPTER TEN

KEEP AN ETERNAL PERSPECTIVE

SEEING OUR LOVED ONES FOR WHO THEY REALLY ARE, NOT SIMPLY FOR THEIR CURRENT CHOICES

But when he was yet a great way off, his father saw him, and had compassion on him, and ran, and fell on his neck, and kissed him.

—Luke 15:20

Our heavenly Father is more liberal in His views, and boundless in His mercies and blessings, than we are ready to believe or receive.

—Joseph Smith[1]

Service in the Lord's kingdom can be demanding. For example, full time missionary work requires constant humility, enduring diligence, unflagging faith, and the ability to handle relentless rejection. It taxes missionaries physically, mentally, emotionally. And it requires deep spiritual depth and purity. So when Corinaton was called to serve with his father and brothers among the Zoramites and approached his assignment boastfully and carelessly, it negatively affected not only his efforts, but those of his fellow servants as well. As his father, Alma, pointedly reminded him, "Behold, O my son, how great iniquity ye brought upon the Zoramites; for when they saw *your* conduct they would not believe in *my* words (Alma 39:11, emphasis added). Unfaithful and reckless conduct on the part of one member of a family can negatively impact (and seemingly undo) the efforts of so many.

But Alma knew his son. Just as one cannot "hide [their] crimes against God," one cannot ultimately hide their sins and transgressions, their mayhem and misdeeds from those closest to them. Alma could certainly be excused for not only delivering a severe tongue-lashing, but, considering the lasting and far-reaching impact of Corianton's mischief, Alma's very public position, and the significance of Corianton's missionary calling, Alma could have turned his back on his wayward son. Just like the rest of us, from time to time (or most of the time), young, inexperienced, questioning, doubtful Corianton made serious mistakes. But this mortal probation is a time for growth, a time of learning and proving. A mistake, though serious, does not need to define a person. Alma knows this. He understands that Corianton is more than his current behavior and choices and helps raise Corianton's site above his present challenges—serious as they are—and provides guidance, perspective, admonition, encouragement, and especially love to his boy. One mistake doesn't derail the promise and potential one has. Neither does two, nor forty.

Alma knows a little about coming back from a less than stellar set of choices. By his own admission, he had "murdered many of [God's] children, or rather, led them away unto destruction." He states, "So great had been my iniquities . . . the very thought of coming into the presence of my God did rack my soul with inexpressible horror" (Alma 36:15). Truly, his pain and his guilt were bitter beyond description—a bitterness and pain that had been earned through years of bad behavior.

But the Lord knew who Alma really was. He knew, despite his current behaviors, there was something more to him. And as exquisite and bitter as was Alma's pain, the sweet joy he experienced at his repentance and return to God's grace was also beyond his ability to fully express.

Sometimes the journey seems more than we can bear. When we've made mistakes, we can feel poignantly the loss of the Lord's proximity (not because He has distanced Himself from us, but rather that we've distanced ourselves from him). Or, we may have subtly, step by step, moved away from our faith and covenants, forgetting the fire we once felt. There are consequences to our actions, and these consequences can be significant.

When our loved ones do the same, it brings a different kind of sorrow. We might feel helpless, hopeless, and without influence. We might tend toward impatience and, ultimately, harsh judgment. We might even close off these important relationships—relationships that were once tender and intimate.

Leadership in our families requires a constant effort to see beyond the present circumstance, to understand the greatness that exists in others, despite their current behavior.

What became of Corianton? Did he wither and shrink in the face of his shortcomings? One of the most encouraging scriptures in our canon comes after Alma's stern reprimand of Corianton. He reminds his son—after all he had done—that he, Corinaton, had been called of God. His charge to do the Lord's work remained. The promises available to him for faithful service were still in force, despite whatever misdeeds he had done.

Well after Alma's passing, Corinaton's work as one of the Lord's ordained servants continues, along with that of his brethren, leading to "continual peace . . . and prosperity in the church" (See Alma 49:30).

There is a way back, a way out of the darkness, a way out of uncertainty and doubt. It can take time—it often does. But the Lord is in charge of the timetable, and it is never too late. There are lessons to learn along the way, with work to do and lives to bless. No one has to be forever lost. The Lord knows who we really are, and our challenge is to see ourselves and others that same way—and not to define ourselves or others simply by current behaviors.

Family relationships can be tricky. Parents, siblings, cousins, grandparents grieve when a loved one strays from the tenants of their faith, or when decisions are made that cause a violation of trust and sacred covenants. This is an issue facing nearly every family in the Church. But remember, it was not by accident that Nephi, Sam, Jacob and Joseph had Laman and Lemuel as their brothers. They belonged together because that's how the Lord established it. Likewise, your family and our family are not together by accident. They are established by divine design.

We don't fully understand the timeline for if or how or when loved ones will come back to full fellowship, at least in this mortal time frame. But we do know the Lord is mindful of all His children. We must remember that the path back to heaven is a long one, that we don't have all the answers all the time. We know that our Heavenly Parents are pretty good at what they do, and that they know us and love us with a perfect love, with perfect understanding.

One of the key leadership challenges (and profound opportunities) for family members (parents, siblings, aunts, uncles, grandparents, grandchildren) is to love each other—not just when the sailing is smooth but when it is turbulent. Camilla Kimball offers this wise advice: "preserve the relationship with family whenever possible."[2] Very little is solved when loved ones are cut off because of differences in faith or choice.

Covenants have binding power. Prophetic council has been consistent on this. Consider the following statements:

Joseph Smith

> When a seal is put upon the father and mother, it secures their posterity, so that they cannot be lost, but will be saved by the virtue of the covenant of their father and mother.[3]

Brigham Young

> Let the father and mother, who are members of this Church and kingdom, take a righteous course, and strive with all their might never to do wrong, but to do good all their lives; if they have one child or one hundred children, if they conduct themselves towards

them as they should, binding them to the Lord by their faith and prayers, I care not where those children go, they are bound up to their parents by an everlasting tie, and no power on earth or hell can separate them from their parents in eternity; they will return again to the fountain from whence they sprang.[4]

Gordon B. Hinckley

I have here an interesting statement by Elder Orson F. Whitney: "The Prophet Joseph Smith declared—and he never taught more comforting doctrine—that the eternal sealings of faithful parents and the divine promises made to them for valiant service in the cause of Truth, would save not only themselves, but likewise their posterity. Though some of the sheep may wander, the eye of the Shepherd is upon them, and sooner or later they will feel the tentacles of Divine Providence reaching out after them and drawing back to the fold. Either in this life of the life to come, they will return. They will have to pay their debt to justice; they will suffer for their sins; and may tread a thorny path; but if it leads them at last, like the penitent Prodigal, to a loving and forgiving father's heart and home, the painful experience will not have been in vain. Pray for your careless and disobedient children; hold on to them with your faith. Hope on, trust on, till you see the salvation of God" (Conference Report, April 1929). If any of you have a child or loved on in that condition, do not give up. Pray for them and love them and reach out to them and help them.[5]

James E. Faust

May I . . . say a word of comfort for the anguished parents of children who have lost their way and have turned a deaf ear to parental pleading and teaching . . . There are some great spiritual promises which may help faithful parents in this church. Children of eternal sealings may have visited upon them divine promises made to their valiant forebears who nobly kept their covenants. Covenants remembered by parents will be remembered by God. The children may thus become the beneficiaries and inheritors of these great covenants and promises. This is because they are the children of the covenant.[6]

Boyd K. Packer

It is a great challenge to raise a family in the darkening mists of our moral environment. We emphasize that the greatest work you will do will be within the walls of your home (see Harold B. Lee, CR, April 1973), and that "No other success can compensate for failure in the home" (see David O. McKay, CR, April 1953, p. 116).

The measure of our success as parents, however, will not rest solely on how our children turn out. That judgment would only be just if we could raise our families in a perfectly moral environment, and that now is not possible.

It is not uncommon for responsible parents to lose one of their children, for a time, to influences over which they have no control. They agonize over rebellious sons and daughters. They are puzzled over why they are so helpless when they have tried so hard to do what they should. It is my conviction that those wicked influences one day will be overruled . . .

We cannot overemphasize the value of temple marriage, the binding ties of the sealing ordinance, and the standards of worthiness required of them. When parents keep the covenants they have made at the altar of the temple, their children will be forever bound to them.[7]

Russell M. Nelson

Rewards for obedience to the commandments are almost beyond mortal comprehension. Here, children of the covenant become a strain of sin-resistant souls. And hereafter . . . children of the covenant, and "each generation [will] be linked to the one which went before . . . [in] the divine family of God" (Joseph Fielding Smith, CR, April 1965, 10). Great comfort comes from the knowledge that our loved ones are secured to us through the covenants.[8]

Do we understand *everything* about the plan of salvation? Of course not. There is so much we don't know. The restoration of the gospel continues to unfold, and greater understanding, light and knowledge will continue to come.

Do we know *everything* about our Heavenly Parents? No. Do we understand *all* the intricacies of the Atonement or the far-reaching and enabling power of God's grace? No.

Simply put, we don't know *everything* about *anything.*

At what level do we really understand the details of the Lord's plan of happiness for each of his children? Thankfully, we have guidance from the scriptures and on-going revelation through inspired leaders. We know enough to make covenants, and that the Lord will honor these covenants. And these covenants are binding. We know enough to know that He has not left us without comfort, revelation, and continual guidance. We know enough to trust Him.

Do we *fully* comprehend the Lord's love for us and for our families? No. But we do know this: our Father loves us *perfectly.* What does it mean that our perfected, all-wise and all-knowing Heavenly Parents love us with their perfect love? Honestly, we don't really know. But it brings immeasurable comfort to know they do, despite our mortal shortcomings and naiveté. Elder Jeffrey R. Holland shared the following counsel pertaining to our sometimes-limited perspective in our families:

> We know there are many of you who for whatever reason struggle with the idea of what is often termed the traditional family of the perfect family. Perhaps abuse has darkened the brightness of what might have been a celestial home. Perhaps divorce has left you on your own, searching for answers about the past and protection for the future. Perhaps you're prayerfully and patiently still waiting for the blessing of being married to your own eternal companion, or having children you cannot bear. For our faithful LGBT friends, perhaps your heart and mind are struggling to find hope, peace, and your place in the eternal picture.
>
> Please, all of you, know this: we see all of you and love all of you. If you will be faithful and keep your covenants with the Lord, I promise you that every opportunity and every blessing enjoyed by others will be afforded you in the Lord's divine timetable—and I mean every opportunity, and every blessing. No matter when, in

> the unfolding of our eternal lives, those future blessings are given to you, you are now, and you will be then, part of the family.
>
> Try to avoid getting tripped up by the phrase "traditional family" and instead replace it with a phrase like "eternal family." With an eternal perspective comes understanding that we are all part of the one big family—the family of God.[9]

Imagine a tennis ball, fresh from its can, smelling new, still tight and firm, springy and vibrant, the green felt still furry and undisturbed from any competition on the courts. If you close one eye and place that tennis ball within 1/16th of an inch from your open eyeball, what do you see? The tennis ball is so close to your eye it blocks the light, and most of what you see is darkness. Now, place that same ball on a beautiful, freshly mowed lawn, and stand 10 feet away. What do you see? You can describe the ball, the lawn, and the surrounding parts of the yard. Suppose you could float 100 feet in the air, over that same ball and lawn. What could you see now? Certainly, you could see the ball—now a tiny speck on a green lawn. But you'd also see extensively beyond the small patch of grass as your home and the entire neighborhood come into view. What if you were one mile in the air? Could you still see the ball? Probably not, but a grand new vista would unfold, and you'd be able to see for miles. What about five miles in the air? What about ten? Now, suppose, by some special power, you were able to go 200,000 miles from earth. What could you see? What would your perspective be?

Here's the point: our Heavenly Father not only sees us where we are today—with intimate detail far greater than our mortal ability can comprehend, he sees us with a perspective far, far broader than we can fathom. Too often our view of the world, of ourselves, and of others is like the tennis ball that's too close to our eye. We only see the here and now, and even that is often jaded by the proximity of our problems and concerns. But our Heavenly Father sees us and knows us with a perspective incomprehensible to us. He sees everything—both near and far. He knows us with an understanding of who we were before we came to mortality, who we are today, and who we will ultimately become. We must trust that *His* understanding of us is greater than our understanding of *us*. We cannot judge ourselves or others simply by what is happening today. Our Heavenly Father certainly doesn't. He brings an eternal perspective that we don't yet fully comprehend. As Paul taught, "For now we see through a glass darkly; but then face to face: now I know in part; but then shall I know even as also I am known" (1 Cor 13:12). What today seems murky will someday become clear. Today we are known perfectly by a loving Heavenly Father. And while some day we will "know as [we are] known," we don't bring the same parental perfection to our loved ones. Our challenge and opportunity is to trust in Him and His perfect love, and see and treat our family members accordingly.

Each of us carries a name—one given to us from our parents, one they also received from their parents. It represents the legacy of our forebears and comes with significant expectations—not just for us as individuals or our immediate families, but those who went before who also carried that name. Certainly, that is true for Thomas Wirthlin McConkie—a hefty name for someone in the Church—a name steeped in a solid, faithful tradition and prominent church leadership.

Thomas grew up in the heart of the Wasatch Front church culture as part of a very active family—his great uncle was Elder Bruce R. McConkie, an apostle, and his grandfather was Elder Joseph B. Wirthlin, also an apostle. At age thirteen, despite a natural inclination towards spiritual matters, Thomas decided the Church wasn't for him and stopped attending. At age nineteen, he elected not to serve a mission. Instead, he went on a global tour, with an agenda to study meditation and explore different cultures. This tour eventually landed him in China.

After a few years, his friends began returning from their missions, and though Thomas had had his own paradigm-expanding and spiritually profound experience, his was not the typical returned missionary profile. Culturally, Thomas felt out of place with them—a self-described street rat. Still, his move to China reinforced his lifelong desire for spirituality, and it felt like a natural place to explore this phase of his spiritual life. He became what he called a "Buddhist rebel." His exploring opened his eyes to new paradigms and new perspectives about God, culture and priorities. Still, the cultural expression of his parents' faith was not one of those priorities, and his lack of church participation was a source of continued conflict with most of the members of his family.

When he was home from his first world tour at age twenty-one, Thomas was invited to meet with his grandfather, Elder Joseph B. Wirthlin, at Church headquarters ("summoned," as Thomas called it). His grandad had always maintained a close and tender relationship with Thomas, and Thomas was excited to meet with him. But as he entered the church office buildings—with hair down to his shoulders—he felt he just didn't fit in this place.

Thomas feared he might get a sermon from his apostle grandfather, something like, "Let me tell you how you should be living, son..." But his experience with him couldn't have been more different. His grandfather simply affirmed his love for his grandson and told him, "I know you'll serve a mission." That was it. Thomas would later admit that everything he felt about himself at that time was the opposite of that affirmation.

Thomas left his grandfather's office confused. He recalls, "I don't know how my granddad knew what to say, what I needed at that time. But somehow, I could sense that he had tapped into a power in his life—something that gave him insight and wisdom. Something that comes with a lifetime devoted to emulating the Savior's love and a lifetime of submitting to the influence of the Spirit." Thomas had experienced something significant.

Elder Wirthlin's expression of faith and love affirmed Thomas' understanding that different people serve missions in different ways and at different times, and in fact, spiritual direction and maturity come in ways tailored to the individual. It underscored a growing understanding that God uniquely knows His children.

Thomas' return to the church wasn't immediate, and his grandfather's interview wasn't the only influence that directed him back to activity. He had, over the course of many years, developed an appreciation for a global perspective, goodness and truth in other cultures, and in particular, an expertise in meditation, which enabled an ability to gain a stillness of heart, clarity of thought and deep spiritual sensitivity. Other forces continued to guide him and instruct and prepare him. One Sunday, when he was thirty-one years old, and living in Salt Lake City again, on a whim he put on a tie and wandered into an LDS meeting house for the first time in nearly twenty years. While his visit to the church conjured some feelings of uneasiness and a recollection of contentiousness with most of his family, it also brought to both his mind and heart a simple, but overwhelmingly powerful message: he felt the Spirit, and it was a marvel to him. He felt he belonged. There was, he describes, "a powerful, living, holy presence in that building" that filled his heart with something that had been missing for so long—an overwhelming sense of love and joy. Subsequent abundant healing and a realization of spiritual gifts has been profound. He began to realize, "I would be totally impoverished if I didn't come back to this." He did so, incorporating perspectives and life-experience that enriched his belief with deep empathy and a broad, full perspective.[10]

Not every story ends this way. And keeping an eternal perspective with loved ones can be demanding to the core—as one friend recently shared, the process of doing so "will stretch me more than all my other assignments, callings and challenges combined." In Thomas' case, pressure from family to live up to the name came from a good place, a place motivated by deep love and conviction. And it was not altogether bad. Thousands of prayers were offered on his behalf. His relationship with his mother, in particular, offered a place where he was welcomed, despite the distance between lifestyles and belief. He learned the human connection becomes the critical component to another's growth—and a critical component to our own growth.

Our Heavenly Father is mindful of each of His children. With whatever distance one might create from Him or their family or loved ones, God does not lose sight of a child. He sees us with an eternal perspective, not bound by present choices or behavior. Our responsibility as leaders (in the family and elsewhere) is to follow suit—to love as He would love and to see others for who they really are.

Unconditional love has immense power to change and to influence, and is certainly what the Savior modeled:

> And the scribes and Pharisees brought unto him a woman taken in adultery; and when they had set her in the midst,
>
> They say unto him, Master, this woman was taken in adultery, in the very act.

Now Moses in the law commanded us, that such should be stoned: but what sayest thou?

This they said, tempting him, that they might have to accuse him. But Jesus stooped down, and with his finger wrote on the ground, as though he heard them not.

So when they continued asking him, he lifted up himself, and said unto them, He that is without sin among you, let him first cast a stone at her.

And again he stooped down, and wrote on the ground.

And they which heard it, being convicted by their own conscience, went out one by one, beginning at the eldest, even unto the last: and Jesus was left alone, and the woman standing in the midst.

When Jesus had lifted up himself, and saw none but the woman, he said unto her, Woman, where are those thine accusers? hath no man condemned thee?

She said, No man, Lord. And Jesus said unto her, Neither do I condemn thee: go, and sin no more. (John 8:3–11)

Some things to consider doing:

1. Avoid preaching to the one who is no longer participating in Church activity. This seldom propels that person to suddenly "come to the light."

2. Love your family member unconditionally. Embrace them. Include them. Communicate openly, frequently, and with empathy. Celebrate their goodness and contributions. This doesn't mean embracing every choice they make as acceptable. But it does suggest the greatest persuasive power in any relationship is love. As Robin Zenger Baker reminds us, "The

[very] essence of love and religion is finding a way to embrace a person no matter what choices they make."

3. Avoid blaming yourself. We cannot control others' choices—only our own. Again, this dynamic is one that touches—and has touched since the days of Adam and Eve—nearly every family.

4. Speak openly about your faith—don't hide who you are or what you believe—and allow loved ones the same privilege.

Note: For additional resources on this topic, see Robin Zenger Baker's book *Finding Peace When a Child Chooses Another Path*; Robert L. Millet's *When a Child Wanders*; Thomas Wirthlin McConkie's *Navigating a Mormon Faith Crisis*.

CHAPTER ELEVEN
LEAD WITH EMPATHY

He that ascended up on high, as also he descended below all things, in that he comprehended all things, that he might be in all and through all things, the light of truth; which truth shineth.

—D&C 88:6–7

This is empathy: Let me hold the door for you. I may never have walked a mile in your shoes, but I can see that your soles are worn and your strength is torn under the weight of a story I have never lived before. So let me hold the door for you. After all you've walked through, it's the least I can do.

—Morgan Harper Nichols[1]

Could a greater miracle take place than for us to look through each other's eyes for an instant?

—Henry David Thoreau[2]

Elder Neal A. Maxwell declared: "None of us ever fully utilizes the people-opportunities allocated to us within our circles of friendship. You and I may call these intersectings 'coincidence.' This word is understandable for mortals to use, but coincidence is not an appropriate word to describe the workings of an omniscient God. He does not do things by 'coincidence' but . . . by 'divine design.'"[3]

Every moment we encounter in the Savior's life provides examples of leadership and communication we should strive to follow. And a prevailing message from His example is how, as a leader, He is focused on the unique needs each individual has. Here's a favorite illustration of that point.

A poor, unnamed widow in the small, impoverished and out-of-the-way village of Nain had just lost her son. Nain was a secluded farming village on the east side of the Jezreel Valley. Of course, the loss of a child is excruciating under any circumstance. In the case of this widow, it has particular long-lasting implications. Professor Keith J. Wilson explains the far-reaching significance of this tragedy for this widow.

> What would it have meant socially, spiritually, and financially to be a widow without an inheritor in ancient Israel? In Old Testament culture, it was believed that when a husband died before old age, it was a sign of God's judgment for sin. Thus, some believed that God was meting out punishment upon this surviving widow.
>
> Not only was there spiritual and emotional pain, but this widow of Nain was also facing financial ruin—even staring starvation in the face. Upon marriage, a woman was assigned to her husband's family for financial protection. If he died, then her care was delegated to her birthright son. Now that this widow's birthright and only son was dead, she was at the end of her rope financially. If her son was in his twenties, she was probably a middle-aged woman, living in a small, secluded farm town, and now found herself spiritually, socially, and financially destitute.[4]

The day just prior to this son's funeral Jesus had been in Capernaum, where he had risen the Centurion's servant from imminent death (Luke 7:1–10). Following that stunningly miraculous event, Luke records, "And it came to pass the day after, that he went into a city called Nain; and many of his disciples went with him, and much people" (Like 7:11, emphasis added). Keith Wilson continues:

> This sequence is very important. Capernaum is situated on the northern shore of the Sea of Galilee, 600 feet (183 m) below sea level. Nain is about 30 miles (48 km) southwest of Capernaum at 700 feet (213 m) above sea level, thus requiring an arduous, uphill climb to Nain. In order to walk from Capernaum to Nain, it would have taken at least one or two days. This means that Jesus probably had to arise very early or possibly even walk during the night in order to intercept the burial procession.[5]

How is it that Jesus knew to leave Capernaum immediately following the miracle with the Centurion's servant? Why was He willing to make the long and demanding journey—on foot—and press on to such an extent that He was able to arrive the very next day? Jesus' encounter with the widow, just at the time the mourners were carrying the lifeless body of her only son, highlights the Savior's remarkable leadership and empathy. Some journeys are not convenient. Some service requires long and taxing effort. Sometimes leaders follow a prompting to act when they don't have the full context. It is often only after the service is rendered the leader understands the larger picture. When guided by the Spirit, what can seem like a coincidence is really a manifestation that the Lord is in charge and that He knows the needs of His children. Surely, He is involved in the details of our lives; surely, He loves us and extends His empathy and understanding towards us, and He utilizes His faithful and obedient leaders—whether called to a formal position or not—to bring about abundant blessings to those in need. Remember the admonitions of President Thomas S. Monson (who likewise lived a life filled with remarkable, even miraculously timely service): "One day, when we look back at the seeming coincidences of our lives, we will realize that perhaps they weren't so coincidental after all."[6]

Keith Wilson concludes:

> Jesus somehow sensed the utterly desperate situation of this widow. Perhaps she had spent the night sprawled on her dirt floor, begging

Heavenly Father to know why. Perhaps she had even openly questioned why He was requiring her to live any longer on this earth. Or perhaps she was terrified of the pending loneliness that she would face. We do not know. But we do know that the Savior chose to leave Capernaum immediately, which could have required Him to walk through the night in order to intercept the burial procession right before they put the body in the ground.

Yes, when He saw her tear-stained face as she walked behind the procession, Jesus felt great compassion for this woman—but it appears that His compassion came from feelings He experienced long before He just "happened" to intercept that burial entourage. He had clearly planned to be there in her moment of need.[7]

"Weep not," Jesus tells the woman, and touches the bier as the procession stands breathlessly still. "Young man, I say unto thee, Arise. And he that was dead sat up, and began to speak. And [Jesus] delivered him to his mother" (verses 14–15).

One of our most significant needs in mortality is to experience the power of being understood. We want to know that we matter. We want to know that we, among all of God's creations, aren't just a compilation of random elements, but instead, a being that is connected—somehow—to something larger, that we have purpose. We want to know that we are known and loved by God, despite whatever current challenge or limiting circumstance we may be encountering. And we are all encountering something. I love this statement: "The deepest need of the human soul is to feel understood."[8] We all want—and need—to feel understood. One of the Savior's great traits is His ability to have empathy with each of us. We feel His understanding of our circumstances because we know He has been there. Alma taught:

And he shall go forth, suffering pains and afflictions and temptations of every kind; and this that the word might be fulfilled which saith he will take upon him the pains and the sicknesses of his people.

And he will take upon him death, that he may loose the bands of death which bind his people; and he will take upon him their infirmities, that his bowels may be filled with mercy, according to the flesh, that he may know according to the flesh how to succor his people according to their infirmities. (Alma 7:11–12)

Empathy is defined as "the action of understanding, being aware of, being sensitive to, and vicariously experiencing the feelings, thoughts, and experience of another of either the past or present without having the feelings, thoughts, and experience fully communicated in an objectively explicit manner."[9] To have empathy means one feels another's feelings. Empathy is not sympathy, though the two words are close cousins. To have sympathy suggests a level of agreement or sharing, while empathy means one has the capacity to experience the emotions of another, whether or not that person actually agrees with the person with whom they are engaged. The well-oiled phrase, "to walk a mile in another's shoes" is a description of what it means to have empathy—to see how another sees something, to feel how another feels something.

Developing the skill of empathy is a particularly critical leadership skill—one that is often counterintuitive. One might assume that because a question is asked or a statement is made, that question or statement deserves a specific answer. Sometimes it does. For example, if your teenage daughter asks, "What is for dinner?" you'll probably want to respond directly. But when emotions are high and there's lots at stake, it frequently does not foster effective communication to engage in harsh probing questions or extensively recounting of your own experience. And so often, that's exactly what we do.

One well-intended but particularly pernicious communication trap so many of us fall into is the tendency to want to "fix" another's problems. This comes from a good place. We care about the person with whom we are communicating, and we have a solution. Pretty simple. We bring to the discussion strong opinions about what a course of action should be, or perhaps we've had a similar experience from which the other could benefit. Certainly, our track record should account for something.

Here are a couple problems with fixing. First, more often than not, those with whom we are talking don't necessarily want or need their problem to be "fixed." Instead, they want to be heard—*truly* heard. Solutions to problems generally reside with the person who has the problem. We seldom need another to fix a circumstance. We do, however, want to feel understood in the process of resolving it.

Second—there is great danger in assuming you know the details of another's concern or issue. Think about how you feel when you engage in conversation with another on an emotional issue, something that has been troubling you. But before you have a chance to get to your concerns, the one with whom you are conversing quickly assumes they understand and launches into their solution for you. Far too often, their assumption is off, and you leave feeling diminished by the interaction.

Here are two primary skills to aid in the fostering of communication, especially when emotions are high or there is a lot a stake: 1) reflect or restate words the other person said back to them, and 2) to reflect to them their emotion. Of the two, reflecting feelings and emotions is the more critical skill.

Imagine going to play tennis. You show up at the courts a few minutes before your partner does. Many courts have a hitting board, which allows a single player to hit and have the ball bounce back. You hit the ball; it comes back to you. That's a little like what it means to listen in this way. When emotions are high, it may not be effective to pin your communication partner to the wall with endless questions or extensive recounting of your own experience of the "old days." The proverbial, "When I was young, we had to walk to school without shoes, in the snow, and uphill, both ways" doesn't usually inspire great communication.

Instead, be a faithful translator of what the other person said and restate or "bounce" their message and their emotions back to them. For example, if your communication partner said to you, "Wow, you can't imagine the day I had to day . . . It seemed I had competing priorities every moment. I was incredibly busy, but I'm not sure I got anything done!" Instead of responding with something like: "I know . . . my day was out of control too! And tomorrow is worse!" you might say, "Your day seems really crazy. Sounds exhausting!"

It's a simple mindset shift—you are listening to come to and convey understanding rather than listening to reply or to share your own story. So often when we are engaged in an emotional or high-stakes discussion, we listen just long enough to form a rebuttal to what the other person is saying, then interrupt them to share our viewpoints. In turn, just as you are embarking on your well-crafted response, your partner doesn't really listen to you either, instead prepares their own rebuttal to your words. So it goes, back and forth, with neither party really listening or showing even the slightest degree of empathy, leading the discussion down a dark and fruitless spiral of miscommunication. It's called the dialogue of the deaf—neither side attempting to understand, instead both parties are listening to reply, and both come away frustrated and feeling misunderstood.

Ninety-five percent of communication is straightforward. A question is asked, an answer is given in response. If someone comes to you in obvious discomfort and asks where the restroom is, you probably don't want to respond with, "You seem uncomfortable and want to know where the restroom is." Instead, you simply point them in the right direction, and off they go, thankful for the advice and direction.

But there are times—especially with those closest to us—where emotions are high, and a deeper understanding is required. When this is the case, remember the two tennis balls—restate or "bounce back" the words they say and the emotion they are conveying.

Several years ago I was invited to speak to both youth and parents at a youth conference. The topic was: "Demonstrating empathy in our relationships between parents and teens." To reinforce the principle of and process for showing empathy, I conducted a role-play with the class. I assumed the role of a disgruntled teenager, while the class—adult leaders and parents as well as the youth—were to assume the role of my parents. I announced as I began the role play that I, their seventeen-year-old son, wanted to quit school. What I didn't share, however, was that I had bigger issues that I was dealing with but didn't reveal because I didn't feel comfortable opening up. I went person to person, expressing my desire to quit school. If their response to me was an empathic one, I revealed just a little bit more of what was really going on in my life. If their response to me was not empathic, I retreated more forcefully into my position that I wanted to quit school (which I really didn't want to do). My objective was to help each participant understand the power of reflecting back to me, without judgement or imposing their own story, my own words and emotions—to practice the skills of listening emphatically. I wanted them to walk, for just a few steps, in my shoes.

A fascinating thing happened. As I said to the adult leaders and parents, "I want to quit school," their response was generally in the spirit of, "No way! Not on my watch!" or "Listen, your sister had tough times, but she persevered, and look at her now!" or "I just don't understand what's going on. Just open up and share!" None of these responses made me feel the slightest bit understood. Instead, I found myself being thrust immediately from my agenda and issues to theirs—in some cases being forced into a recounting of their own hardship when they were young. None of this was helpful.

However, as I shifted my role-pay to the teenagers (among whom was my own seventeen-year-old son), something changed. These youth grasped the concept of empathy very quickly. They responded with understanding hearts, saying things like, "That must have been frustrating to you" or "Wow, you must be in a difficult spot right now." They didn't try to "fix" me or my circumstance. Nor did they agree with my irrational and emotional conclusions. They simply listened and reflected my emotions. They sensed how I was feeling, and "bounced" those feelings back. As they did so, I began to feel understood. I felt safe in opening up to them what my real concerns were—concerns and fears that caused me to feel embarrassed and that I was not willing to share openly in an unsafe environment. But once I began to feel their level of genuine interested in my feelings, I opened up.

It was a fun session, one where I could point out to the adult leaders how our experiences and years of scripting can deter real communication. We laughed together at how badly they had blown any attempt to empathize, while I lauded these great youth participants on their ability to develop mutual understanding and show real empathy. The process was simple—just restate my words and express an appreciation for the emotions I had been feeling. They were wonderful, and the adults were not so much. It was a humorous learning moment.

Fast forward from that experience a few weeks. I was having a discussion with my son—the same son who had participated in that youth conference—about his use of my car. To say it was a discussion is probably not fully accurate. It might be better to refer to it as a somewhat heated, one-way lecture on the virtues of driving safely and of respecting my property. This interchange was prompted by my belief that he was either not careful enough or grateful enough, or both.

My son, Cameron, had a different perspective of his driving prowess. His view was that he was conscientious and careful, and he articulated this position at the same volume I was lecturing him. Back and forth we went—neither side really listening, both just preparing our rebuttal as the other was speaking. We were both listening only to respond. Then, while I was talking, saying something like, "Listen, in this home, driving is a privilege, not a right," Cameron paused, bit his bottom lip just a little, took a deep breath, and said quietly and sincerely (mostly), "Dad, this must be really frustrating to you."

I immediately realized what he had just done. In an emotional moment, he had the presence of mind to pause from his legal defense and express a little empathy. I realized at that moment, that I was doing exactly what the adult leaders had done at the recent youth conference, actions which I had gently mocked and used as a teaching moment. Just like at the youth conference, it was the teenager who came to the rescue and provided a needed healing moment.

His moment of self-awareness brought a bit of levity to an otherwise unproductive communication and allowed us to quickly resolve both our issues with ease and understanding.

Sometimes demonstrating empathy simply means we show up, that we are present for another person. We may not always know what to say. But we don't always need to say anything. To minister is to be empathic—to meet another where they are, to understand their pain and particular needs. Then, to lift them, to succor them, to genuinely love them as the Savior loves them. One of my favorite teachers, Kristin McQuivey, reminded me of this. She taught:

> God made us to need each other. He made us so that we crave and need connection. We need to know each other. We need to care. We need to love. He wants us to truly be there for each other in essential ways. He wants us to minister to each other.

Consider this day in the life of Jesus, taken from Matthew 9.

- His day began as He left a ship and entered into own city.
- He spent morning teaching, then healed a man sick of palsy.
- As he left that place, He saw a man called Matthew and invited him to "Follow me."
- He took a moment to sit and eat, surrounded by disciples but also joined by publicans and sinners.
- He held a discussion with Pharisees who questioned His choice of friends.
- During this conversation, a man named Jairus came and asked the Lord to come heal his daughter who was near unto death.
- On the way there, the Savior walked down a very crowded street.
- A woman sick for twelve years came behind Him and touched His garment.
- The Savior stopped, took time to find the woman.
- She came forward fearing, trembling. He blessed her saying, "Thy faith hath made thee whole."
- He finally arrived at Jairus' home. He passed through room of people who laughed Him to scorn.
- He entered the room of Jairus' daughter and raised her from dead.
- Leaving, He met two blind men, asked if they believed, touched their eyes and they were healed.
- He was approached by others who brought unto Him a dumb man. He cast out the devil.

Quite the day! He stopped where He was needed. He met people where they were. Which of those things do you think were on his "to do" list for the day?

> The chapter ends with a verse that is a perfect definition of how the Savior's days were filled, "And Jesus went about all the cities and villages, teaching in their synagogues, and preaching the gospel of the kingdom, and healing every sickness and every disease among the people. But when he saw the multitudes, he was *moved with compassion* on them.[10]

Jesus' attention to the unique and individual needs of the people he encountered are what Emily Freeman, calls "Compassionate Detours,"[11] and begs the following questions:

- Do I make room in my crowded and complicated schedule to notice the needs of others?
- Do I recognize the subtle promptings I receive about another's needs?
- What do I do about those promptings?
- Do I make time for compassionate detours in my life?

Bonnie D. Parkin, who served as the general Relief Society president, reminds us, "Most ministering opportunities are spontaneous, not planned in advance. Much of the Savior's ministering seemed almost incidental, happening while He was on His way to somewhere else, while He was doing something else. He gave us the example of ministering as He went."[12]

To show compassion is to show empathy. To minister is to show empathy. To set aside our busy schedules for the benefit of someone in need is to show empathy. To listen to another without imposing your own story is to show empathy. Audrey Hepburn provides this wisdom: "Nothing is more important than empathy for another human being's suffering. Nothing—not career, not wealth, not intelligence, certainly not status. We have to feel for one another if we're going to survive with dignity."[13]

Here's one final example of the power of empathy. Jodi Orgill Brown grew up in the Washington, D.C. area as a precocious, overachieving child. She was a top performer academically, and an ambitious, social and outgoing student. Her parents had instilled in her the belief that she could do anything she set her mind to, and that vision matched her natural type-A personality. She was someone who moved fast, worked hard, had faith, and got things done. As Jodi describes her personality, "In first grade, my teacher would leave the room and leave me in charge at the head of the class. Which is exactly the way I liked it." If there was a class president position available, she had her hat in the ring. And while she didn't always win, more often than not she found herself on the winning side. Her vision, energy, and passion for life was contagious and captivating. Her love for others radiated in all she did and consistently drew others to her.

Jodi came to BYU with a goal to earn her four-year degree in three years, which she did. While there, she met her husband, Tolan. Four children came, one after the next, and with her beautiful family, loving and supportive husband, fulfilling work, Jodi was living the life she had always dreamed of. In fact, just as her parents had promised, the good things she had hoped for as a young girl had come about because of her drive, her goodness, her hard work and her abundant faith.

Then the dizzy spells started. She had difficulty walking. Her balance was askew. She described to me how headaches and nausea soon began to dominate her daily life. They began to interfere with the most basic of tasks and invaded the special moments she cherished with her family.

Repeated visits to the doctors didn't provide much solace until she had an MRI, after which she received the devastating news of a mass on her brain. This news was made even more devastating when she learned from her neurosurgeon the location of the tumor was situated in a precarious and nearly inoperable position.

Her first brain surgery was successful in that the physicians were able to remove most of the tumor, but the effect of the surgery was that most of her face was now paralyzed. Her head was shaved, exposing staples left over from the surgery, drool dripped from the side of our mouth, her eye bulged and was not able to blink, and she had spinal fluid leaking from her nose and down the back of her throat. Jodi recalls this stage of her treatment with this troubling statement:

"It didn't take long for me to realize not all people are treated the same way."

A young man once entered her hospital room to clean up, looked at Jodi, and immediately gave her a look of pity. Jodi then recalled the words from the Savior's teaching in Matthew 25: "In as much as you have done it unto one of the least of these, my brethren, ye have done it unto me." "The least of these!" Jodi thought. "When have I become one of the least of these?" This once unstoppable and driven force for good, who volunteered for every opportunity to lead and serve, was now laying on her hospital bed garnering the pity of the hospital staff. "When did people stop seeing me, and started seeing just a body on a bed?" She wondered.

Jodi could no longer care for herself, not to mention her husband or her children. That is when she learned this penetrating truth: every interaction is an opportunity to change someone's life. The interactions she had while in this state left her with one of two emotions: first, she had some that left her feeling helpless, hopeless and all alone. Other times, however, her interactions with others help her to feel lifted, empowered, and surrounded with love.

Jodi recalls in her own words this experience:

> One day a Certified Nurse's Assistant (CNA) entered my hospital room. She didn't share her name, only that she was there to bathe me. She placed me on a plastic mattress and wheeled me down to a shower room. The CNA then shut the door to the shower room and proceeded to yank the gown from my body and dropped it on the floor. She then grabbed the shower hose and sprayed me off with cold water. I could feel all my humanity and dignity spiraling down with each drop of my tears and the icy water. I felt I might as well have been a car in a car wash, a body in a bed, a name on a chart.

Indeed, every interaction is an opportunity to change a life. And this particular interaction left Jodi feeling hopeless and invisible and wondering if she should give up her fight.

Nine days later, with a renewed drive to persist in her life's fight, she determined once more to have a shower—once a perfunctory duty but now, based on her previous experience, something that required all the strength she could muster.

Jodi continues:

> A young man walked into my room. He marched immediately over to the whiteboard which was titled, "CNA on shift," and wrote his name: "Lucas." "Great," I thought—"the day I finally determine to try this miserable experience again, I get a male CNA!" I quickly decided that if I could just get my hair washed, it would make all the difference—it would give me a sense of strength and just a touch of normalcy. So I asked Lucas, "Are any of the girls on duty today who could come help me wash my hair?" Lucas looked at me with a humorous expression and responded, "I can help you wash your hair!" So I gritted my teeth and determined to move ahead with my plan.
>
> Lucas left my room to gather some supplies, retuning a few minutes later with a cart filled with what was needed. He helped me scoot to the bottom of the bed. He then draped black garbage bags all over the bed, over the pillow, then cascading down to a garbage bin such that it would allow the water to drain without soaking the bed. He then scooted me back up to the head of the bed and told me to relax while he began washing my hair. With significant trepidation for me, the process began. Lucas started by pouring water over my stubbled scalp. It felt so luxurious! He very tenderly massaged the shampoo into my scalp, careful not to touch the sutures or staples or do anything that might compromise me or cause me harm. When he was done, he started the process all over again, this time with conditioner.
>
> In what otherwise should have taken about five minutes, Lucas kindly, carefully and gently took thirty minutes massaging not only the shampoo and conditioner into my scalp, but also a sense of my humanity. His every action told me that he did not see me as maimed or as an outcast or as sick. He saw me as a whole person, but one who was hurting. When he was finished, I felt like I had had a day at the spa.[14]

Lucas was not a physician or a nurse. His placement on the healthcare pecking-order was near the bottom of the list. But he was a man who acted with great stature. His every action emboldened Jodi to continue the fight for her life and to return to her family, to love herself and embrace her new life.

After numerous more surgeries, Jodi eventually returned home to continue her fight and today stands as a stirring reminder of enduring strength, inspiring faith, and a literal manifestation of God's love for His children.

Lucas' behavior reminds us that every soul is great in God's sight, and that, regardless of our title or position, we can show our love by our actions. We may not be able to "fix" every problem we see—and, indeed, we shouldn't try. But we can express empathy, and that empathy will make all the difference. Jodi concluded her recounting of her experience with this challenge: "When Christ encouraged his disciples to love and serve the least of these, it was not an insult. It was an invitation—an invitation to stop seeing imperfection and start seeing the divine individuals we truly are."[15]

That's what it means to show empathy. And effective leadership requires it.

Some things to consider:

1. Practice the skills of empathy today. Try setting aside the natural tendency to immediately fix another's problems or dispel wisdom from your own story. Instead, simply listen to their circumstance. Remember the two tennis balls — "Bounce back" to them their own words and feelings.

2. Pray to better hear and understand the promptings from the Holy Ghost on how you can serve another in need.

3. Act on those promptings.

CHAPTER TWELVE
LEARN TO HEAR HIM

If thou shalt ask, thou shalt receive revelation upon revelation, knowledge upon knowledge, that thou mayest know the mysteries and peaceable things—that which bringeth joy, that which bringeth life eternal.

—D&C 42:61

I can't think of anything more important for any of us in this day than to have the promise that we can hear Him, that we can receive His guidance, His reassurance, His protection in our lives.

—Elder David A. Bednar[1]

Near the end of his life, as he was passing the mantle of leadership to his son, Mosiah, King Benjamin instructs Mosiah to gather the Nephites for his final address. This address—one of the great and significant sermons recorded in any scripture—was given to him by an angel (Mosiah 3:2) and provides beautiful and poignant direction.

King Benjamin was a leader who engaged personally with his people and provided a powerful framework for coming unto Christ.

Counsel and direction from the Lord's prophet and other inspired leaders really takes root as mothers, fathers and other family members turn their hearts and homes to the Lord. In the case of the Nephites, faithful family members gathered to hear King Benjamin's words as a unit. These families pitched their tents with the door facing toward the temple to hear their prophet-leader's council, "that thereby they might remain in their tents and hear the words which king Benjamin should speak unto them" (Mosiah 2:6). Their instruction, their faith, and even their safety as a family unit came because they gathered and learned together—as a family unit. Their spiritual and physical attention was toward the words of the prophet and the symbol of the temple. This was their focal point, reinforcing in their lives the spirit of continuing revelation through the Lord's chosen vessels and the strength of the temple and the covenants made therein.

To help the vast multitudes hear his words, King Benjamin erected a tower from which he gave his address. But even that was not fully sufficient: "And it came to pass that he began to speak to his people from the tower; and they could not all hear his words because of the greatness of the multitude; therefore he caused that the words which he spake should be written and sent forth among those that were not under the sound of his voice, that they might also receive his words" (Mosiah 2:8).

Just as in King Benjamin's time, proximity and circumstance may make physical gathering impractical or even impossible. The global pandemic of the spring of 2020 brought this potential into sharp reality as businesses, temples, weekly services all closed, requiring the home—our "tents"—to become not only places where we gathered, ate, and slept, but also our offices, our gyms, our schools, our theatres, our daycare centers, our restaurants. And they became, in a very real and formal sense, our places of worship. Families gathered to read the words of the Lord and to partake of the sacred sacramental emblems. Our homes became places where, through the blessings of inspired technology, we heard and read the words of the Lord's prophets, despite the inability to physically gather. Our homes became places where our spirits received strength and where we testified—together—of hope and of eternal truths.

Leadership in the home—where and how we "pitch our tents"—provides the foundation for every other aspect of our lives, including the opportunity to receive revelation as it comes from the spoken and written words of the prophets, from our experiences with the temple, and through the whisperings of the Holy Ghost.

President Boyd K. Pack taught:

> Every man, woman, and child of every nation, creed, or color—everyone, no matter where they live or what they believe or what they do—has within them the imperishable Light of Christ . . . The Light of Christ in everyone is a testimony that God is no respecter of persons (see D&C 1:35). He treats everyone equally in that endowment with the Light of Christ.[2]

In addition to the Light of Christ, that wonderful teacher every one of God's children can feel, as members of The Church of Jesus Christ of Latter-day Saints, we are offered a remarkable gift when we are baptized and confirmed: The Gift of the Holy Ghost. Elder David A. Bednar taught of the meaning of this gift:

> The simplicity of this ordinance may cause us to overlook its significance. These four words—"Receive the Holy Ghost"—are not a passive pronouncement; rather, they constitute a priesthood injunction—an authoritative admonition to act and not simply to be acted upon (see 2 Nephi 2:26) The Holy Ghost does not become operative in our lives merely because hands are placed upon our heads and those four important words are spoken. As we receive this ordinance, each of us accepts a sacred and ongoing responsibility to desire, to seek, to work, and to so live that we indeed "receive the Holy Ghost" and its attendant spiritual gifts. "For what doth it profit a man if a gift is bestowed upon him, and he receive not the gift? Behold, he rejoices not in that which is given unto him, neither rejoices in him who is the giver of the gift" (D&C 88:33).[3]

All that we have and enjoy as members of the Church comes as a result of this gift, but activating it requires effort. In 1839, The Prophet Joseph had an audience with the President of the United States. His purpose in meeting the President was to discuss and ask for redress for the wrongs suffered by the Saints in Missouri. During his meeting, President Buchanan asked the Prophet what the difference was between Joseph's religion and all the others. According to Elias Higbee, who accompanied Joseph, his response was simple:

> Brother Joseph said we differed in mode of baptism, and the gift of the Holy Ghost by the laying on of hands. We considered that all other considerations were contained in the gift of the Holy Ghost."[4]

The structure of the Church, the saving ordinances, the gifts found in the temple—everything that encompasses who we are, what we do, and the blessings that flow from our membership come from the influence of the Holy Ghost. That is the key differentiator we enjoy.

So how can we access this great gift more purposefully? Elder Richard G. Scott instructed us on this point:

> One must be ever mentally and physically clean and have purity of intent so that the Lord can inspire. One who is obedient to His commandments is trusted of the Lord. That individual has access to His inspiration to know what to do and, as needed, the divine power to do it.
>
> For spirituality to grow stronger and more available, it must be planted in a righteous environment. Haughtiness, pride, and conceit are like stony ground that will never produce spiritual fruit.[5]

Learning how the Holy Ghost works is a requirement for any leader—for guidance in our individual decisions and direction, in our callings, and certainly in our families. The Holy Ghost won't likely show us every detail of every problem or concern. Sometimes we need to take a few steps into the darkness.

One evening I was wrestling with some concerns at work. These concerns were complex and felt all-consuming. I had stewed on these problems for some time, and my path forward was not clear. That night, as I knelt by my bed, I poured my heart out to my Heavenly Father. I believed at the time that He know my circumstances, and that He could provide the direction I needed. I approached Him with that faith. It was an exhausting experience, but after some time, after I felt I had clearly articulated the issues I was experiencing, I paused to listen to whatever counsel I might get. After a bit of silence,

I embarked again on the recitation of concerns. While I didn't immediately receive an answer, what I did immediately and poignantly feel was my Heavenly Father's understanding. Then, as clearly as if someone had whispered in my ear, I heard these simple words: "Have faith!" That was it. I didn't receive a detailed solution that guided my every action. In this instance, I *did* receive a clear message that the Lord was aware of my struggle, that He heard my petitions, and that He would guide and assist me in my efforts as I moved ahead with my work. I left my prayer that evening with the assurance that all would be well, and, in fact, it was. I had received just enough, and just what I needed.

Clarity in the midst of on onslaught of information

When my daughter, Mallory, was fourteen years old, she served in student government on her junior high student council. Her specific assignment that year was to plan the school's annual talent show. I cannot think of anything closer to the seventh ring of Dante's Inferno than that assignment, but she was thrilled with it and approached her task with her typical fervor and enthusiasm. Mallory has a beautiful singing voice, and it was her plan to conclude the talent show by playing the guitar and singing a Taylor Swift solo for her classmates. It was a great plan that had only one flaw: she had never played the guitar and didn't know a single chord. Undaunted, Mallory did what so many of her generation do when they need to learn a new concept or skill—she turned to YouTube. In a matter of hours, Mallory had mastered the necessary skills to play her selected song, and the event came off without a hitch. She sang and played beautifully and received a thunderous ovation from her fellow students.

Access to seemingly unlimited information—any topic—wherever we are and just when we need it, stands as one of the remarkable hallmarks and blessings of our modern age.

Yet it also represents one of the great paradoxes of our time: Just as our immediate access to unlimited information can bless our efforts to learn, grow and contribute, it has also proven to be a source of overwhelming stress, intense contention, and unnecessary distraction. A 2009 Harvard Business Review article by Paul Hemp revealed:

Most organizations unknowingly pay a high price as individuals struggle to manage the information glut. For one thing, productive time is lost as employees deal with information of limited value. In the case of e-mail, effective spam filters have reduced this problem. Still, a survey of 2,300 Intel employees revealed that people judge nearly one-third of the messages they receive to be unnecessary. Given that those same employees spend about two hours a day processing e-mail (employees surveyed received an average of 350 messages a week, executives up to 300 a day), a serious amount of time is clearly being wasted.

- Ringing phones and e-mail alerts lower IQs by 10 points
- Knowledge workers average 20 hours a week managing e-mail
- Information overload costs the U.S. economy $900 billion a year
- 60% of computer users check e-mail in the bathroom
- A typical knowledge worker turns to e-mail 50 to 100 times a day
- 85% of computer users say they would take a laptop on vacation
- Employees consider 1 in 3 e-mails unnecessary[6]

That was in 2009. In 2020, the statistics were even more stunning:

- 1.7 MB of data were created every second by every person.
- Between 2018 and 2020, 90% of the world's data was created.
- 2.5 quintillion bytes of data are produced by humans every day.
- 463 exabytes of data will be generated each day by 2025.
- 95 million photos and videos are shared every day on Instagram.
- 44 zettabytes make up the digital universe.
- 306.4 billion emails are sent each day, with 5 million Tweets.[7]

And these numbers will only increase with each successive year. Indeed, with innovation expanding at nearly light speed, the technology we use today to access and disseminate information is obsolete before it hits the market.

The great Samuel Taylor Coleridge penned these memorable words in his epic poem, *The Rime of the Ancient Mariner*, describing the abundance of sea water surrounding his becalmed ship, while a lack of available drinkable and life-sustaining water nearly led to the sailors' demise (something that could also describe our ever-increasing flood of information):

> Water, water, everywhere,
> And all the boards did shrink;
> Water, water, everywhere,
> Nor any drop to drink.[8]

The onslaught of information we both create and relentlessly access as a function of modern life opens the door to new kinds of communication—a lot of which is positive. Because of the blessings of technology, we're able to make and sustain connections to loved ones regardless of our physical proximity. We can share ideas, impressions and inspiration that lift so many. We're nearly always accessible (day or night) and can be counted on to offer an encouraging word or provide critical insight. Indeed, technology is a significant means for building the Lord's kingdom in our fast-paced and ever evolving society. It comes in direct fulfillment of prophecy. President Spencer W. Kimball declared in 1974 the magnificent technology that would transform the Church's missionary efforts:

> The Lord will lay in our hand inventions which we can scarcely conceive whereby we will be able to bring the gospel to the peoples of the world. . . . I have faith that the Lord will open doors when we have done everything in our power. I believe that the Lord is anxious to put into our hands inventions of which we laymen have hardly had a glimpse. . . . We shall use the inventions the Lord has given us to awaken interest and acquaint people of the world with the truths, to ease their prejudices and give them a general knowledge.[9]

In addition to all the good we gain from technology and connectivity we also experience the "opposition in all things" Lehi discussed (2 Nephi 2:11). Far too much of what is communicated via digital and social platforms or other technological modalities is vicious, cowardly and without regard to any standards of civility. Our political climate has polarized us to such an extent we are experiencing father pitted against son, brothers and sisters arguing, and close friends taking anonymous and mean-spirited potshots against each other. Those who otherwise admire and love one another are finding ways to contend, compete, and criticize with staggering cynicism, creativity, and frequency.

Do you ever feel overwhelmed with the contentious "war of words" and "tumult of opinions" (JSH 1:10) that prevail in our society? Does it feel this war's pace increases in volume and fury with every passing day? Do you find, with all the various voices shouting loudly from any and all directions, the clarity on what to do, how to act, and what to feel can become clouded by the unrelenting noise?

We all need answers to the big things and the little things in our life. And in the midst of the pounding surf of ever-expanding but not always reliable data there is one constant source of information, direction, assurance, and peace that is always available—whenever we ask and as often as we need. And it doesn't come because of the number of megabytes per second we can access. The source is the same One the Prophet Joseph turned to: personal revelation.

President Russell M. Nelson has taught, "It has never been more imperative to know how the Spirit speaks to you than right now. He is the comforter. He will bring a feeling of peace to your heart. He testifies of truth and will confirm what is true as you hear and read the word of the Lord . . . Do whatever it takes to increase your spiritual capacity to receive personal revelation. Doing so will help you to know how to move ahead in your life, what to do during times of crisis."[10] Revelation is, as David Butler has taught, "where God meets you in your story,"[11] and He is certainly aware of our story.

Consumed with his own conflicted feelings brought about by his own contentious and disruptive community environment, fourteen-year-old Joseph Smith decided to gain clarity by the only means he felt would penetrate the fog—he turned to God. Though expressed nearly two centuries ago his questions "What is to be done?" and "How shall I know it?" (JSH 1:10) strike a profoundly relevant tone to our lives today. We all are faced with questions like these, which remain some of the prevailing, universal quandaries of morality. Notice the pattern for cutting through the contentious clutter we face today, modeled by the young, inexperienced but sincere and faith-filled Joseph Smith, which outlines for us how we can increase our access to this great resource.

1. Be willing to invest the time necessary to obtain divine guidance. Joseph pondered and discussed and wrestled with his questions. Clarity on his course of action came "In process of time" (JSH 1:8). Understanding the Lord's will for each of us may require patience. This is not to suggest He doesn't know the answers we need even before we ask the questions. However, the process we engage to learn his answers—even if and especially because it takes time and effort—is a significant benefit to us. This can take days or months or years, and regardless of the timetable, we are enriched by the experience.

2. Seek direction from the scriptures. Reading the scriptures opens our hearts. Joseph came across the well-known passage in the Book of James because he had spent time reading the Book of James (JSH 1:11). Elder David A. Bednar taught:

> One of the ways I hear him is in the scriptures. The scriptures are the pre-recorded voice of the Lord. And it's not hearing an audible voice, per say, although that can happen. It's hearing the scriptures in a feeling—a feeling in your mind, a feeling in your heart. Revelation is thoughts to the mind, feelings to the heart. The scriptures, for me, are the key in being able to have those thoughts and feelings"[12]

At one point in my mission, I was given the assignment to assist my mission president. I remember feeling totally unprepared and inadequate for the position, and those feelings became more acute when I learned the prophet, President Ezra Taft Benson, was coming to visit our mission. It was the time of the bicentennial of the constitution, and he was coming to speak at Valley Forge to commemorate the event. We were to be his hosts for his stay in the Philadelphia area. I was excited to meet him, eat breakfast with him, and hear him teach all the missionaries of our mission. But I was also a bit unnerved. We were to have a mission leadership conference that same day, and my mission president asked me to teach all the mission leaders. I asked him what he wanted me to speak on, and he simply said, "Follow the Spirit." Great. I would have been so much happier if he had given me a topic. I spent the next couple weeks praying and fasting to know what I should say. I got absolutely nothing—no inspiration whatsoever. I talked again with my mission president, asking again (pleading) for counsel, and he simply said again (this time with a little smile), "Follow the Spirit." So helpful. I will never forget the night before I was supposed to meet the prophet and conduct the training. I had nothing prepared and nowhere to go. It was not as if I had not put in an effort. I had for days. I remember kneeling beside my bed, pouring my heart out in prayer, pleading for answers. Then, as if someone was speaking directly in my ear, I heard so clearly the words, "Elder Moon, you teach your investigators every day that they will gain answers to their prayers by reading the Book of Mormon. Read the Book of Mormon!" Revelation that direct and that clear doesn't always happen to me, but that night it did. I jumped off my knees and began to read. I don't remember where I was reading. I don't think it mattered. As soon as I started reading, I became filled with the great spirit of that book, and then, just like that, I knew what I was supposed to say. It all came to me at once, every thought and every detail. It was a remarkable experience and poignant reminder of the power of reading—even immersing yourself—in the scriptures.

President Benson taught us:

> One of the most important things you can do...is to immerse yourselves in the scriptures. Search them diligently. Feast upon the words of Christ. Learn the doctrine. Master the principles that are found therein . . . Few other efforts . . . will bring greater dividends to (you.) Few other ways (will result in) greater inspiration... "You must . . . see that studying and searching the scriptures is not a burden laid upon (us) by the Lord, but a marvelous blessing and opportunity."[13]

3. Ponder your questions in the context of the scriptures you read—not just once, but continually. Joseph recalled that he "reflected on [what he had read] again and again" (JSH 1:12), and this became a catalyst for his actions.

4. Act on impressions, even if it prompts you to do things you haven't done before. In Joseph's case, he had never prayed out loud (JSH 1:13). But his study and pondering led him to the "determination" to do just that. Which leads to the next insight . . .

5. Pray intentionally and vocally. Could there be a correlation between how frequently and effectively you are praying and your feelings of "connectedness" with the Spirit? For those who have served missions, think back on your mission's morning routine: How many times did you pray? You likely had personal prayer when you awoke; you prayed silently as you studied your scriptures, language and lessons; you had prayer with your companion as you studied together; you offered a blessing on your breakfast (meager as it probably was), and you knelt with your companion in prayer before you left your apartment for the day. Think about it—by 9:30 or 10:00 a.m. you prayed five or more times before you opened your front door! Your prayers were targeted, specific and efficacious. But when this pattern of prayer changes, and daily prayer is lost in the shuffle of other activities, it is natural to expect a diminished spiritual sensitivity.

Pray vocally where possible. This can be a very powerful and wonderful experience. It will help clarify thoughts and feelings. Elder Jeffrey R. Holland has taught, "As Joseph did, I believe it is important for us to pray out loud. It is basic to what God intends for us in our communication with Him. He invites a conversation, if you will, and wants so much to 'hear us.' We should make every effort to let Him hear us — literally."[14]

6. Find your sacred places. Praying throughout the day and retaining a constant prayer in our hearts is essential. But sometimes it is worthwhile to go to our sacred places to have a planned, deliberate prayer. Temples are places of revelation where many go with specific questions and where sacred prayer and contemplation occur. Enos went to the woods, setting aside his hunting, and devoted significant time for his pleadings. In Joseph's case, he had determined beforehand a specific place (JSH 1:14–15) in the grove behind his home to offer his petitions to the Lord. These places become sacred ground to us, and can help us be more thoughtful, more focused, and more determined in our efforts. Find your own sacred places—places where you can have your individual experiences.

7. Pray fervently. Joseph's prayer was not a passive, passing thought, but instead an impassioned pleading both for his deliverance and to know God's will, "exerting all my powers" as he described it (JSH 1:16). There was energy behind his prayer. It was, as Elder Jeffrey R. Holland taught, a "muscular" prayer. Joseph was fully committed and deeply engaged in his efforts to commune with God. Mormon also counsels us to "pray unto the Father with *all the energy of heart*" (Moroni 7:48, emphasis added), suggesting that meaningful prayer can be an active, deliberate communication.

8. Persevere through opposition. Part of mortality is experiencing opposition. Sometimes seeking the Lord's guidance on important matters follows that same pattern. For Joseph, the opposition he faced was so extreme he felt he wound "sink into despair and abandon myself to destruction" (JSH 1:16). It was this moment when he felt he'd gone beyond a place where he could return that he experienced his deliverance, when he saw his pillar of light. So it can be with us. Sometimes our answers come immediately, and sometimes we wade through difficulty so extreme we don't know if we will ever emerge or if we'll ever feel or see the light again. Often, this is the moment of our illumination; this is the moment the light comes.

9. Learn to listen. In Joseph's case, his experience with revelation was a two-way conversation. Now, of course, if your experience is, like Joseph's, a visitation from the Father and the Son, you most certainly would listen to whatever is said! But the Holy Ghost's role is, in fact, to communicate the will of the Father and the Son, in and through a variety of means and modalities, all of which requires us to listen in order to hear him. Set time aside to be quiet and to listen to the whisperings and subtle thoughts the Spirit provides. Remember how the Lord spoke to Elijah:

> And he said, Go forth, and stand upon the mount before the Lord. And, behold, the Lord passed by, and a great and strong wind rent the mountains, and brake in pieces the rocks before the Lord; but the Lord was not in the wind: and after the wind an earthquake; but the Lord was not in the earthquake:
>
> And after the earthquake a fire; but the Lord was not in the fire: and after the fire a still small voice. (1 Kings 19:11–12)

The answers we receive through the still small voice are from our Father in Heaven and are just as efficacious as if they were received in more dramatic fashion. The challenge we have is to recognize them for what they are.

Answers can come immediately, and sometimes they "descend gradually," bit by bit, insight upon insight and revelation upon revelation. Elder David A. Bednar describes two different experiences most of us have with light as a template for how revelation can flow to us. The first occurs as we enter a dark room and turn on a light. Immediately we experience a "flood of illumination" that fills the entire room. The second experience happens as we watch the rising sun gradually ascend over the distant horizon, its light ever so slowly but surely warming the earth, turning the dark night into the day. This second experience with light is more subtle, but just as powerful as the first. Elder Bednar teaches:

> A light turned on in a dark room is like receiving a message from God quickly, completely, and all at once. Many of us have experienced this pattern of revelation as we have been given answers to sincere prayers or been provided with needed direction or protection, according to God's will and timing. Descriptions of such immediate and intense manifestations are found in the scriptures, recounted in Church history, and evidenced in our own lives. Indeed, these mighty miracles do occur. However, this pattern of revelation tends to be more rare than common.
>
> The gradual increase of light radiating from the rising sun is like receiving a message from God "line upon line, precept upon

precept" (2 Nephi 28:30)). Most frequently, revelation comes in small increments over time and is granted according to our desire, worthiness, and preparation. Such communications from Heavenly Father gradually and gently "distil upon [our souls] as the dews from heaven" (D&C 121:45).[15]

10. Be willing to learn the Lord's will, even if it is different than your hope or intent for the prayer. For Joseph, his query was simple: "Which of all the sects was right?" (JSH 1:18). Every account of the First Vision shows the Lord's answer went considerably beyond Joseph's initial question, as important as that question was. The Lord had something significant in store for Joseph, and His answer to a simple question began a long-anticipated and much prophesied series of events. And He has answers for each of us as well. The Lord knows you. He knows your needs. He knows who you were before you came to this mortal experience, and he knows who you must become. Have faith that He will direct your life. Certainly, you can and will receive answers to specific questions. You should establish personal patterns where this becomes part of your everyday experience. But be open to answers that may be different than your initial question.

11. Continue to seek revelation. We don't know every detail of Joseph's instruction that sacred day. But we do know that it was just the beginning of the revelations he was to receive as the restoration began to unfold. An answer to a prayer one day often requires new petitions and subsequent answers the next day. And the next. Sometimes we learn just what is needed for today, for our immediate next step. Often what we learn through prayer to just enough for now. But tomorrow we'll need the next step. Don't be like the man who, as his wife was dying, said, "I loved her . . . and almost told her once." Take advantage of the moment while realizing there will be other moments needed—tomorrow, and the day after, and so on.

12. Repent. Every day. Make the effort to acknowledge your shortcomings and sins and ask to have them forgiven. Prior to Joseph Smith's vision of Moroni, he plead with the Lord for this forgiveness of his sins. He wrote: "I often felt condemned for my weakness and imperfections; when, on the evening of the above-mentioned twenty-first of September, after I had retired to my bed for the night, I betook myself to prayer and supplication to Almighty God for forgiveness of all my sins and follies" (JSH 1:29). Seeking forgiveness was the impetus for his prayer and the catalyst for profound revelation.

Elder Bednar further instructs us:

> We more readily receive and recognize the Spirit of the Lord as we appropriately invite Him into our lives. We cannot compel, coerce, or command the Holy Ghost. Rather, we should invite Him into our lives with the same gentleness and tenderness by which He entreats us (see D&C 42:14). Our invitations for the companionship of the Holy Ghost occur in many ways: through the making and keeping of covenants; by praying sincerely as individuals and families; by searching the scriptures diligently; through strengthening appropriate relationships with family members and friends; by seeking after virtuous thoughts, actions, and language; and by worshipping in our homes, in the holy temple, and at church. Conversely, casualness about or the breaking of covenants and commitments, failing to pray and study the scriptures, and inappropriate thoughts, actions, and language cause the Spirit to withdraw from or to avoid us altogether.
>
> As King Benjamin taught his people, "And now, I say unto you, my brethren, that after ye have known and have been taught all these things, if ye should transgress and go contrary to that which has been spoken, that ye do withdraw yourselves from the Spirit of the Lord, that it may have no place in you to guide you in wisdom's paths that ye may be blessed, prospered, and preserved" (Mosiah 2:36).[16]

If we want to feel a closeness to the whisperings of the Spirit, we must eliminate activities that repel that Spirit and engage in activities that invite it. Elder Neal A. Maxwell taught, "Each of us must not only renounce evil, disengaging from doing wrong, but we must also engage anxiously in doing much good. Only then can a mighty change occur. Even then, our moral appetites seem to persist, for perfection is a direction to be pursued in the process of time."[17]

Be conscious of the music you embrace and the movies you watch. Be cautious of the amount of time you spend streaming mindless TV. And avoid the easily accessible but destructive influences of pornography.

President Russell M. Nelson has occasionally challenged members of the church to experience a "media fast." That is, going a period of time without participating in media of any kind, other than what is critical for required professional endeavors. While I was serving as a bishop, our ward accepted the challenge to go a full month on this fast. It was tough work. It meant no popular music, movies, video games, streaming, television or DVD's, and no Internet unless specifically required by a school or work assignment—for a full thirty days.

For the first week or so, those who participated in this challenge struggled to find things to do. Media is such a pervasive part of our lives and has become the default activity for many of us. But after a very short time, the participants in the challenge began to lose their desire for these influences. More time was spent with friends. More attention was given to scripture study. Individuals who were struggling with the addictive pull of pornography simply cut off their access to this vile practice. Some of these individuals had been struggling for years to eliminate this temptation, and after a few weeks, gained a new hope that pornography did not have to rule them. It was an amazing experiment as we learned how much we are influenced by the media. Don't fool yourselves into thinking that what we listen to or watch has no impact on our spiritual sensitivity.

We were given the gift of agency, which allows us to be tested, to grow and learn. In giving us this gift, our Father knew we would exercise it against His will from time to time, so He provided a Savior for us, through whom we can repair and repent. He invites us to turn to Him, hear His voice, and allow Him to heal us. Elder Dale G. Renland testified to this truth:

> Our Heavenly Father, referring to His Beloved Son, said, "Hear Him!" As you act on those words and listen to Him, remember, joyfully and reverently, that the Savior loves to restore what you

cannot restore; He loves to heal wounds you cannot heal; He loves to fix what has been irreparably broken; He compensates for any unfairness inflicted on you; and He loves to permanently mend even shattered hearts.[18]

13. Expect the Lord to hear and answer your prayers. Joseph's prayer for forgiveness was accompanied by an expectation that the Lord would hear him: "For I had full confidence in obtaining a divine manifestation, as I previously had one." His prior experience, like our prior experiences, remind us that we are not alone, that, regardless of who we are, where we are, what we have or don't have in terms of physical possessions, God is there. His arms are continually stretched out to accept and embrace us (Isaiah 9:12). He wants to communicate His Love to us. He invites us to hear Him.

14. Be willing to share your conviction. Despite the intense and abusive opposition he faced, Joseph boldly declared:

> I had actually seen a light, and in the midst of that light I saw two Personages, and they did in reality speak to me; and though I was hated and persecuted for saying that I had seen a vision, yet it was true; and while they were persecuting me, reviling me, and speaking all manner of evil against me falsely for so saying, I was led to say in my heart: Why persecute me for telling the truth? I have actually seen a vision; and who am I that I can withstand God, or why does the world think to make me deny what I have actually seen? For I had seen a vision; I knew it, and I knew that God knew it, and I could not deny it (JSH 1:25).

Bearing your testimony is one of the most powerful ways of opening the channel to revelation. We hear His voice as we testify of truth. This process is tied to the principle that the more you give, the more you receive. Alma taught, "For that which ye do send out shall return unto you again." (Alma 41:15). On this point, President Boyd K. Packer writes:

> Oh, if I could teach you this one principle. A testimony is to be found in the bearing of it! Somewhere in your quest for spiritual knowledge, there is that leap of faith, as the philosophers call it. It is the moment when you have gone to the edge of the light and

stepped into the darkness to discover that the way is lighted ahead for just a footstep or two. The spirit of man, is as the scripture says, indeed the candle of the Lord. (Prov 20:27)

It is one thing to receive a witness from what you have read or what another has said; and it is a necessary beginning. It is quite another to have the Spirit confirm to you in your bosom that what you have testified is true. Can you not see that it will be supplied as you share it? As you give that which you have, there is a replacement, with increase.

Bear testimony of the things that you hope are true, as an act of faith. It is something of an experiment that the prophet Alma proposed to his followers. We begin with faith—not with a perfect knowledge of things. That sermon in the thirty-second chapter of Alma is one of the greatest messages in holy writ, for it is addressed to the beginner, to the novice, to the humble seeker. And it holds a key to a witness of the truth.

The Spirit and testimony of Christ will come to you for the most part when, and remain with you only, if you share it. In that process is the very essence of the gospel.

Is not this a perfect demonstration of Christianity? You cannot find it, nor keep it, nor enlarge it unless and until you are willing to share it. It is by giving it away freely that it becomes yours."[19]

How can I know if I am receiving revelation?

For over two decades I have worked closely with the youth and young single adults of the church. A common question I received throughout this service (and continue to receive) is this: How do I know if I am getting revelation? How can I tell if it is the spirit or just how I want to feel?

In May of 1829, Hyrum Smith, older brother of the Prophet Joseph, received the following which provides a wonderful answer to the question and introduces six filters to guide our recognition. The Lord told Hyrum:

> And now, verily, verily, I say unto thee, put your trust in that Spirit which leadeth to do good—yea, to do justly, to walk humbly, to judge righteously; and this is my Spirit.
>
> Verily, verily, I say unto you, I will impart unto you of my Spirit, which shall enlighten your mind, which shall fill your soul with joy;
>
> And then shall ye know, or by this shall you know, all things whatsoever you desire of me, which are pertaining unto things of righteousness, in faith believing in me that you shall receive. (D&C 11:12–14)

Again, here are six filters we can use to determine the source of our inspiration:

1. Is what you're feeling telling you to do good? If so, it is the Spirit (D&C 11:12).

2. If it is telling you to "do justly"—in other words, to treat others with fairness and equity or to lift them up—it is the Spirit (D&C 11:12).

3. If it is telling you to walk humbly in a situation and to place God's priorities over everything else, it is the Spirit (D&C 11:12).

4. If you're in a circumstance where you need to judge righteously—to weight in between good and not so good, and you're drawn to the good—it is the Spirit (D&C 11:12).

5. If your mind is enlightened or an idea has come to your mind guiding you to do good, that's the Spirit (D&C 11:13).

6. If it makes you feel joy when you contemplate doing what you are feeling, that's the Spirit (D&C 11:12).

Inspiration comes in many ways

While serving in a stake presidency of a young single adult stake, our presidency would prepare for our ward conferences each year by meeting with each ward council prior to our formal Sunday ward conference session. It was always a wonderful time to hear from the amazing members of our stake—some of whom where students carrying tremendous academic loads, while others were at the beginning stages of their professional careers, with all the pressure and demands that are associated with that time in one's life. Some had served missions while others hadn't. Some were actively dating, while others were hoping for that event in their lives. All of them had the financial pressures of being on their own, and many had multiple jobs just to make ends meet. And all of them stood as shining examples of discipleship as they worked to establish foundations for their successful future. During this meeting, I posed a question that led to a robust and enlightening discussion: "How does the Holy Ghost communicate with you? How do you hear Him?" Their answers were both wonderful and diverse, and included the following:

- When needing guidance on a critical decision, I feel peace and calm about a particular course of action.

- I have instructive dreams. I think of the counsel from Elder Richard G. Scott, who taught us that "revelation can also be given in a dream when there is an almost imperceptible transition from sleep to wakefulness. If you strive to capture the content immediately, you can record great detail, but otherwise it fades rapidly. Inspired communication in the night is generally accompanied by a sacred feeling for the entire experience. The Lord uses individuals for whom we have great respect to teach us truths in a dream because we trust them and will listen to their counsel. It is the Lord doing the teaching through the Holy Ghost. However, He may in a dream make it both easier to understand and more likely to touch our hearts by teaching us through someone we love and respect."[20]

- I feel him when I read the scriptures. Sometimes it is a specific verse that addresses my very question. I may have read a particular verse many times, but this time it seemed to speak directly to me. Other times, it is not a particular verse, but a clarity of thought and feeling as I read and feel the power of the scriptures in general.

- I feel His influence when I listen to and participate in uplifting music.

- I feel direction as I engage in gospel-related discussions with others.

- I feel His presence when I serve. When I extend myself to others, I feel love for them. And when I feel love for them, I also feel my Heavenly Father's love for me. That's when I feel His spirit.

- I hear a voice speaking to both my mind and my heart. I can't tell if it is an audible voice, though it could be. Either way, it is clear and undeniable.

- I gain direction and understanding when I watch (and reread) the messages from our inspired leaders in General Conference and other meetings.

- I get impressions as I pour my heart out to my Father in Heaven in prayer—especially in the quiet moments of my prayers. Too often I get so busy or distracted or tired, my prayers seem like checklists that I have to work through, and once I've gone through my list, I finish and go to sleep. But when I am more thoughtful and deliberate with my prayers—when I take time not only to share what I want but to listen to what He is trying to tell me—I get thoughts and impressions that initially seem to pull me away from what I am saying. Then I realize that thought is precisely what I have been praying about.

- Fasting helps me set aside my otherwise seemingly unrelenting physical needs and tunes me more carefully to subtle but powerful spiritual impressions. I love what Elder Wirthlin taught about fasting when he said, "Fasting, coupled with mighty prayer, is powerful. It can fill our minds with the revelations of the Spirit. It can strengthen us against times of temptation. It can help develop within us courage and confidence. It can strengthen our character and build self-restraint and discipline. Often when we fast, our righteous prayers and petitions have greater power. Testimonies grow. We mature spiritually and emotionally and sanctify our souls."[21]

- I feel the Savior's love as I thoughtfully and reverently partake of the sacrament and consider both His sacrifice for me and the wonderful covenant I am privileged to participate in.

- I am better able to hear Him when I am grateful. When I feel disconnected from the Spirit, I pause for a moment and think of all the abundant blessings I have received. Really, everything I have is a manifestation of the Savior's love, and that helps me feel more open to the Spirit's influence.

- I feel a warmth pour over my body, bringing the sweet assurances that I am known and loved.

As each person in the room shared their own experience in receiving revelation, several things became clear. First, each shared a different way that the Spirit communicated with them. Their experiences were diverse, yet each experience had power and personal relevance.

Second, these wonderful people had each developed a pattern of doing the things that regularly invited divine communication, and this communication was familiar to them. They expected it, and it had become second nature, part of how they lived their lives.

And third, as I listened to each of these wonderful ward council members share how they received revelation, I had one of my own. It was the simple realization that I, too, have had all those same experiences.

As we went around the table sharing our thoughts and experiences, we realized that getting answers to prayers is not the same every time for every person, but that the Lord works with us in unique ways and in ways we will personally recognize. We all left that discussion with the overwhelming sense that we are not on this mortal journey alone, that the Lord is aware of each of us and is involved in the details of our lives, and that His communication with us through His Spirit is pervasive, timely and more abundant that we might normally realize.

Sometimes inspiration comes through others

The Lord instructed Hyrum Smith that he would "be the means of doing much good in this generation" (D&C 11:8). The same instruction applies to all leaders, who provide guidance and direction for those they serve. Indeed, often the answers we seek are presented through a key relationship or interaction with another. As a brand-new missionary, I watched closely the other elders in the mission. I wanted to learn what they knew, follow how they worked, and study how they led. A few provided examples of attributes I did not want to follow, but most offered sterling models of leadership and diligence. One of these elders was my second district leader, Elder Campbell. On an exchange one day we talked as we worked. Elder Campbell asked questions about my family, my schooling, my hobbies, etc. Then, out of the blue, he said, "You need to write your grandfather a letter." I hadn't mentioned my grandfather to that point in the conversation, but he had, in fact, been ill (which, of course, Elder Campbell knew nothing of), and I agreed it would probably be a good idea to send him a note. So I did. In my letter I shared my love for my grandfather and of his example of goodness throughout his life. It was a simple but sincere expression of gratitude for a rich and faithful heritage, one that had helped shape me, one I had seen at close quarters. Not many weeks after sending the letter, my grandfather passed away. I'm not sure how Elder Campbell received the inspiration to prompt me to write. But I do know the feelings of gratitude that washed over me when I received word of my grandfather's passing.

The Comforter, "which is the Holy Ghost" (John 14:26), does indeed provide comfort

My daughter, Mallory, is a gifted ballerina. She began her early dance training when she was three, then at age six, she commenced her formal ballet instruction from some gifted and dedicated teachers. For Mal, it required several hours every day, six days every week, for many years. Ballerinas are tough athletes who move with a well-earned grace and discipline brought on by years of detailed and demanding refinement, and Mallory has experienced both the pain and the joy of that refinement. She has loved every minute of her experience.

When she was a young dancer, she idolized the older, more experienced and polished ballerinas. They performed the principal parts in the productions, and she watched each of the dancers closely in every one of those productions. But the role she admired most was that of the Snow Queen in *Nutcracker*. The choreography was gorgeous, and the scene ended with the Snow Queen and her prince dancing the Pas de deux as snow fell onto the stage. "One day," my daughter dreamt, "I will dance that part." It was her quintessential role.

Indeed, the day did come. All her years of intense training were culminating with this part, at this moment, in front of a theatre packed with eager patrons. But as the days lead up to her debut performance, her nerves began to fray, and her confidence waned. "Am I good enough?" she asked herself over and over. "Can I do the lifts and the turns? Will I be as graceful as all those I watched and admired for so many years? Will I be a credit to the patient efforts of my teachers, whom I have grown to love?"

The closer the day came, the more she worried, until she wasn't sure she could proceed. She had put in the work. She was strong and graceful. She was ready. Despite this, her anxiety nearly overcame her. But she had learned over the years to rely on her Heavenly Father. She had confidence that He would hear her pleadings, and that He would provide whatever guidance and revelation she needed in order to proceed. She knew that He knew her, and that she could turn to Him in her times of need. So she did just that. As she was waiting in the wings to go on, she prayed fiercely that her confidence would match her preparation, and just as she was going on, in her most desperate time of need, she was overcome with a profound sense of warmth, starting at the top of her head and flowing down throughout her entire being. She knew, at that moment, that she would be buoyed by His strength. She then heard a voice, strong and familiar, saying a phrase she had heard hundreds of times, "Honey, you're going to be ok." She learned the truth of President Joseph F. Smith's testimony, when he stated:

> I believe we move and have our being in the presence of heavenly messengers and of heavenly beings. We are not separate from them . . . We are closely related to our kindred, to our ancestors . . . who have preceded us into the spirit world. We cannot forget them; we do not cease to love them; we always hold them in our hearts, in memory, and thus we are associated and united to them by ties that we cannot break . . . If this is the case with us in our finite condition, surrounded by our mortal weaknesses . . . how much more certain it is . . . to believe that those who have been faithful, who have gone beyond . . . can see us better than we can see them; that they know us better than we know them . . . We live in their presence, they see us, they are solicitous for our welfare, they love us now more than ever. For now they see the dangers that beset us . . . their love for us and their desire for our wellbeing must be greater than that which we feel for ourselves.[22]

Mallory learned, once again, that her Heavenly Father is aware of her. Nothing is beyond His view, and what matters to her matters to Him—because it matters to her. She had reinforced to her that He does listen and that He does answer. The Comforter, "which is the Holy Ghost" (John 14:26), does indeed provide comfort.

The Lord has established the means whereby He will provide revelation to us, and He has invited us to hear Him. And effective leadership demands it.

Things to consider doing:

1. Find your own sacred places to commune with your Heavenly Father.

2. Pray vocally when possible. Identify a time and location where you can pour out your thoughts and feelings and questions out loud.

3. Combine prayer with fasting. Look forward to the fast. Don't see it is a burden, but rather as an opportunity to focus and to feel.

4. Express your gratitude to your Heavenly Father. Go beyond the simple and sometime rote statements we all make and think deeply about the abundant blessings you enjoy. If you were to dedicate a full hour to prayer, and that entire hour would be spent in expressing gratitude, what would you say? Consider holding a fast dedicated wholly and completely to expressing gratitude and have your prayers throughout that experience be centered on that gratitude.

5. Include some quiet listening time in your prayers.

6. Keep a notepad close by and write down the impressions you receive.

PART IV
LEADERSHIP IN MY CALLING

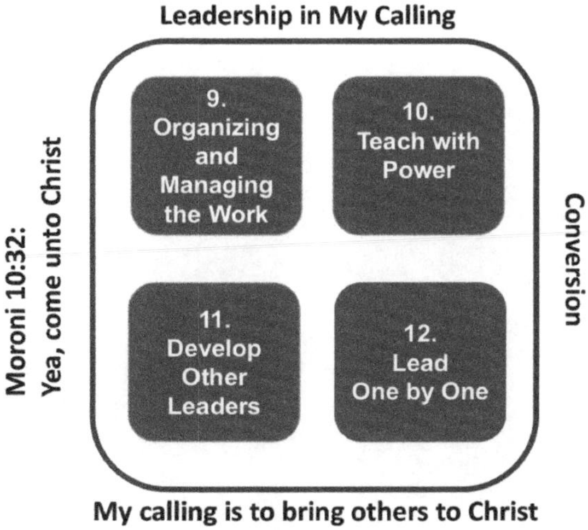

Leadership Level	Foundational Scripture	Governing Principle	How I Think	Practices
Leadership in my calling	Moroni 10:32: "Yea, come unto Christ, and be perfect in him, and deny yourselves of all ungodliness."	Conversion	In every action, in every word, and in every program, my job, regardless of a specific calling, is to help others come closer to the Savior and to make and keep sacred covenants. There is no other agenda.	**Practice 9:** Organizing and Managing the Work **Practice 10:** Teach with Power **Practice 11:** Develop Other Leaders **Practice 12:** Lead One by One

CHAPTER THIRTEEN

ORGANIZING AND MANAGING THE WORK

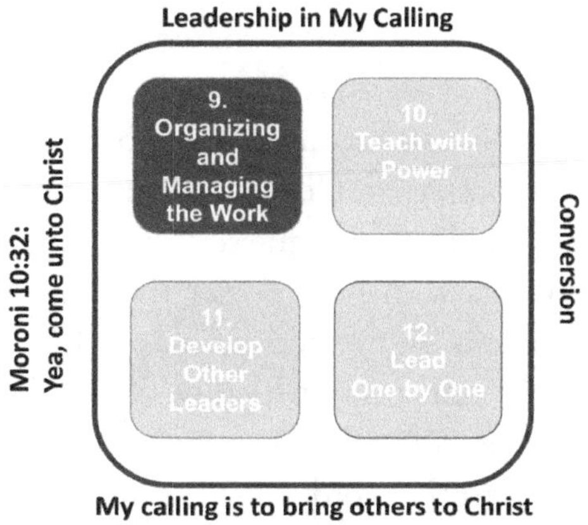

But be ye doers of the word, and not hearers only.

—James 1:22

Do all the good you can,
By all the means you can,
In all the ways you can,
In all the places you can,
At all the times you can,
To all the people you can,
As long as ever you can.

—John Wesley[1]

When one considers the great leaders in the scriptures, those remarkable souls who followed their divine mandate to set aside everything else for the building of God's Kingdom, many names spring to mind, conjuring up images of courage, vision, endurance, resilience, and unwavering conviction: Elijah, Elisha, Samuel, Jeremiah, Isaiah, Paul, Stephen and Peter. The Book of Mormon introduces King Benjamin and Mosiah, Alma and Alma, Helaman and Captain Moroni, Ammon and Samuel the Lamanite. Modern-day scripture reminds us of the great sacrifice and transcendent inspiration of the prophets and leaders of the restoration, whose willingness to give their all for the cause of Zion stands as a monument for our lives today. Indeed, everything we enjoy as blessings from heaven today comes from their sacrifice. All these examples are worthy of admiration and deep study. As we do so, we will learn of God's individual and intimate love for us as His children. Our faith in Jesus Christ and His ability to save becomes clearer because of the goodness and example of our prophets and leaders—both ancient and modern. And of all the influential leaders in the scriptures—the great prophets who testified boldly and with such power their words penetrate our hearts to this day—one must include Sariah on their list.

When Lehi beheld a dream in which he was commanded to leave his home, his lands, his gold and silver, and all his precious possessions, he was obedient to the words of the Lord and left to dwell in a tent—leaving a life of familiar comfort and embarking on a life of a tent-dwelling nomad. Nephi gets credit for expressing his willingness to "go and do." But Nephi had the example of his father—who also "went and did." And while both Lehi and Nephi ultimately had the benefit of having visions, dreams and heavenly manifestations, there is no record of Sariah having the same experience. Still, she acted on faith. She endured the loss of worldly wealth. She kept the commandments, even when she did not have a full perspective. She exercised faith in the words of the prophets. She overcame intense doubt. She endured hunger and uncertainty. She experienced childbirth in the wilderness, away from familiar comforts and without the benefit of those who sustained and assisted her in previous experiences. She stood as a beacon of strength when her daughters and daughters-in-law had the same experience. She was the mother of prophets, and her blood ran through their veins. Today, as thousands of missionaries testify thousands of times each day of the truthfulness of this great work, they honor this great leader whose enduring faith and resilient strength has impacted millions upon millions of truth seekers, whose testimonies and subsequent blessings stem in no small part from the great matriarch of the Book of Mormon, who, with her husband, "went and did."

The Lord has been explicitly clear on how He expects us to perform in our callings. Whether we're called as a bishop, relief society president, a primary teacher, or secretary of the Sunday school, an essential job in organizing and managing the work is to understand the significance of the responsibility, and that our leadership in doing so is critical to the overall efforts in building the kingdom. Where we serve isn't important. President Dieter F. Uchtdorf shared the following:

> Some years ago in our meetinghouse in Darmstadt, Germany, a group of brethren was asked to move a grand piano from the chapel to the adjoining cultural hall, where it was needed for a musical event. None were professional movers, and the task of getting that gravity-friendly instrument through the chapel and into the cultural hall seemed nearly impossible. Everybody knew that this task required not only physical strength but also careful coordination. There were plenty of ideas, but not one could keep the piano balanced correctly. They repositioned the brethren by strength, height, and age over and over again—nothing worked.
>
> As they stood around the piano, uncertain of what to do next, a good friend of mine, Brother Hanno Luschin, spoke up. He said, "Brethren, stand close together and lift where you stand."
>
> It seemed too simple. Nevertheless, each lifted where he stood, and the piano rose from the ground and moved into the cultural hall as if on its own power. That was the answer to the challenge. They merely needed to stand close together and lift where they stood.[2]

President Dieter F. Uchtdorf admonishes us to "cease to aspire and cease to retire!" In whatever capacity, for as long as the Lord asks, our job is to lead bringing our finest and most determined leadership initiative. "Our Heavenly Father asks," President Uchtdorf continues, "that we represent Him in the noble work of reaching out and blessing the lives of His children. He asks us to stand firm . . . and give the calling we have at this moment our best efforts."[3]

While it doesn't matter where we serve, how we serve, including how we organize and manage the work, matters a great deal. President Ezra Taft Benson taught, "The Lord expects each of us to have a calling in His Church so that others may be blessed by our talents and influence."[4]

Note the sense of urgency about how we serve in the following scriptures:

> Wherefore, now let every man learn his duty, and to act in the office in which he is appointed, in all diligence. He that is slothful shall not be counted worthy to stand, and he that learns not his duty and shows himself not approved shall not be counted worthy to stand. (D&C 107:99–100)
>
> And we did magnify our office unto the Lord, taking upon us the responsibility, answering the sins of the people upon our own heads if we did not teach them the word of God with all diligence; wherefore, by laboring with our might their blood might not come upon our garments; otherwise their blood would come upon our garments, and we would not be found spotless at the last day. (Jacob 1:19)
>
> Now, my beloved brethren, I, Jacob, according to the responsibility which I am under to God, to magnify mine office with soberness, and that I might rid my garments of your sins, I come up into the temple this day that I might declare unto you the word of God. (Jacob 2:2)
>
> Magnify thine office. (D&C 24:3)
>
> And now, my beloved son, notwithstanding their hardness, let us labor diligently; for if we should cease to labor, we should be brought under condemnation; for we have a labor to perform whilst in this tabernacle of clay, that we may conquer the enemy of all righteousness, and rest our souls in the kingdom of God. (Moroni 9:6)

> Verily I say unto you, behold how great is your calling. Cleanse your hearts and your garments, lest the blood of this generation be required at your hands. (D&C 112:33)

As the CEO of the Polynesian Cultural Center (PCC), Von Orgill would meet regularly with the First Presidency to review the PCC's vision and strategy, address financial plans and performance, and outline priorities for the coming months. During his first meeting with President Hinckley in Salt Lake City, where the eighty-nine-year-old prophet had just returned the night before from a two-week trip to Australia and the Pacific, President Hinckley appeared exhausted from his travels.

Somewhat lightheartedly, Von said to the prophet, "We'd love to have you come to the PCC any time." President Hinckley jokingly responded something like, "Well, you know I've been to the PCC many times and that drive from the Honolulu airport to the PCC is a long one. If only you could move the PCC closer to the airport that would help. And you know that flight from Salt Lake to Hawaii is a long one too. If only you could move Hawaii a little closer to California it would be so much easier to make that trip."

At that point, President Hinckley, his counselors, President Monson and President Faust, and Von were each chuckling. Surely, it would have been difficult to even think about taking another trip after having just completed the arduous two-week journey he had.

President Hinckley then paused, looked down, and was quiet for several moments. Almost as if the spirit was whispering to him that he should be careful not to leave an inappropriate impression, he looked up, now serious, and shared something like, "I want it to be clear that I would never hesitate to do whatever the Lord asks me to do, no matter what it would require."

President Hinckley visited the Polynesian Cultural Center many times, each time he was an example of energetic and enthusiastic devotion to the Lord and to the Lord's work and purposes.[5]

Leadership in our callings is not about being overly dynamic, giving the funniest talks or having the biggest personality in the room. In fact, it's not about being anything or anyone other than yourself. It is about being authentic, prayerful, humble, diligent, and filled with faith. Here are a few areas to consider as you approach your callings:

1. Leaders (and remember—that's all of us) need to examine our motive—the "why" of our service as well as the "what" and the "how."

2. Leadership requires that we love both those for whom and with whom we serve.

3. Leaders at all levels and in every calling need to establish and/or connect to a vision for what needs to be done.

4. In every role and calling, effective leadership also depends upon our followership.

5. We have to learn to balance the requirements of our service with the other priorities in our life.

6. We need to establish goals that are consistent with our vision and then execute those goals with precision, despite the obstacles that arise (and they will arise!).

7. We need to meet consistently with those with whom we serve in order to effectively engage them in a manner that is consistent with the vision.

8. And ultimately, we need to get to work—and inspire others to do the same. We have to both "Go" and "Do."

9. Learn as we go. Not everything is spelled out at the beginning. In fact, usually very little is. The Lord will provide answers along the way.

Let's briefly explore each of these:

1. Examine your motive

As a bishop of a large young single adult ward, I always looked forward to tithing settlement. While it occasionally took some creative scheduling to meet individually with every ward member, it was my favorite time of the year. Most of those I met with were actively involved in the ward, attending their meetings and attending to their callings. But not all. Some were still "feeling their way" down the path but were doing so humbly and sincerely. As we discussed their individual circumstances, they each had the opportunity to declare their status as a tithe payer. After their declaration, I asked each of them—given the practically desperate financial circumstances they nearly all faced as poor students—why they paid their tithing. Initially, I expected their responses to be something like, "I pay because I need the blessings that come with paying tithing!" But that was never what they said. It was always something to this effect: "I pay my tithing because I love the Lord. I have been so abundantly blessed; it is my privilege to participate." While that may not be an exact quote, it's pretty close, and I received it over and over by nearly every person, regardless of their current activity status. Certainly, blessings come with the payment of tithing, and I had the opportunity to testify of how the Lord would open the windows of heaven and pour out blessings so great they would not have room to receive them all. But they already knew and had experienced that. Their motive was not to pay because of what they would receive in return. Instead, it was about following a commandment because they loved the Lord.

That is why we serve. That is why we accept responsibilities that are, at times, inconvenient and often uncomfortable—because we love the Lord. All aspects of our leadership are influenced by that over-arching motive.

2. Love those you serve and those with whom you serve

Jesus taught that the first and greatest commandment in the law is to "Love the Lord thy God with all thy heart, and with all thy soul, and with all thy mind. And the second is like unto it, Thou shalt love thy neighbour as thyself. On these two commandments hang all the law and the prophets" (Matt 22:37, 39–40). They also represent the blueprint for success as a leader. Take time to get to know those with whom and for whom you serve. As you build relationships of love and trust, your ability to lead will accelerate, and your capacity to address your challenges will increase. You will invite the Spirit in rich abundance as you work together synergistically, and your service will become a deep joy for you and those with whom you serve. Elder M. Russell Ballard reminds us: "Leadership based on love brings incredible power. It is real, and it generates lasting results in the lives of our Father's children."[6]

3. Establish a vision

A vision describes a future state of being, and effective leaders convey this sense of vision. In Proverbs it states: "Where there is no vision, the people perish" (Proverbs 29:18). As I have studied visionary leaders, I have come to the conclusion that there are few things more powerful than a bold and compelling vision. In 1831, when the restored Church was still in its infancy, with just a few hundred members in New York, Pennsylvania, and Ohio, with persecution and resistance building from all corners, the 26-year-old Prophet Joseph declared to the world, "And this gospel shall be preached unto every nation, and kindred, and tongue, and people" (D&C 133:37). Though at the time his vision may have been viewed as outrageous, it was inspired, and tens of thousands would soon join in the cause. Today, that vision is being fulfilled, as through various means and modalities the gospel is available in nearly every language and every culture across the world.

As you establish your vision, remember the principle of "no involvement, no commitment." When a leader merely dictates the team's purpose without involving others in the process, that leader will find a low level of commitment and a high level of burnout from others.

At the same time, you can't just rely on the input of others as the sole basis of your direction. A leader is more than a census-taker. In fact, you will learn if you haven't already that it is difficult to please all the people all the time. So don't even try. Involve people in key decision-making processes, let them help you clarify the direction of the team or the initiative, but be prepared to take a stand once you have gathered data and input.

Think for a moment about the great leaders in your life. My personal experience with inspiring leaders in my life is that they each had a unique ability to provide a sense of direction and purpose, a sense of clarity about who I was and a vision for what I could do, often causing me to reach for and achieve results I might otherwise not have considered. This is one of the most inspiring traits of a leader—the ability to inspire others to achieve well beyond what they initially think they can do.

On July 4, 1952, Florence Chadwick, who had previously swum the English Channel, now attempted the twenty-one-mile swim from the Southern California mainland to Catalina Island. The water was a freezing forty-eight degrees. The fog was thick and visibility almost nil. Finally, only a half mile from her destination, she became discouraged and quit. The next day reporters clamored around her asking why she had quit. Had it been the cold water or the distance? It proved to be neither. She responded, "I was licked by the fog." She then recalled a similar experience while swimming the English Channel, where the fog had likewise been engulfing. She was exhausted. As she was about to reach out for her father's hand in the nearby boat, he pointed to the shore. She raised her head just long enough to see the land ahead. With new vision, she pressed on and became the first woman to conquer the English Channel.[7]

With increased vision comes increased motivation. And that's our job as leaders—to create and communicate that vision and then to lead in such a way that it comes to pass. Business author and leadership expert Warren Bennis has said: "The first job of a leader is to define a vision for the organization...Leadership is the capacity to translate vision into reality."[8]

4. Understand the importance of followership

During his visit and ministering to the people in the Land Bountiful, Jesus called his disciples, instituted the sacrament, healed their sick, and prayed for and blessed their children. He then defined His gospel:

> Behold I have given unto you my gospel, and this is the gospel which I have given unto you—that I came into the world to do the will of my Father, because my Father sent me. And my Father sent

> me that I might be lifted up upon the cross; and after that I had been lifted up upon the cross, that I might draw all men unto me, that as I have been lifted up by men even so should men be lifted up by the Father, to stand before me, to be judged of their works, whether they be good or whether they be evil—And for this cause have I been lifted up; therefore, according to the power of the Father I will draw all men unto me, that they may be judged according to their works. And it shall come to pass, that whoso repenteth and is baptized in my name shall be filled; and if he endureth to the end, behold, him will I hold guiltless before my Father at that day when I shall stand to judge the world. (3 Nephi 27:13–16).

Jesus is the *Perfect Leader.* His example of love, service, and compassion transcends adequate expression. His Atonement is both infinite and eternal. It is broad and all-encompassing. And it is also deeply personal. As incomprehensible as the vastness of His atoning sacrifice is, one feels—individually and intimately—Jesus' concern for each of us. He did it because He loves us—collectively and individually. And He did it because His Father sent Him. In His leadership, Jesus is also the *Perfect Follower* of all His Father asked. Elder Jeffrey R. Holland taught:

> Throughout His ministry, Jesus constantly made clear His unbending loyalty, His total obedience, and His unique loving relationship to His Father. Indeed, this undeviating bond the Savior has with the Father is one of the sweetest things in the scriptures to have grown on me in recent years. In His youth, Jesus said He was to "be about [His] Father's business," and He didn't mean His stepfather's carpentry trade. He continually sought out His true Father in prayer. He told the people He did only what He had seen His Father do and taught only what He had heard His Father teach. He could tolerate a great deal in life but was furious over the desecration of His Father's house. When He wanted unity, He prayed the Twelve would be "one" with the Father as He and the Father were already one. In Gethsemane, He said it was the Father's will that must be done, not His. In the end, at Calvary, His ultimate relief is expressed in the humble phrase "Father, into thy hands I commend my spirit." Maybe I am making a case here that is obvious to everyone already, but to love as Christ loved—"as I have loved you"—is to love the Father best of all, to obey Him to the

end, and therein find the divine motivation to love our neighbors as ourselves. This was indeed a "new idea."[9]

You may have opportunity to serve in a position as the president of an organization, where it becomes your responsibility to organize and establish vision and direction. And in another calling, you may serve as a counselor or a teacher. And you may have opportunity to do both at different times. Your ability to both lead, as the calling requires, and follow, as the also calling requires, will be necessary. Aristotle said, "He who has never learned to obey cannot be a good commander."[10] Effective leadership requires we follow the inspired direction set forward by our leaders.

5. Practice balance

King Benjamin declared: "And see that all these things are done in wisdom and order; for it is not requisite that a man should run faster than he has strength. And again, it is expedient that he should be diligent, that thereby he might win the prize; therefore, all things must be done in order" (Mosiah 4:27). The scriptures provide a recurring theme about how the Lord will magnify us as we seek to magnify our callings. He can make an offering of five loaves and two fish feed 5,000, with abundance to spare. With His influence, seven loaves and a few small fish provide for 4,000. After fishing all night with no success, the Savior's disciples learn that, with His guidance, their nets become so full, they cannot "draw it for the multitude of fishes" (John 21:6).

We are asked to give all we can. For one bishop, who may be retired and with grown children, He can devote full-time hours to his calling. Another bishop may be busy with work—in the prime of his career—with significant family duties, frequent travel, and other pressing responsibilities. In ministering to the needs of his ward, he may spend significantly less time. Both can be effective leaders; both can be significant blessings in the lives of their ward members. With the Lord's help, one is not more effective than the other. He understands our unique circumstances and works with us regardless of our individual weaknesses or limitations. As we reach for His hand, He reaches for ours and magnifies our efforts. We are asked to do all we can. We are not required to do more than we can.

6. Determine goals

Setting goals is an essential habit for any leader to develop. The Lord commanded us: "Thou shalt not idle away thy time, neither shalt thou bury thy talent that it may not be known" (D&C 60:13). Goals have tremendous power. A leader must provide vision and direction, but that vision and direction has to quickly translate to action. As Peter Drucker, the father of modern management development, wrote, "Plans are only good intentions unless they immediately degenerate into hard work."[11] Setting goals and then vigorously working toward the accomplishment of those goals is critical to achieving any desired result. Pablo Picasso reminds us, "Our goals can only be reached through a vehicle of a plan, in which we must fervently believe, and upon which we must vigorously act. There is no other route to success."[12] Dreams are about vision; goals are about action. Author Curtis Morely has written:

> You may dream of climbing the mountain, but without effective goal setting you'll never make it all the way to the top. Remember that goals are:
>
> - Never achievable if they haven't been articulated first.
> - 42% more likely to be achieved if you write them down.
> - Stronger if accompanied by a commitment to action.
> - More likely to be achieved if the goal setter is accountable to others.
> - Kept on track through a cadence of regular updates.
> - Need to be more than just an easy win; they need to be significant.

- Better realized if they focus on the process, not just the outcome.

- More powerful if framed positively versus negatively.

- Subject to setbacks, so prepare for failure and make learning from them a part of the plan.[13]

Two days into the Apollo 13 mission, a routine stir of an oxygen tank ignited a damaged wire, causing an explosion that vented the contents of both of the ship's service module's oxygen tanks, preventing the Apollo 13 crew from attempting their planned lunar landing. NASA's objective quickly shifted from landing on the moon to getting astronauts Jim Lovell, Fred Haise and Jack Swigert home safely. Oxygen was needed to provide life support, of course, but also to generate electric power. Needing to conserve energy in the command module for re-entry, the crew transferred to the lunar module to survive. But the lunar module was designed to support only two astronauts on the lunar surface for two days, so NASA's Houston Control had to design both equipment and processes to allow the three men to survive, navigate, and eventually return safely to the earth's surface. Further, they could only access the limited resources available on the ship to create the equipment and processes. The phrase uttered by Commander Jim Lovell is now well known: "Houston, we have a problem." And certainly, they did—one that had few answers and required new, better, innovative thinking. The circumstances they all faced were not in their control. But their response to their circumstances was. One of NASA's greatest achievements was actually deemed a "successful failure," because while they did not land safely on the moon's surface, the crew did, in fact, return safely.

I am continually amazed by the power of focus, and in the midst of all the ambiguity and chaos that surrounds our current business environment, the need for focus has, perhaps, never been greater. Sometimes our goals and well-established plans—created with valued input and with the best of intentions—can teeter on the precipice of impossibility.

But what if we were to ask ourselves this one question: "What if it were *not* impossible to accomplish what we set out to do?" I have seen the power of this question repeatedly. When a goal is agreed upon with a team or a council or a family, it moves from the realm of something we *hope* to do to something we *commit* to do. That word "commitment" is not a small word. It becomes something we are passionate about. We go to bed with it on our minds and hearts. We dream about it. We wake up with it in the morning. We treat it with firm resolve, as a promise to deliver. And we are people of our word, regardless of challenges—even significant ones—that arise.

I have had multiple experiences working with teams who have identified a goal, and in the process of working to achieve that goal, have encountered barriers. Sometimes these barriers are small, and in the course of doing the work, we plow through them. But more often than not, and especially when the goal is significant and really matters, the barriers we encounter feel insurmountable. These barriers are frequently out of our control. Things like economic downturns, foreign exchanges, an unforeseen change in a client's business, a health crisis, or even a global pandemic. All these seem to make the goal's accomplishment impossible. In a perfect, unencumbered world, one without extreme challenges, a goal's accomplishment likely requires new and different behaviors on the part of everyone at every level to achieve it. It was never a "lay-up" to begin with. It was always heroic and achieving it under normal circumstances would push us to our limits. But when new barriers assault the process, goal achievement can seem too daunting to obtain.

The process of achieving goals in a turbulent, uncertain, and barrier-ridden environment requires a deliberate effort and new thinking. It demands collaboration, innovation and synergy. But these things are in our control. As the team meets to address the challenges, they will likely reach an impasse as to what to do. When this happens, stay in the process. It often requires long hours and a commitment to remaining engaged in discussions. These discussions can be intense, though they do not need to combative or contentious. Involve as many stakeholders as is required. Challenge yourselves to be innovative, and ensure the team is unified in their commitment toward the goal—the very thought that not achieving the commitment is neither acceptable nor open for discussion. If there is a shared paradigm that "it is NOT impossible to achieve this goal," new levels of creativity will emerge. You will explore questions like: How do we need to see and approach the problem differently? And who else needs to be involved that isn't currently?

The process includes the following steps:

1. Clarity on the goal. Is everyone on the same page? Do they articulate the objective the same way, and does everyone understand their individual roles and responsibilities?

2. Team commitment. Does the team see the goal as something that is nice to do, or is it viewed as a commitment, a promise?

3. Willingness to engage in the discussion. Is the team willing to engage in vigorous, thoughtful, ego-less discussion? Does this discussion include the mindset that not achieving the goal is not even on the table? Does the team have all the rights brains in the game—or does the team need to include the thinking of others—perhaps across multiple organizational levels?

4. Adopt the mindset that goal achievement is not impossible. Is the team willing to challenge their own mindsets on how the problem is viewed?

5. Willingness to do what is necessary to get it done. Is the team willing to stay engaged in the process until a viable plan is identified, with clarity on roles and responsibilities?

Insurmountable problems are part of a leader's daily diet. If the problems we face were routine and easy, our leadership would not be necessary. But with a steeled resolved and a unified and committed team, you will be amazed at what can be accomplished. Mindsets will shift. Rich, intense and often extended discussion will follow, creativity will flow, ideas will emerge that you hadn't considered, and the path forward will become clear. It starts with a sense, not just of a goal, but with the mindset that that goal is, in fact, a commitment—a moral bond—that no one is willing to break. And the Lord will magnify to your efforts; He will expand your capabilities, bring insights to you and those with whom you work, and help you capture creativity.

Perrin Walker served as a mission president in Northern France and Belgium in the mid 80s. During his time of service, the mission had established a goal to create a stake. As the mission president, President Walker served as the priesthood leader for the district in addition to his stewardship with the missionaries. The goal of creating a stake required everyone's focus—both the members of the districts and the full-time missionaries. The entire district was clear on the objective, and they organized and planned so that every leader knew his or her role. With the great faith and remarkable diligence of both the missionaries and the members of the district, they did, in fact, eventually meet the requirements to become a stake.

Elder Russell M. Nelson was assigned to facilitate the new stake's organization. As is generally the case when an apostle visits a stake, he had sent President Walker a list of preparation items, including a challenge to have twenty brethren prepared to receive the Melchizedek Priesthood and be ordained elders as part of the conference weekend. That was most certainly a daunting goal, but one President Walker, the missionaries, and district members accepted and rallied around. They met together to create a plan. They prayed in every meeting for guidance and inspiration. They exercised their faith. Then they got to work. When the long-awaited weekend of the conference finally arrived, President Walker, the missionaries and the members of the various branches across the district were thrilled to report, as part of the momentous happenings of that magnificent weekend, that they had, in fact, nineteen men who were prepared to be ordained.

During dinner the evening prior to the conference, President Walker happily reported this to Elder Nelson. Elder Nelson was thrilled for each of these nineteen brethren, of course, but kindly reminded President Walker, "I challenged you to have twenty brethren prepared, not nineteen."

The goal for twenty men to receive the priesthood was not new to President Walker. They did, in fact, have a plan. President Walker mentioned this to Elder Nelson, saying, "We do have a worthy brother ready, but we need your permission. He's only been a member less than two weeks."

Elder Nelson shared with President Walker the vignette from the life of Brigham Young who was baptized in a creek that flowed through a nearby wood on a frigid day in April 1832. Immediately after he was baptized, with his wet clothes still clinging to his body, Brigham was confirmed and member of the Church and ordained an elder.[14] Elder Nelson then said, "If it was good for Brigham Young, it's good enough for me." So they proceeded. A new stake was created, and twenty wonderful men were ordained as elders that same weekend.[15]

Your goals and circumstances are different, certainly. Nevertheless, this example shows the power of having a plan, exercising faith, working as hard as you can, and expecting miracles.

7. Use meetings as a time to lift, instruct, and counsel

In any calling, whether as a Primary president, stake president, young women's president, a counselor, a teacher, a secretary or clerk, a minister, a librarian, assistant young women's camp cook, or whatever our responsibility is, our imperative is to bring others to Christ. While the specific duties and responsibilities with the different callings are varied and occasionally complex, the ultimate object for all who serve in any calling is the same. So how can we enlist and engage those with whom we serve in this imperative? How can we hold effective meetings that help move the work forward? The Lord declared to the prophet Isaiah: "Come now, and let us reason together." (Isaiah 1:18). And to Joseph Smith, He reiterated: "Let us reason together, that ye may understand" (D&C 50:10). That admonition helps clarify the purpose of our coordination and meetings. We must work and counsel together. Effective councils enlist the best thinking and experiences of others. The old-school command and control style of handing out orders will not bring out the best ideas. Inspiration from the Spirit begins to flow as all council participants prayerfully attend and openly share their ideas.

A friend of mine was called to work with the young men of his ward. In his initial meeting with his new presidency, the president announced, "I hate these meetings and don't intend to hold one again. Here is your responsibility. Just go do it." This comment took my friend's initial enthusiasm and squashed it. The president missed an initial opportunity to provide vision, set a positive tone and clear direction, create a forum to discuss and counsel around the needs of the ward's youth, and to invite the spirit to guide the work that needs to accompany the prayerful discussion that should occur in those important and sacred meetings. And he missed on-going opportunities to do the same. Few of us want one more meeting to attend, and no one wants to meet endlessly on any topic, especially when meetings are poorly organized or a spirit of resentment for the work exists. But effective meetings provide essential inspiration, training and encouragement necessary for the work to succeed. They are an opportunity to counsel together.

President Stephen L. Richards taught: "The genius of our Church government is government through councils. I have had enough experience to know the value of councils. Hardly a day passes but that I see . . . God's wisdom, in creating councils . . . to govern his Kingdom . . . I have no hesitancy in giving you the assurance, if you will confer in council as you are expected to do, God will give you solutions to the problems that confront you."[16]

President M. Russell Ballard has provided important and inspired direction on how to hold effective counsels. I recommend a careful study of his book, *Counselling with our Councils.* In it, he addresses how to plan and conduct effective meetings, how to draw upon the Spirit by tapping the combined wisdom and experience from all the women and men who serve on the council, and how to engage family, ward and stake councils to bring others to Christ.

In an address to the brethren of the Church, President Ballard taught: "We have an urgent need in the Church for leaders, particularly stake presidents and bishops, to harness and channel spiritual power through councils. Family, ward, and stake problems can be solved if we seek solutions in the Lord's way." Elder Ballard continues:

> This is the miracle of Church councils: listening to each other and listening to the Spirit! When we support one another in Church councils, we begin to understand how God can take ordinary men and women and make of them extraordinary leaders. The best leaders are not those who work themselves to death trying to do

> everything single-handedly; the best leaders are those who follow God's plan and counsel with their councils.[17]

Involvement inspires commitment and captures the hearts of everyone involved. "But what if I am not the bishop or relief society president?" You might ask. "What's my responsibility as a member of a meeting or council?" Let me share a personal lesson on the power of offering my full participation.

I was once asked to attend an extensive leadership training as part of my calling. This particular training required six full days out of my incredibly busy schedule. My business was leadership development, and in my arrogance, I was confident that what I was going to experience was going to be far below what I considered my standard. I was resentful and resistant, and made my feelings known broadly to my family and close friends. Never mind the fact that faithful women and men, my sisters and brothers in the gospel, had been preparing for this event for nearly a year. They had been prayerful and diligent in this preparation. They had communicated clearly and often about the purpose of this experience. They had generated an impressive level of enthusiasm for this experience (except for with me, of course). So, reluctantly, I determined I would go, but wasn't committed or excited about it. For me, it was about fulfilling my duty, not about making any kind of meaningful contribution.

As the event began, however, I felt something. I could sense the significant level of effort and intense preparation that had gone into this event. I was touched by the prayers that were offered, and the diligence demonstrated by those who were leading the effort. I noticed the genuine, positive reaction from others in the event, and realized very quickly that I was completely missing the purpose of the event. I needed to be present. I needed to show up more than just physically. I needed to see this as something more than checking an obligation off my list. I needed to engage mentally and spiritually. I needed to offer my best efforts as a participant. I needed to repent and humble myself and be willing to learn. I came away from that experience changed. Yes, the training was good and uplifting. But more than that, we united our focus, our thoughts and our prayers toward a common purpose. Because we did, we felt the Spirit. It was an edifying experience, one made possible by the faith and tireless efforts of so many, despite my initial bad attitude and arrogance. I was grateful for the opportunity to repent and allow the Spirit to teach me. I learned the power of Elder Ballard's insight: "When we act in a united effort, we create spiritual synergism which is increased effectiveness or achievement as a result of combined action or cooperation, the result of which is greater than the sum of the individual parts."[18]

8. Go and Do!

Establishing a vision and direction for the work is a critical leadership responsibility. As noted earlier, a clear and compelling vision unifies and engages people, it enlists their hearts and minds in the importance of a cause. But at some point, leaders—at every level—must engage in the work. They must "go and do"; they must get to work.

Stephen Burnett and Eden Smith, both early converts to the Church, received important direction from the Lord as they began their missionary service. Captured pointedly in one of the shortest sections of the Doctrine and Covenants, the Lord instructs Stephen and Eden to:

> Preach the gospel to every creature that cometh under the sound of your voice. Wherefore, go ye and preach my gospel, whether to the north or to the south, to the east or to the west, it mattereth not, for ye cannot go amiss. (D&C 80: 1–3)

In other words—get to work. Go and do. The details of where to go and what to say will be given, but we need to understand that, as leaders, there is work to do at every turn, with every person, and in every circumstance. Engage in the work and we cannot go amiss. As we do so, the Lord has promised us He will go before us; He will be our on right hand and on our left; His Spirit will attend us, and His angels will be with us to bear us up (D&C 84:88).

It can be a trap to become so anxiously engaged in talking about the work, in meeting about the work, and planning the work that we never actually get to the work. It is one thing to go. It is another thing to do. They are two sides to the same coin, and when combined, become a powerful force for good. But when one simply just goes, the actual work is left undone.

Elder Dallas V. Merrell related a couple of experiences that demonstrate the significant good that can occur as leaders get to work:

> While assigned to the Pacific Area Presidency I visited two small stakes in Perth, Australia, the last stake having been organized seventeen years earlier. For years, they were hoping for a third stake, but were barely qualified for two. We knew that the growth of the Church required considerable individual spiritual progress. We discovered that many members were lost, and their addresses were unknown. Others had requested that the Church not contact them. Others were part-member families. Too many families were headed by prospective elders and were without the Melchizedek Priesthood.
>
> The two stake presidents and the mission president in Perth, Australia committed to find and invite all of the lost or wavering souls, to come and receive essential priesthood ordinances.
>
> After just a few months, many families had been found and invited to come and complete all priesthood ordinances. A large majority of those newly contacted families were taught the missionary discussions, and more than half of those families came back to the Church. Miracles were evident. In just five months they were qualified for the third stake. After two years there were four stakes in Perth, and they are now preparing for a fifth.

In this case, it was a matter of identifying, of finding, and of reaching out. Significant work on the part of Relief Society leaders, young women and men leaders, bishops, and elders quorum leaders was required. All had to get on their knees, then get in their cars and get to work. That's when then miracles began to happen.

Here's another example from Elder Merrell:

> In a priesthood leadership meeting at stake conference, I learned that there were about 100 prospective elders in that stake. I asked the president, "How would you feel about making assignments so that every one of those prospective elders would be invited to come tomorrow to receive the Melchizedek Priesthood?

He thought about it, and then said, "We'll go do it."

That night in our Saturday evening session of conference we had a young mother speak. She had been through the temple just a month or two before, and she spoke of what a wonderful spiritual experience it was for her. As she finished she said, 'The greatest desire of my heart is that my husband would come and go with me to the temple.'

We were all touched by that. Little did we know that in that very hour, two brethren were inviting him to come in for an interview with the bishop for the Melchizedek Priesthood. In conference the next morning, her husband was approved to receive the Melchizedek Priesthood and [The stake president] called on him to bear his testimony and on her to speak again a second time.

She spoke first and said, "I told you all last night how wonderful I feel about the temple and the greatest desire of my heart is that my husband would come with me." She said, "Thank you for inviting him. Thank you for interviewing him."

Then the husband stepped up to the microphone. He said, "I've been running from the Church for ten years. Thank you for your patience. Thank you, brethren, for coming last night and inviting me. I'm going with my wife to the temple."

It wasn't a matter weeks or months. It was a matter of inviting him. Those spiritual forces of heaven, his earlier premortal decisions, his nurturing in his home, and the Holy Spirit came to bear on that moment when he was invited: will you come for an interview with the bishop tonight to receive the Melchizedek Priesthood?

They had six who received the Melchizedek Priesthood who were invited that day, and the stake president said they had eighteen more who were invited that they would be able to approve soon.[19]

In the October 2007 Priesthood session of General Conference, President Henry B. Eyring offered this important counsel, suggesting three keys to service and leadership: First, remember the Lord and how He has sustained you in the past. Be assured He will do so in your current and future assignments. Second, pray for those you serve. Said President Eyring: "When you forget yourself to pray for the circle of others, your service will be extended in your heart. It will change not only your service but your heart. That is because the Father and His Beloved Son, whom you are called to serve, know and love so many people your service will touch, however limited to a few it may seem to be to you." Third, go to work. President Eyring reminds us that our job as leaders is to bless others,

> And that always takes moving out and doing something, usually something hard to do. So you can expect, in addition to assurance of God's help and the command to forget yourself, the clear prompting by the Holy Ghost to go and do something which will bless someone's life. That may be as obvious as going prayerfully to visit a person or a family or a quorum member to whom you are assigned to serve. For a father it may be to correct one of his children.
>
> Whether what you do is to correct or to teach the gospel of Jesus Christ, you will do it better if you remember what success will be. You are to help Heavenly Father and His Son, Jesus Christ, make eternal life possible for those you serve. To do that, the Spirit must take a testimony down into their hearts. And that testimony has to lead them to choose to keep the commandments of God, whatever storms and temptations may come.[20]

Here's a bit more context on Nephi's determination to both "go" and "do." The border of the Red Sea is approximately 180 miles (290 Km) from Jerusalem. Even with camels to assist in the travel, it is unlikely Lehi and his party could have covered that distance in just three days. The "three day" distance may not represent a total chronological account of the trip. The authors of the Book of Mormon Central research team have written:

> Lehi would likely have fled Jerusalem as quickly as possible, pushing his traveling party much faster than under normal travel conditions, but the journey of three days does not refer to the distance from Jerusalem to the Red Sea. Rather, their party first departed from

> Jerusalem and came down near the Red Sea, and after that traveled three more days until they reached their first campsite in the Valley of Lemuel. It makes clear sense to understand the three-day journey as a reference to the specific segment of wilderness travel "near the shore of the Red Sea," which had just been mentioned in the previous verse. Thus, the most likely interpretation, based on sound textual analysis, also happens to be the most geographically realistic.[21]

With a potentially expanded distance beyond our traditional "three day" understanding, Nephi's willingness to "go and do" becomes more significant. Going and doing requires a lot of actual work. One must be prepared to go beyond simply an initial attempt.

9. Learn from the Journey

Leaving the comforts and privileges of their Jerusalem home and familiar hearth must have been an excruciating experience for Lehi, Sariah and their family. After Lehi's dream, wherein he receives the commandment from the Lord to depart into the wilderness, Lehi's and Sariah's obedience is on full display. The family doesn't dawdle. They don't take time to carefully pack their most valuable items. Instead, they gather only the critical items they need to survive and go and do as the Lord had commanded as they depart the land of their inheritance, leaving their gold, silver, and all the rest of their precious possessions and journey into the harsh and unforgiving wilderness.

What was the conversation like as they travelled? What information did they have that caused them to be willing in the first place to go on this open-ended, undefined and uncertain excursion? Never mind the subsequent teaching and admonitions, the guidance and murmuring that will occur. What a remarkable example of immediate obedience to the Lord's commandments. No wonder, when Nephi is faced with his own journey, he responds in kind—to go and do—because he had seen his mother and father do it.

Just as the traveling party reaches their hard-earned destination, the Lord informs Lehi, again through a dream, that Nephi and his brethren are to return to Jerusalem to obtain the brass plates. Of course, these plates have significant value to Lehi and his posterity. It is where his genealogy is recorded, where the word of the Lord is inscribed, and will become the means through which their language and spiritual culture will be perpetuated. But why doesn't Lehi receive instruction about the plates prior their initial departure? Certainly, the Lord, who knows the end from the beginning, could have instructed Lehi before they travelled a significant distance from their home that the plates were an important thing to have. Leaders face this dilemma constantly—if we're on the Lord's errand, why isn't path forward more clearly delineated?

Did Lehi simply overlook the importance of the plates as he and the family were rushing to obey the Lord's directive? Could he have ignored an important prompting as he was busily on the Lord's errand? Or did the Lord know that Nephi and his brethren—because of their new task—would learn critical lessons about themselves because they were required to go back?

Sometimes (or all the time) there is power in the journey. It galvanizes faith, instructs on critical learning points, and fortifies and strengthens resolve.

Nephi and his brethren approach Laban three times: first, with reason. Certainly, Laban will understand the need for Lehi to possess these plates. Except Laban isn't reasonable. Second, they approach him with their exceedingly great amounts of gold and other valuable property. But money doesn't always solve the problem. In Laban's case, he confiscates the gold and other precious possessions (the money) but remains unwilling to part with the plates. Dejected, discouraged and disheartened, Lehi's older brethren are ready to concede defeat after their first two attempts. Nephi, however, is emboldened. He goes beyond his initial "go and do" sentiment as he declares to his brethren, "As the Lord liveth, and as we live, we will not go down unto our father in the wilderness until we have accomplished the thing which the Lord hath commanded us" (1 Nephi 3:15). When reason and money don't work, Nephi is required to rely on a third approach: *faith*.

For Nephi, he was willing to be "led by the Spirit, not knowing beforehand" what he should do or where he should go. "*Nevertheless*," he declares, "I went forth" (1 Nephi 4:6–7, emphasis added).

Leadership often requires a step into the unknown—a "nevertheless" moment. Like Nephi, we are often asked to move forward—to *go and do*, even when the direction is unclear, or worse, unknown.

"Be not weary in well-doing" (D&C 64:33), the Lord admonishes. We are to "waste and wear out our lives in bringing to light all the hidden things of darkness (D&C 123:13). As leaders, we are to be about the Lord's work, to be a kingdom builder. Among all the important and urgent things in your life—things that require your very finest efforts—choose to be part of the great work of building the Lord's kingdom.

Some things to consider doing:

1. As you organize around your calling, read the following general conference addresses by President M. Russell Ballard: 1) "Strength in Counsel," October 1993 and 2) "Counseling with Our Councils," April 199.

2. Deliberately spend time getting to know those with whom you serve. Find ways to serve them and get to know their family.

3. Craft a statement that captures the vision of your calling. Consider these questions as you do so: How, specifically, do you intend to help others come unto Christ? What do you want to have accomplished when your time in this specific calling has ended? How will others' lives be blessed because of your service?

CHAPTER FOURTEEN
TEACH WITH POWER

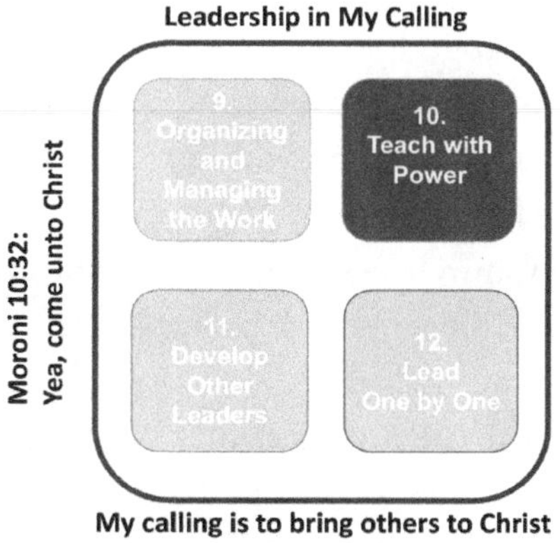

And I give unto you a commandment that you shall teach one another the doctrine of the kingdom.

Teach ye diligently and my grace shall attend you, that you may be instructed more perfectly in theory, in principle, in doctrine, in the law of the gospel, in all things that pertain unto the kingdom of God, that are expedient for you to understand.

—D&C 88:77–78

Effective teaching is the very essence of leadership in the church. Eternal life will come only as men and women are taught with such effectiveness that they change and discipline their lives. They cannot be coerced into righteousness or into heaven. They must be led, and that means teaching.

—President Gordon B. Hinckley[1]

In the early days of the restored Church of Jesus Christ, the Prophet Joseph and other leaders had a monumental task on their hands. After the Church's formal organization on April 6, 1830, its leaders quickly assumed responsibility to provide structure, direction, and inspiration to a rapidly growing group of believers, where just months before, no organization of any kind existed. What a task! From an organizational design perspective, it's overwhelming just to think about all that was immediately required. Thankfully, revelation poured in, providing critical guidance on several issues—though the list of issues seems to have grown daily. One of the more important issues they addressed involved providing effective teaching to one another. The need to get together in some kind of structure was more than just a nice thing to do. It had become a scriptural mandate—to "meet together oft, to fast and to pray, *and to speak one with another concerning the welfare of their souls*" (Moroni 6:5, emphasis added).

The nature of the Church now required involvement from more than just a few trained preachers or orators. Instead, teaching one another, preaching to nonmembers, and testifying whenever and wherever required became the responsibility of many—most of whom had little to no formal training on the pedagogy for such an effort. In a revelation given amid this context, the Lord poignantly asks the new church, do we teach by the "Spirit of truth or some other way? And if it is by some other way, it is not of God" (D&C 50:17–18).

We must teach; and we must have the Spirit when we do so.

When the Spirit becomes a partner in our teaching, speaking and testifying, it has a remarkable effect on all involved. Understanding is shared, and edification and enlightenment occur—for both those in the class or congregation as well as the one teaching or speaking. It becomes a time where not only do we learn together and lift one another, we "rejoice" together (see D&C 50:22).

Are we rejoicing often enough with our classes and in our sacrament instruction? We have an obligation, as Elder Jeffrey R. Holland has taught, to be spiritually stunning in our teaching.

The adversary unrelentingly both shouts loudly and whispers subtly to us and those we teach, attempting to divert our attention and sway us from an understanding of God's plan. Distraction is one of his primary strategies. Our devices, our addictions to posts and tweets and dings and reminders, our constant and instant access to news and information—some worthwhile and a lot not so much—all compete for space, relegating any kind of connection to heaven or scripture as a distant activity or a token effort for too many.

For some, the only connection to and reminder of God's plan is their interaction with their leaders—who are also their teachers. With all that the world offers to distract us from our understanding of our Heavenly Father, from Jesus Christ and His endless mercy for us, and from the magnificent plan of happiness, we simply cannot afford to squander the opportunity to teach and testify of eternal truths.

Regarding the need to teach and testify of Jesus Christ, President Henry B. Eying, shared the following:

> I was once invited to speak at graduation services at a university. The university president had wanted President Gordon B. Hinckley to be invited but found that he was unavailable. So by default I got the invitation. I was then a junior member of the Quorum of the Twelve Apostles.
>
> The person who invited me to speak became anxious as she learned more about my obligations as an Apostle. She called me on the phone and said that she now understood that my duty was to be a witness of Jesus Christ.
>
> In very firm tones she told me that I could not do that when I spoke there. She explained that the university respected people of all religious beliefs, including those who denied the existence of a God. She repeated, "You cannot fulfill your duty here."
>
> I hung up the phone with serious questions in my mind. Should I tell the university that I would not keep my agreement to speak? It was only two weeks before the event.
>
> My appearance there had been announced. What effect would my failing to keep my agreement have on the good name of the Church?
>
> I prayed to know what God would have me do. The answer came in a surprising way to me. I realized that the examples of Nephi,

> Abinadi, Alma, Amulek, and the sons of Mosiah applied to what I was. They were bold witnesses of Jesus Christ in the face of deadly peril.
>
> So the only choice to be made was how to prepare. I dug into everything I could learn about the university. As the day of the talk grew closer, my anxiety rose and my prayers intensified.
>
> In a miracle like the Red Sea parting, I found a news article. That university had been honored for doing what the Church has learned to do in our humanitarian efforts across the world. And so in my talk I described what we and they had done to lift people in great need. I said that I knew that Jesus Christ was the source of the blessings that had come into the lives of those we and they had served.
>
> After the meeting the audience rose to applaud, which seemed a little unusual to me. I was amazed but still a little anxious. I remembered what happened to Abinadi. Only Alma had accepted his witness. But that night, at a large formal dinner, I heard the university president say that in my talk he heard the words of God.[2]

So how can we become more effective in our efforts to teach with power? Whether we're teaching a formal class, or in our informal influence with others, our example will be the best teacher. Author Patrick Mason reminds us of Jesus' consistent use of three metaphors describing his disciples both ancient and modern. There are: "light, yeast, and salt (See Matthew 5:13–14; 13:33). Particles of light are so small they are invisible, but they overpower the darkness. Other ingredients are far more substantial, but it's the tiny amount of yeast that causes a lump of dough to rise. And only a pinch of salt transforms a dish from bland to savory."[3]

In our formal teaching efforts, the Lord has declared, "I will give unto you a pattern in all things" (D&C 52:14). His promise to provide a pattern extends to how we teach, speak, and testify. At the conclusion of their mission to the Zoramites, Alma shares important counsel with his son, Shiblon, giving him (and us) a pattern for effective teaching:

1. "And now, my son, I have told you this that ye may learn wisdom, that ye may learn of me that there is no other way or means whereby man can be saved, only in and through Christ. Behold, he is the life and the light of the world. Behold, he is the word of truth and righteousness." (Alma 38:9)

Center your life on Jesus Christ. To be an effective teacher, we must make His example and light foundational to all our efforts. We must know Him and feel of His love for us.

2. "And now, as ye have begun to teach the word even so I would that ye should continue to teach; and I would that ye would be diligent . . . " (Alma 38:10)

We must be diligent in our efforts to emulate Him. Of course, we won't be perfect at this, but our daily efforts to let the Savior's light and love shine through us will be, perhaps, the single greatest preparation we can do as a teacher.

3. " . . . And temperate in all things." (Alma 38:10)

Be careful to avoid extremes in personal opinions or positions. Recognize that those you are teaching will bring their own perspectives and experience, and those might not always match yours. The key to having influence with others lies in first being open to influence from others. When those you teach feel this desire from you, their openness will immediately increase. Extremes from a teacher shut down participants' discussion and willingness to listen or engage. Remember the wisdom from Spanish critic and philosopher George Santayana, "Fanaticism is redoubling your efforts when you have forgotten your aim."[4] The goal for our teaching and speaking efforts must be to bring people to Christ. Extremes beyond that singular goal are counterproductive.

Barnacles are crustaceans that live, usually, in shallow, tidal waters. They often attach themselves to hard substrate, like the hull of ships, with cement glands and can be very difficult to remove. Wherever the ship goes, the barnacle goes, almost as if it's a formal part of the ship.

But it's not. Barnacles can be damaging to the ship, and in some cases, can cause additional hull-drag that significantly reduces fuel efficiency. According to one study, "The U.S. Naval Academy estimates that biofouling creates enough hull-drag to increase the Navy's petroleum bill by about $250 million every year."[5] Removing barnacles can be a challenging task, and it is best to do so quickly. It requires carefully working a scraper under the edge of the barnacle to work it free from the surface. In the Church, like with ships, we have barnacles—those teachings that have attached themselves to the beautiful and pristine doctrines of the gospel of Jesus Christ. Wherever the Church goes, the barnacles seem to follow. But they're not doctrine and need to be scraped. Stick to the doctrine and be careful to avoid pet theories or unfounded and sensational stories.

Remember to facilitate involvement. People will remember what they say. Your job as a teacher is not to dispense all your great wisdom or pontificate on a particular soap-box issue. It is to facilitate a rich discussion where others can ask their questions and share their experiences and testimonies.

Note that in Alma's great sermon captured in Alma 5—first to the people of Zarahemla and later throughout all the land—he poses at least 47 questions (perhaps you'll find more)! His poignant teaching comes as people consider their own answers to his questions, not just in his own brilliance as a lecturer.

4. "See that ye are not lifted up unto pride; yea, see that ye do not boast in your own wisdom, nor of your much strength." (Alma 38:11)

Be wary of pride or boastfulness. It might be tempting, after giving a talk or lesson you feel went well, to think to yourself, "I am pretty good at this." Be careful; this is a very slippery slope. An effective talk or lesson comes with the aid of the Spirit, and we can't take any credit for that.

5. "Use boldness, but not overbearance; and also see that ye bridle all your passions…" (Alma 38:12)

Testify clearly, confidently and powerfully of eternal truths, without apology. At the same time, be mindful of another's unique experiences. I love the maxim: "Seek to bless, and not impress!" So much of our ability to connect with others while teaching rests with our motive—our intent. Technique is good and important. Your intent is more important and counts more than technique. If your motive is to bless others, you will be blessed with the Spirit. If your intent is to impress others, you won't.

If you think you can do it on your own, you will be, in fact, on your own. There is no more lonely feeling than teaching without the assistance of the Spirit.

6. " . . . That ye may be filled with love." (Alma 38:12)

Love those you teach. There simply is no substitute for this. "Pray unto the Father," as Mormon taught his son, "with all the energy of [your] heart" for this love (Moroni 7:48). Find ways to serve those you teach—especially when it is hard to do. Love is the currency you deal with when you teach. Remember this definition of leadership: "Leadership is seeing and communicating another's worth and potential so clearly they begin to see it in themselves." I think this definition applies to teaching as well, with just one minor adaptation: "Teaching is seeing and communicating another's worth and potential so clearly they begin to see it in themselves."[6] When you are teaching or speaking, remember you are teaching or speaking to a real person, a person who has their own feelings, concerns, issues, ideas, hopes, dreams, etc. Take time to ponder the needs, concerns, issues of those you teach. Remember C. S. Lewis' observation: "You have never talked to a mere mortal."[7] Be prayerful about them as part of your preparation. As you do this, you will significantly increase your ability to connect directly with them, and those who receive your message will feel your love, and more importantly, the Lord's love in powerful ways.

7. "See that ye refrain from idleness." (Alma 38:12)

Be diligent in your efforts. Pay the price in your preparations. Ponder deeply the doctrines and principles you are teaching and their application in your own life. Don't simply just show up. Having a desire to teach by the Spirit does not give you the excuse to not prepare. You will find your ability to understand that what the Lord wants you to say comes in direct proportion to the work you put into preparation. You may not always teach or say what you have prepared—that's an entirely different matter—but your ability to feel the Spirit's guidance will begin during your preparations.

8. "Do not say: O God, I thank thee that we are better than our brethren; but rather say: O Lord, forgive my unworthiness, and remember my brethren in mercy—yea, acknowledge your unworthiness before God at all times." (Alma 38:14)

Be humble and prayerful. Seek the Lord's guidance as to what you should say and teach. Acknowledge your dependence on Him and His mercy, and He will not abandon you in the moment. As you prepare, be prayerful. Ask for the guidance of the Spirit such that you might be an instrument in the Lord's hands to say what He wants you to say. Follow the promptings you receive, and don't get too caught up in your outline. If you have the Spirit, both you and those you are teaching will be edified. Pray as you speak that you might be attentive to the specific messages others need to hear. And when you are done, pray again and give thanks for the opportunity to share your testimony. When you are given the privilege to teach or to give a talk, remember whose errand you are on—His. This is His work and His message. It is not about you. It is about blessing others. (Alma 38:14)

Think of a time when you've heard a memorable and moving talk or participated in an edifying lesson. What did you feel? What was impactful? What did the speaker or teacher do?

Not every teacher or speaker is alike—and they're not supposed to be. Some speak directly to some while others speak to others. You'll experience this phenomenon every six months in general conference.

I love discussing the various talks we've heard with my family and friends at the conclusion of each conference. I am always a bit surprised (though I shouldn't be) that not everyone had the same experience with the talks and messages as I did. What stands out to me doesn't always stand out to others. And what is meaningful to them doesn't always register with me. And that's ok. Each speaker has a different personality and background, each brings a different style and approach. But all of them are inspired and directed by the Spirit, and I have every confidence that what they say comes to us from a base of intense spiritual preparation guided by fasting and prayer. They are vehicles through which the Lord speaks to us. What they say becomes scripture: "Whether by mine own voice or by the voice of my servants, it is the same" (D&C 1:38).

Occasionally, however, we feel a more direct connection to a particular message. Perhaps because it connects to a specific need in our lives.

I vividly recall as a young child that when the prophet spoke during General Conference, everything else stopped. The entire family listed with rapt attention, as his words became indelibly etched on our hearts. It was a message from the Lord through his prophet. And we knew it.

I have similar reactions today when I hear the inspired words of our leaders—not just the prophet, but many others as well. I feel five distinct things when I hear an inspiring, edifying talk. They are:

1. I receive a confirmation of my testimony of the restoration of the gospel of Jesus Christ—in no uncertain terms.

2. I am reminded of the Lord's love for me as an individual—that His grace is sufficient for me.

3. I want to be better. I feel intrinsically motivated to improve my behavior and develop new habits.

4. I feel his or her—the speaker's—love for me.

5. I feel the speaker is on the Lord's errand. It is not about him or her, but about what the Lord wants them to say.

Again, this is not about any one particular speaker. I have experienced this countless times with various speakers and teachers—each possessing a different background and teaching style. But the common element is that the message in not centered on the speaker or teacher. The edification comes through the Spirit, with the speaker/teacher as the vehicle.

The Savior declared, "Teach ye diligently and my grace shall attend you" (D&C 88:78). And the Prophet Joseph Smith reminds us, "The things of God are of deep import; and time, and experience, and careful and ponderous and solemn thoughts can only find them out. Thy mind, O man! if thou wilt lead a soul unto salvation, must stretch as high as the utmost heavens, and search unto and contemplate the darkest abyss, and the broad expanse of eternity—thou must commune with God. How much more dignified and noble are the thoughts of God, than the vain imaginations of the human heart! None but fools will trifle with the souls of men. How vain and trifling have been our spirits, our conferences, our councils, our meetings, our private as well as public conversations—too low, too mean, too vulgar, too condescending for the dignified characters of the called and chosen of God, according to the purposes of his will, from before the foundation of the world!"[8]

Our charter as leaders is to be teachers. And the Lord has set forth the pattern for doing so that will prepare us "in all things" that we "can magnify the calling whereunto I have called you, and the mission with which I have commissioned you" (D&C 88:80).

Some things to consider:

1. For your next talk or lesson, review in your mind the pattern Alma presented to Shiblon (focusing on Christ, striving to be diligent in emulating Him, avoiding extremes, being wary of pride or boastfulness, testifying confidently, loving those you teach, preparing diligently, exercising humility and remembering whose errand you are on).

2. Introduce a theme scripture as a foundational concept for your message.

3. Include a brief recap of a supporting scripture story.

4. Share a personal experience that relates to your theme.

5 Invite those you are teaching to make a commitment.

6. Testify boldly and confidently both of the truths of the gospel and of the theme you have presented.

CHAPTER FIFTEEN
DEVELOP OTHER LEADERS

Therefore, strengthen your brethren in all your conversation, in all your prayers, in all your exhortations, and in all your doings.

—D&C 108:7

The simple fact is that our Father did not recommend Eve or Moses or Nephi or countless other magnificent exemplars for this dispensation—He recommended you and me. Do you think God would have left the last days to chance by sending men and women He couldn't count on? A common theme of patriarchal blessings given to men and women your age is that you were sent now because our Father's most trustworthy children would be needed in the final, decisive battle for righteousness. That is who you are, and it is who you have always been.

—Sheri Dew[1]

Leaders are duty-bound and obligated to prepare others to take their place at some future time.

—Elder Spencer J. Condie[2]

The final night of Jesus' mortal journey provided profound teaching moments for Peter, the chief apostle, on whom the mantel of leadership was soon to fall. Peter was walking ground no mortal had walked before. He had been privy to the Savior's transcendent teachings and miraculous experiences, but he encountered those teachings and experiences through the lens of his own mortality and didn't always understand them fully. Like the rest of us must, Peter saw through "a glass darkly," and didn't, at the time, have the full context or eternal perspective he would ultimately gain. When Jesus knelt and gently washed the dust off His apostles' feet, Peter resisted. The Savior's stern but loving rebuke was followed by Peter's bold response to have his entire body washed. One of the meaningful messages Jesus left Peter was that, as leaders, our job is to love and to serve. "He that is greatest among you shall be your servant," Jesus declared (Matt 23:11), as that sacred moment foreshadowed what was to come, when Jesus would descend below all so that we could eventually rise above. Leaders serve. This is a preeminent responsibility. "He that is greatest among you, let him be as the younger," Jesus states, "And he that is chief, as he that doth serve . . . I am among you as he that serveth" (Luke 22:26–27).

Jesus had provided critical instruction to his chief apostle throughout his ministry, and slowly, Peter begins to comprehend his role. Peter's impetuous and reactive response in cutting the ear off the servant of the high priest is met with yet one more miraculous healing and a poignant reminder of Jesus' mission—which was not to take up the sword at that moment, as justified as that might have felt to Jesus' disciples. A leader, Jesus shows, remains true to his or her purpose and calling, despite the opposition one almost always encounters.

Toward the end of that final evening, while the disciples were still in the upper room, after the institution of the sacrament but before the migration to and the transcendent happenings at Gethsemane, Jesus tells Simon Peter,

> And the Lord said, Simon, Simon, behold, Satan hath desired to have you, that he may sift you as wheat:
>
> But I have prayed for thee, that thy faith fail not: and when thou art converted, *strengthen thy brethren* (Luke 22:31–32, italics added).

Notice the distinct shift in the use of different pronouns: in the first part of Jesus' statement, He declares: "Satan hath desired to have *you*." Not just "you," singular, but "you," plural, meaning all of God's children. Jesus pointedly reminds Peter that Satan has his own clear purpose, namely, the destruction and misery of everyone. He desires to have us all. To counteract that, Jesus prays specifically for Peter, the soon-to-be new leader of God's church and kingdom on earth. "But I have prayed for *thee*," Jesus tells Peter, "That *thy* faith fail not: and when *thou* art converted, strengthen *thy* brethren." As He prepares to pass the baton of leadership to His chief apostle, Jesus prays specifically for Peter, and charges him that when he is converted, he must devote his time to strengthening and lifting and guiding all those whom Satan desires to have.

What a sacred privilege to have experienced that last night with Jesus, and to know that the Savior himself prays for His leaders! We learn so many things through this significant moment, including the fact that a critical role of any leader is to guide, mentor, and develop other leaders.

So much of what was being taught would be understood more fully later. Indeed, Peter would experience profound learning moments that very night and subsequent day as Jesus was imprisoned, whipped, tried, ridiculed, spat upon, tortured, and ultimately crucified. Peter was to learn a lot about Peter, and despite his denials—perhaps in part because of them—Peter's grasp of his new role as the leader of the Lord's church began to settle in. He had experienced divine leadership mentoring at the hands of the Master Teacher.

There is sufficient, renewable nuclear energy in seawater to power the world indefinitely. They key is unleashing it.[3] As leaders, our task is to unleash the extraordinary potential of the people with whom and for whom we serve—to recognize the leadership potential of others and to help enable and magnify this potential. You can help those you serve discover their potential by having a conversation with them around these questions: Imagine meeting yourself when you leave your current calling:

- How have you changed?

- What contributions have you made?
- How do you know?
- Have you made a real difference to those you serve? And how would you define and measure that difference?
- Have you given the best that's in you? Have you brought your best talents, gifts, and creativity to the calling? In what ways?

In your own leadership responsibilities, have you felt yourself stretching, growing, and learning? How have you grown? What is the most important thing you've learned?

Everything a leader does communicates something—whether you, as the leader, want to communicate or not. Others are constantly watching what you do, what you say, how you solve problems, how you express love, how you treat your family, how you serve, how you handle difficult situations. And since what you do as leaders communicates, it is prudent to be deliberate and conscientious about what you communicate rather than leave anything to chance. A few years ago, some colleagues and I collaborated on a book entitled, *Talent Unleashed.* In it, we wrote about the purposeful communication leaders can have to nurture, mentor and develop other leaders. How we communicate with those we lead and serve can have a profound impact on how they grow and develop as leaders.

Here are four specific leadership conversations related to our service in the Church you might consider as you seek to emulate Jesus' powerful example of developing leadership skills with and among those you serve: the Trust Conversation, the Contribution Conversation, the Delegation Conversation, and the Barrier Removal Conversation.

1. The Trust Conversation: Express confidence and extend trust to those within your stewardship. Allow others to grow in their callings. Give them room to maneuver, to explore their own ideas, to pray for inspiration and revelation for their calling, to struggle a bit, and then to pray again. Carefully avoid the temptation to micromanage.

Have confidence that the Lord will hear them and answer their prayers. Remember, He has called them to their respective responsibilities, and, as President Monson so wonderfully taught, whom God calls, God qualifies.[4] "Be thou humble," the Lord said, "and the Lord thy God shall lead thee by the hand and give the answers to thy prayers" (D&C 112:10). Regarding our callings, President Henry B. Eyring taught, "You are called of God. The Lord knows you. He knows whom He would have serve in every position in His Church. He chose you."[5] Have confidence in those who serve under your leadership that the Lord, will, in fact, follow through on this divine promise, and express that confidence to them often.

2. The Contribution Conversation: Part of helping individuals develop their own leadership skills comes with helping them make connections between what they're asked to do and the unique spiritual gifts, talents and capabilities they possess. Each of us is given certain gifts, Moroni explains, and these gifts are given that they might both "profit" us individually (Moroni 10:8), but also that we might use them to elevate and bless all of God's children (D&C 46:26). Our spiritual gifts, talents and capabilities represent ways that God manifests Himself in our lives (including the great Gift of the Holy Ghost). Discussing these gifts with those within your stewardship helps create awareness and action around them, and might include:

- Engaging with them about what they love to do and what they're good at. What are their gifts? How might they seek for and develop these gifts in order to better serve and lift others?

- Reminding them of their previous opportunities to serve and lead, and how they have accomplished important objectives, despite difficult and challenging circumstances.

- Providing them with a vision for who they really are and helping them tap into that vision as they begin their work.

Serving provides opportunities to grow and develop in ways that otherwise might not be known. Talents emerge, capabilities strengthen, and connections with a larger purpose become a driving force for action that is both compelling to those who serve and contagious for those around them. Remember the discussion about the young, untested sons of Helaman—those 2,060 stippling warriors (Chapter Three). Their driving force was not a well-honed military skill set, but rather, a deep and abiding hope to contribute whatever gifts they had to the effort. That desire to connect to a broad and significant purpose became the impetus that ultimately made a meaningful difference in the war. They proved that each part matters to the whole. Leaders need to help those with whom they serve understand and realize this, and to bring their gifts to the work.

3. The Delegation Conversation: Learn to delegate effectively. During the forty years in the wilderness, Moses' duties became nearly overwhelming. When his father-in-law, Jethro, witnessed the overwhelming nature of Moses' daily responsibilities, he asked Moses:

> What is this thing that thou doest to the people? why sittest thou thyself alone, and all the people stand by thee from morning unto even?

Moses responds:

> Because the people come unto me to inquire of God:
>
> When they have a matter, they come unto me; and I judge between one and another, and I do make them know the statutes of God, and his laws.

In other words, when the people have a problem—any problem—they come to me (Moses) to provide judgment.

Jethro's wisely counsels his son-in-law:

> The thing that thou doest is not good. Thou wilt surely wear away and this people that is with thee: for this thing is too heavy for thee; thou art not able to perform it thyself alone.

> Hearken now unto my voice, I will give thee counsel, and God shall be with thee . . .
>
> Thou shalt provide out of all the people able men, such as fear God, men of truth, hating covetousness; and place such over them, to be rulers of thousands, and rulers of hundreds, rulers of fifties, and rulers of tens:
>
> And let them judge the people at all seasons: and it shall be, that every great matter they shall bring unto thee, but every small matter they shall judge: so shall it be easier for thyself, and they shall bear the burden with thee. (Exodus 18:14–22)

Moses needed to develop and establish other leaders who could assist in the great work. But he needed them to function with clarity on the specific jobs that needed to be done, with wisdom and with judgment.

Delegating requires the establishment of boundaries and accountability processes. Leaders must provide a consistent forum for people to return and report on their assignments and stewardship and help establish a vision for the purpose or "Why" of the assignment. Here are some topics to discuss:

- Are the outcomes or goals for the calling compelling and clear? Is the vision understood and shared among all who need it? If not, work to create clarity so there is no guessing on the goals. An objective—perhaps the singular objective—of nearly any calling is to bring people unto Christ. Is that objective crystal clear?

- What are the guidelines for accomplishing the goal? Are there watch-outs or boundaries that need to be discussed?

- What resources are available for accomplishing the goal? Is there a budget? Who else needs to be involved? What other resources can be brought to bear to accomplish the goal?

- How will you hold each other accountable for commitments? When will you meet to discuss? Is this a ward council agenda item or presidency meeting item? Remember President Monson's insightful direction: "When performance is measured, performance improves. When performance is measured and reported back, the rate of improvement accelerates."[6]

- Is there a process to continuously reinforce the vision of a successful outcome? What are the consequences of doing the assignment well? What happens if the goal is missed? Is everyone clear on what's at stake?

Providing clarity on these items does not suggest a lack of trust. Rather, it engages those with whom you serve around the proper priorities. In my professional experience, I have spent a significant part of my career coaching other leaders on how to hold others accountable, how to execute properly around the critical goals—goals that are clear, understood, and shared. A bit of a surprise learning for me occurred throughout this process. I have seen repeatedly, that, on the teams where accountability is high, engagement is measurably higher than on teams where the goals are muddy or vague, with limited or no accountability. People inherently want to be successful. They want to make a difference. They want to contribute their finest efforts. Coaching around these simple but critical elements will bring a sustained level of engagement and increased joy in the work.

When God created the earth, He did so in orderly manner. Here's one portion of the account:

> And I, God, said: Let the earth bring forth grass, the herb yielding seed, the fruit tree yielding fruit, after his kind, and the tree yielding fruit, whose seed should be in itself upon the earth, and it was so even as I spake.
>
> And the earth brought forth grass, every herb yielding seed after his kind, and the tree yielding fruit, whose seed should be in itself, after his kind; and I, God, saw that all things which I had made were good (Moses 2:11–12).

We can surely infer from this and other accounts of the creation that there was clarity around the goals with and among all who were involved, a process, with involvement, assignments, and accountabilities.

We are a covenant people. That is, a people who make promises with God, and a people who believe in a God that will deliver on His promises to us. Our covenants bring clarity to eternal goals and establish an agreement with God. The scriptures really are about the saga of making and keeping covenants and the consequences for keeping (or not keeping) them. The Delegation Conversation—bringing clarity to the goal or desired outcomes, establishing guidelines, understanding the available resources, holding each other accountable, and reinforcing the vision for success—is simply following a pattern the Lord has established and has communicated throughout the scriptures.

4. The Barrier Removal Conversation: Two extremes exist for many leaders. The first is the leader who has all the answers, who wants to dictate or micromanage every detail. These leaders assume the paradigm that leaders supervise because they have "super vision." Because they've done it before, they want to ensure they control every detail. The impact of this, however, is limiting. Those who would otherwise be magnified by their service are diminished and left to follow only the direction they receive from you. Their growth as a leader will be stunted.

Another extreme is the leader who abandons those they serve, assuming that, "their calling is their calling . . . they need to fulfill it." While it is true, too often these leaders leave those within their stewardship feeling alone and lonely, without anyone to turn to for counsel. Of course we need to allow others to serve in their respective roles without constantly looking over their shoulder. But remember, a little coaching can go a long way.

Here's is a third alternative to consider. Rather than the micromanager or abandoner, be a leader who coaches and mentors, one who asks the question, "What barriers can I remove for you?" Be the leader who runs alongside those they serve, who asks what they are learning and feeling, who removes obstacles that only you, in your role, can uniquely remove. Then watch how those for whom you have stewardship soar.

The ultimate example of this behavior is, of course, the Savior, who removed the barriers only He could remove. Without his atoning sacrifice, "all mankind must unavoidably perish; yea, all are hardened; yea, all are fallen and are lost, and must perish except it be through the atonement which it is expedient should be made" (Alma 34:9). We simply cannot do it on our own.

As leaders, be mindful of the barriers you can remove to allow those you serve to do more than they otherwise could. Their growth and development as individuals and leaders will be magnified by your involvement at this level.

I served with a stake president who provided a marvelous model of these behaviors. In preparation for a major activity—one that included all the youth of a very large stake as well as dozens of adult leaders and required many months of planning and the coordination of hundreds of details—he tasked us with planning something that would be aligned with what the Lord wanted for our stake. He didn't give us every detail (because he didn't have every detail), but simply said, "The Lord knows the needs of our stake. Go to the Him, make a plan, then go to Him again and see where you need to adjust. Keep doing that. When it's right, we'll all know it." He respected our callings and the inspiration to which we were entitled. He expected us to pay the price to learn and understand the Lord's will. He constantly expressed confidence in our abilities to plan and organize. He gently prodded us when we were off course. He constantly reminded us to seek the Lord's counsel. He ensured we were clear on the guidelines and available resources and engaged with us frequently on these topics. We had weekly accountability meetings. When we hit a barrier that needed his attention, he addressed it. The end result was a profound experience for all who participated. As leaders, we emerged from that experience with a greater sense of both the Lord's interest and involvement in the lives of our stake members and in our abilities to do whatever is asked of us. We had grown meaningfully in our assignment.

I have always enjoyed traveling and exploring the beauty of the world. I love the rich tapestry of diverse thought and culture, the sound of an unfamiliar language, the cadence of commerce that just feels different than what I am accustomed to and the different aromas that accompany exotic foods in various places around the world. Some time ago, my wife and I traveled to the Holy Land. Toward the end of our extraordinary trip, we visited the Garden of Gethsemane. Following a sacred experience at the Church of the Agony, we transitioned to a secluded garden, enclosed by a large fence. The garden was quiet and serene, but even as we sat there, we could hear the sounds of humanity just outside the garden wall. We heard the call to Muslim prayer. We could hear clear evidence of pulsating traffic, with its hustle and bustle and constant and unrelenting activity—each sound representing a person, a family, a business. I loved the garden's peaceful serenity as I sat and pondered in the shade of a large and ancient olive tree. But the garden's beauty was accentuated by the sounds of life on the other side of the wall. It was a wonderful contrast.

The global pandemic of 2020 brought an abrupt halt to my travel and introduced the longest stretch of time in my life *not* on an airplane in the previous thirty years. Instead of looking for beauty and adventure in the far-flung reaches outside my neighborhood, I found myself looking more closely at my most immediate surroundings. I did so because I had to—I no longer had the option of looking elsewhere. I took time to enjoy the quiet.

I was reminded of my seventh grade English teacher, Mr. Carter, who took us on a field trip where we were required to write poetry. Each student was assigned an isolated corner of a mountainside, all alone. Our assignment was simply to listen, then write about what we had heard and seen. Initially, with no one with whom to converse, I wasn't hearing anything. But once I got past the initial quiet, I began to hear and see all kinds of things that otherwise escaped my attention. I could hear the sound of the gentle breeze in the leaves of the trees. I noticed minuscule insects going about their business in the small detail of the soil and undergrowth. I noticed the veins in the leaves on the nearby plants, and the constant comings and goings of birds to and from the trees' branches. I noticed immense activity, which was normally outside my attention, that happened all the time, every day. I witnessed the power and beauty in that small corner of our ecosystem—something that happened right before me, but without my notice.

Something similar happened during the COVID-19 crisis. Separated from my usual interactions and regular activities, I began to appreciate the importance of close friendships, the friendly back and forth with our neighbors, the healing balm of a freshly mowed lawn or carefully weeded flower bed. My wife and I took regular evening drives—something neither of us would normally have time to take. This time unencumbered by our normal routines and commitments became something we cherished, despite the uncertainty that accompanied the crisis. I began to notice, all around my immediate locale, the remarkable greatness that surrounds my everyday life—both the people and the physical location.

As leaders, do we see the greatness that is right in front of us? Do we take time to first see, then develop that greatness in others?

Once, when speaking with a group of business leaders, I asked the question: who in your life saw and communicated something to you that, at the time, you didn't yet see? One particular leader's hand shot up, very eager to share his experience. He recounted that he had come from a highly dysfunctional family. His home environment was toxic and as a result he had made some less than productive personal choices and ended up in a youth detention facility when he was fourteen years old. One day, while he was sitting in the center's cafeteria, a leader—one of the counselors at the facility—came up to him, put his hand on my friend's shoulder, looked in him the eyes, and asked, sincerely, "What would you like to do in your life?" My friend said that normally, that very question might have set him off, but for whatever reason that day, he was open to the question. He replied, "I don't know." The leader then remarked, "I believe in you. You can do anything you set your mind to." Then he got up and left.

My friend told me that he just sat there in silence. He had never even considered that he would (or even could) do anything with his life. He'd had no vision. And now, all of a sudden, and because of this leader's comment, one started to emerge.

His counselor stayed with him. My friend told me that it was often "tough love." He helped him make certain commitments and held him accountable for those commitments. But in every interaction, he reaffirmed his love for my friend and his vision for him that he could and would do important things. My friend said, "I believed him. I began to see myself differently. I began to apply myself more deliberately. I eventually graduated from High School—the first person in my family to do so. I became introduced to the Church and was happy to learn my counselor was also a member. I was baptized, and later served a mission. I then went to college and eventually earned my bachelor's degree. I met a beautiful girl, whom I married in the temple. I then went back to school and earned my master's degree. Today, I am leading an innovative team that does remarkable work. Our team is part of a cutting-edge and industry-leading organization. I have a terrific and loving family who are doing great things. I look back on where I started and have to pinch myself from time to time at how my life has ended up, and I can trace it all back to that day in the cafeteria when that leader expressed his belief in me."

In 1834, the Lord commanded Joseph Smith to form Zions Camp, a military expedition designed to reclaim lands and possession taken from the saints in Missouri. The group consisted of 207 men and approximately thirty women who were called away from their families in a precarious time and marched 1,000 miles over six weeks. Zions Camp was difficult, came at great sacrifice on the parts of the participants and the families they left behind. The men and women suffered with blistered feet, oppressive heat, heavy rains, excruciating humidity, unrelenting hunger and thirst, coarse bread and rancid butter, raw pork, rotten ham, maggot infested bacon and cheese. They didn't fight a single battle, and from an outside perspective Zions Camp might be considered a failed mission.

However, military might was not the Lord's objective. He was building and refining a new generation of leaders. The Lord used this occasion to create a cohesive, committed group of disciples who were prepared through this experience to lead the Church for the rest of their lives—where much was to be required of them. Through the Zions camp experience these men and women learned to overcome adversity, work together, serve one another, exercise faith, demonstrate courage, and listen to and obey the guidance from their living prophet. In the years to come, they would be called upon to lead a western migration that helped define an entire century, shape a country, and provide a haven for The Church of Jesus Christ of Latter-day Saints. This church would be positioned, because of their leadership, to gain strength and prominence in preparation for the second coming of the Lord.

Of this group, Joseph Smith said, "God did not want you to fight. He could not organize His kingdom with twelve men to open the Gospel door to the nations of the earth, and with seventy men under their direction to follow in their tracks, unless He took them from a body of men who had offered their lives, and who had made as great a sacrifice as did Abraham."[7]

Speaking of the remarkable influence this event had on his ability to lead, Brother Brigham spoke of the mentoring he received from the Prophet Joseph: "I have travelled with Joseph a thousand miles, as he has led the Camp of Israel. I have watched him and observed everything he said or did . . . For the town of Kirtland, I would not give the knowledge I got from Joseph from this Journey . . . This was the starting point of my knowing how to lead Israel."[8]

The impact of this leadership development experience was far-reaching. Nine members of the soon to be called Quorum of the Twelve came from this group, as did 70 members of the First Quorum of the Seventy. Wilford Woodruff later declared, "We gained an experience that we never could have gained in any other way. We had the privilege of beholding the face of the prophet, and we had the privilege of traveling a thousand miles with him and seeing the workings of the spirit of God with him, and the revelations of Jesus Christ unto him and the fulfilment of those revelations. . .. Had I not gone up with Zion's Camp I should not have been here to-day [Salt Lake City, December 1869], and I presume that would have been the case with many others in this Territory. By going there, we were thrust into the vineyard to preach the gospel, and the Lord accepted our labors. And in all our labors and persecutions, with our lives often at stake, we have had to work and live by faith."[9] Joseph knew of this important nature of this experience and understood that part of his leadership role at that time was to develop other leaders. He said, in reference to this, "If I should now be taken away, I [have] accomplished the great work the Lord [has] laid before me."[10] Indeed, we continue to feel today the positive impact of the leadership skills developed during this critical moment in history.

Leaders have the significant responsibility to develop a compelling vision and then a strategy to achieve that vision. They need to establish a productive an engaging culture—a culture where people feel valued, respected, and where a spirit of trust abounds. They must then manage the work and ensure the right things are getting done by the right people at the right time. Leaders must deliver results—or someone else will be asked to fill their role. Certainly, being a leader is not for the faint of heart! In additional to all the critical things associated with these leadership roles and responsibilities, one of a leader's most critical and essential roles is that of developing other leaders—those around them who possess great potential, but sometimes need a leader or mentor to see their latent greatness and help bring that greatness forward. Leaders must see and communicate the greatness that is constantly around them.

Some things to consider:

1. Think of a leader who made a difference in your service—someone who helped you become a better leader. Find a way to express your gratitude to them.

2. Identify someone within the scope of your service who could benefit from your mentoring.

3. Hold one of the leadership conversations with this individual (the Trust, Contribution, Delegation or Barrier Removal conversation).

CHAPTER SIXTEEN
LEAD ONE BY ONE

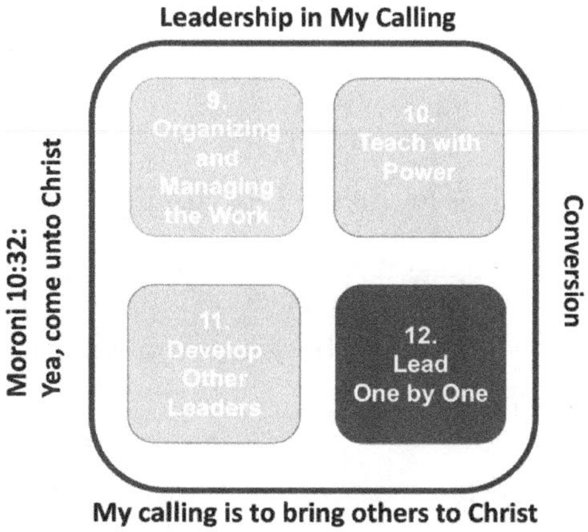

What man of you, having an hundred sheep, if he lose one of them, doth not leave the ninety and nine in the wilderness, and go after that which is lost, until he find it?

And when he hath found it, he layeth it on his shoulders, rejoicing.

And when he cometh home, he calleth together his friends and neighbours, saying unto them, Rejoice with me; for I have found my sheep which was lost.

—Luke 15:4–6

Friendship is born at that moment when one person says to another: "What! You too? I thought I was the only one."

—C. S. Lewis[1]

What are the notable events that transpired 600 years ago? What happened then that significantly impacts our lives today? Who were the leaders? What were the societal conflicts or issues of the day? What was family life like? What did people read, and what did the education process entail? How did people spend their leisure time? What made them laugh? What made them cry?

Resources exist that, if one were inclined to learn, provide information about this time period. Here are some highlights, for example, of some major events that occurred between 1420 and 1430:

- March 1420 — The Celebi Sultan Mehmed Mosque in Didymoteicho is inaugurated
- March 1421 — The French defeat the English in the Battle of Bauge
- August 1422 — Henry VI becomes the King of England at the age of nine months
- July 1423 — Arnold van Egmont becomes Dule of Gelre
- November 1424 — Storm flood ravages Dutch coast
- August 1425 — Countess Jacoba of Bavaria escapes from jail
- August 1427 — Valais witch trial proceedings begins in Valais Canton, Switzerland, first organized witch trials
- April 1429 — Joan of Arc arrives at the siege of Orleans
- January 1430—Jews of Sicily are no longer required to attend conversionist services

There are, I'm certain, individuals who have devoted their professional lives to studying and teaching what life was like in the early 1400's. And I'm equally confident that events occurred then that still impact our modern life. But, truthfully, it's not something I think about. Perhaps I should be more well-versed on those historical details. It's just so long ago that my focus lies in more pressing contemporary issues.

As a point of context, 600 years is the time frame between when Lehi and his family, under direction from the Lord, left Jerusalem and journeyed to a new land and all that entailed, and when Jesus appeared to the people at the Land Bountiful. For six centuries, prophets had testified that Jesus Christ would come. Nephi taught: "For according to the words of the prophets, the Messiah cometh in six hundred years from the time that my father left Jerusalem; and according to the words of the prophets, and also the word of the angel of God, his name shall be Jesus Christ, the Son of God" (2 Nephi 25:19). Not only would Jesus come to Jerusalem, but He would also visit the posterity of Lehi in the new world: "And after Christ shall have risen from the dead he shall show himself unto you, my children, and my beloved brethren; and the words which he shall speak unto you shall be the law which ye shall do" (2 Nephi 26:1). This prophecy was repeated by other prophets throughout the subsequent 600 years. Alma taught his people "that he would appear unto them after his resurrection; and this the people did hear with great joy and gladness" (Alma 16:20).

But 600 years is a long time. The Book of Mormon reveals an often-repeated pattern of periods of righteousness followed by periods of pride-induced wickedness, followed by periods of chastening, then repentance, then righteousness, then pride, then wickedness again. For centuries, this cycle continued. I'm sure, throughout this ongoing cycle, there were times when even the righteous had to question whether they had been forgotten, and if the long-anticipated appearance of Jesus Christ would ever come.

And then, finally, after 600 years it happened. Signs of Jesus' death were ubiquitous, and no one was spared from the influence of these signs as the earth mourned His crucifixion. Tempests, earthquakes, fires, whirlwinds and upheavals of all kinds occurred. Cities were burned, buried in the earth and sunk in the depths of the sea. A thick darkness came upon "all the face of the land, insomuch that the inhabitants thereof who had not fallen could feel the vapor of darkness" (3 Nephi 8:20). But the righteous in the Land Bountiful and other locations survived. One morning, as 2500 people were gathered in the Land Bountiful, the people hear a voice "as if it came out of heaven." They describe it as neither harsh nor loud, yet it did pierce "them that did hear it to the center, insomuch that there was no part of their frame that it did not cause to quake; yea it did pierce them to the very soul, and did cause their hearts to burn" (3 Nephi 11:3).

Three times they hear the voice, and on the third time, the Nephites finally understand: this is the voice of the Father: "Behold my Beloved Son, in whom I am well pleased, in whom I have glorified my name—hear ye him" (3 Nephi 11:7). They then witness the glorious descension of the Son of God, clothed in white. After Jesus declares Himself to the people of Bountiful, they fall to the earth, overcome.

Imagine being there that morning! After 600 long years, you have the opportunity to be a first-hand witness to what was about to unfold! You are, as it says in *Hamilton*, "in the room where it happened."[2] What would Jesus say? What would he do? What would He teach?

What Jesus does is something that for me, is one of the great illustrations of His love and examples of His remarkable leadership. He invites each of the 2,500 people there that day to approach him and to "thrust their hands into his side" and "feel the prints of the nails in his hands and in his feet; and this they did do, going forth *one by one* until they had *all* gone forth" (3 Nephi 11–15, emphasis added). Only after they have this individual experience and personally feel of His love for each of them does He teach them.

The image of "one by one" reminds us that he knows us and leads us one by one—despite the vastness of His creations, the expanse of His heavens, whose greatness and glory is ever increasing as His curtains are being "stretched out still" (Moses 7:30). He knows us *individually* and *personally.* If, in this Land Bountiful experience, each person, including the transition time required to move from person to person, were to take just ten seconds with the Savior, this would have required almost seven hours to complete! And this is precisely what occurred.

Jesus' example provides significant insight to His character. And it should give direction on how we should approach our leadership responsibilities, in any role and at any level. Each leader, regardless of the calling, has many pressing responsibilities, many of which are administrative in nature. For some, their calling actually is administrative—clerks, executive secretaries, and other quorum and organizational secretaries work to keep things organized, facilitate communication, and ensure the reporting and other work is properly managed. But even those roles have an underlying job description—to bring others to Christ. Regardless of our calling, that imperative is realized as leaders understand that the work of the Church is manifest in the work with individuals. Elder Jeffrey R. Holland has taught: "That is how the kingdom of God is built—one person at a time, one covenant at a time."[3]

Like the people in the Land Bountiful, Moses learns the nature of the Lord's individual love for His children when he is transfigured before the Lord and is given the opportunity to glimpse the greatness of God's creations. He beholds "worlds without number," and sees Adam and the inhabitants of this earth and other worlds. The Lord tells him, "But an account of this earth, and the inhabitants thereof, give I unto you. For behold, there are many worlds that have passed away by the word of my power. And there are many that now stand, and innumerable are they unto man; but all things are numbered unto me, for they are mine and I know them" (Moses 1:33,35, emphasis added). We cannot comprehend how this happens, but with all God's creations, we are numbered and known. I truly stand all amazed. C. S. Lewis wrote, "God has infinite attention to spare for each one of us. You are as much alone with him as if you were the only being he had ever created."[4] And Elder Neal A. Maxwell testified of God's intimate love for each one of us:

> In the expansiveness of space, there is stunning personalness, for God knows and loves each of us! (see 1 Nephi 11:17). We are not ciphers in unexplained space!
>
> While the Psalmist's query was, "What is man, that thou art mindful of him?" (Psalm 8:4), mankind is at the very center of God's work. We are the sheep of His hand and the people of His pasture (see Psalms 79:13; 95:7; 100:3). His work includes our immortalization—accomplished by Christ's glorious Atonement!

> Think of it, brothers and sisters, even with their extensive longevity, stars are not immortal, but you are.[5]

Jesus' long-anticipated appearance to the righteous Nephites and Lamanites introduces several leadership patterns that emphasize how we can focus our efforts more specifically on the needs of the one. Below is one example of a pattern, with five parts: 1) Testify Boldly, 2) Remember Those We Serve, 3) Love Those We Serve, 4) Remain Flexible, and 5) Seek Those Who are Missing.

Part One: Testify Boldly

In 3 Nephi 11:10–11, the Savior declares: "Behold, I am Jesus Christ, whom the prophets testified shall come into the world. And behold, I am the light and the life of the world; and I have drunk out of that bitter cup which the Father hath given me, and have glorified the Father in taking upon me the sins of the world, in the which I have suffered the will of the Father in all things from the beginning." Jesus states boldly that He is, in fact, the "Light of the World," He who has been prophesied of from the beginning. The people of Bountiful know, unequivocally, that God lives.

Leadership Lesson: Do we, in our leadership efforts and responsibilities, declare boldly and without apology at every opportunity that we know that God does, in fact, live, that Jesus Christ is the Messiah, He whom we all look to and look for with great anticipation? Do we recognize that we are representing His name in all our service?

Part Two: Remember Those We Serve

In verse twelve of that same chapter, those present at Jesus' appearance then fall "to the earth; for they remembered that it had been prophesied among them that Christ should show himself unto them after his ascension into heaven." Their recollection of those many years of prophecy underscores a critical element of leadership—that the God of Heaven knows them, that he hasn't forgotten them. They know that they are known.

Leadership Lesson: Do we, in our leadership responsibilities, remember those we serve? Do we truly get to know them and their families? Do we know what their challenges are? Do we know what brings them joy? Do we remember that they are daughters and sons of Heavenly Parents, just as we are, and do we serve them accordingly? Do we understand their capabilities and tap into their unique abilities to contribute?

One bishop had a sister in his ward who didn't fit the traditional mold. In what was once an industrious logging town, factory closures brought economic struggles to his small ward. But the members were dedicated and served in their callings with distinction. This sister served as the Second Counselor in the Relief Society Presidency. A former anti-Mormon evangelical, she was a convert who had joined the church four years prior when her husband, a lifelong but less active member, was reactivated. This sister was passionate about the gospel and had seen immeasurable blessings enter her life as a result of joining the church. She was quick to share her testimony to all with whom she came in contact, and every six weeks, she and her husband loaded up their old Suburban and drove the missionaries to their transfer meeting three hours and two bridges each way. She magnified her Relief Society calling and had developed a reputation in the ward for being one of those people who just gets things done. And, she smoked. Before joining the Church, she had been a lifelong smoker, and although she embraced the Word of Wisdom principles, she struggled to quit the habit. After nearly a year of working with missionaries and counseling with her bishop, she was baptized. But despite the fasts, prayers, patches and programs, her smoking habit persisted. She would, on occasion, get discouraged as she was painfully aware that there were more blessings awaiting her at the temple that she could not obtain until she quit smoking. Nevertheless, she persisted in her service in the Kingdom and continued to be a blessing to all she encountered—an example of choosing holiness, even in the face of discouragement. Her bishop and relief society president recognized this sister's unique circumstances, her particular gifts, and her ability to contribute. They sought her out and helped her understand that she was vital to everything that was occurring in the ward, that others could be warmed by the fire of her testimony. They helped her understand that her strengths were needed, and that the ward was lifted by having her part of the work. In turn, she offered all that she had in service to others, often at great sacrifice, and blessed the lives of every member of that ward. The one-by-one ministry of the bishop and relief society president resulted in one-by-one service from this sister, whose contributions were needed and meaningful. All were lifted and magnified by this process.

Leadership in the kingdom requires we seek those who are missing and that we welcome those who don't fit an exact mold. Each one has an ability to contribute, and each one is needed.

Part Three: Love Those We Serve

Jesus then invites them to "arise and come forth unto me, that ye may thrust your hands into my side, and also that ye may feel the prints of the nails in my hands and in my feet, that ye may know that I am the God of Israel, and the God of the whole earth, and have been slain for the sins of the world" (3 Nephi 11:14). Each person then, as noted above, has a "one by one" experience with the Savior. They learn the depth of His love for them, as unique individuals, is penetrating, consuming, and overwhelming.

Leadership Lesson: Do we, in our leadership responsibilities, truly love those we serve? Do we pray for them? Do we serve them? When they are in crisis, do we feel their pain? When they experience joy, do we share in that joy? Do we help them understand their individual uniqueness matters? Do we extend the hand of friendship when it is convenient and when it is not?

How we treat the individual will determine our ultimate effectiveness as a leader with larger groups. My brother-in-law has made a habit of writing his extended family an occasional letter. This letter serves as his personal and family journal, and he graciously shares it with all of us. In this letter he recounts the happenings of each week and adds his insight, feelings, and musings. I always look forward to receiving his letters. Some time ago he sent a note that particularly touched me, which, I believe, is relevant to this leadership principle. He writes of one of his son's missionary experiences when, on preparation day, he and his companion were visiting a family in a rural part of their area. He and his companion decided to ride their bikes to visit another family, some ten miles away. My brother-in-law writes:

> One of the older boys of the member family wanted to go with the Elders on this bike excursion and so the household was searched for a bike that he could use. All he could find was a little pink bicycle that his little sister sometimes rode that really didn't fit him well and didn't have all the nifty gears to help accommodate the ups and downs of the journey. The tires were low, the chain was rusty, but the young man was excited to ride with the Elders. Both Elders had nice ten-speed bikes with good bearings, fully inflated tires, lubed chains, and stylish paint.
>
> For the first few miles they all biked the rural roads together, but it became clear after four or five miles that the young man on the little pink bike was at a serious disadvantage and had fallen behind. At a point about midway through the ride the trio stopped for a rest. The young man on the little pink bike was obviously winded and struggling. It occurred to my son that he might be able to help things along by letting the young man ride his bike while he took a turn on the smaller bike. As they proceeded down the rolling country road my son began to realize what a challenge it was to ride this bike. When the "up" side of the hill came, there was only one gear to use. When the "down" side of the hill came, the under-inflated tires and poor bearings didn't allow for much coasting. It was a constant struggle. My son's legs grew very weary as they neared their destination.
>
> After arriving and taking care of business, the young man faced the grim prospect of riding the little pink bike back to his home. My son, feeling the need to ease the burden, traded time on the little pink bike on the return trip.
>
> As my son related this story he drew an analogy of those who come into this world saddled with "little pink bikes." Their self-esteem might be low, their social skills are rusty, and it's a struggle for them to handle the ups and downs of life. These are not the "beautiful people" of the world with whom we like to associate. These are they that have many needs and are very often overlooked.

Yesterday afternoon I was the only one home when a phone call came in. I looked at the caller ID and saw it was from an out-of-state psychiatric hospital. I picked up the phone and heard a young woman's voice on the other end. She identified herself and asked for my son. I recognized this young woman's name and remembered that she was one of those in High School whom my son had gone out of his way to befriend. I remembered she was short, plump, had thinning hair, heavy acne.

I found myself—all of a sudden—becoming protective of my son's time. After talking for a minute, I became more and more agitated at her persistence that I get her number to my son. Ultimately, however, I agreed to do it.

As I called my son to talk with him, I hatched a way that he could call her but be able to end the call in short order. She had told me she couldn't talk after 9:00 p.m., so I suggested to my son that he call her after 8:30, thus assuring a shorter call. My son listened, then told me that he knew how to let the young woman know when he had to leave and that he would be ok. "Not to worry, dad," he said. "She is one that has been given a little pink bike to ride through life." He told me that he loved me and then we hung up. I sat and pondered his words.

I have been listening to audiotapes of a fictional account of a family living at the time of Christ and of their interactions with the Savior. As I was listening this morning, the narrator told of one of the story's characters that happened to be near the Savior as he recited the following parable:

But he, willing to justify himself, said unto Jesus, And who is my neighbour?

And Jesus answering said, A certain man went down from Jerusalem to Jericho, and fell among thieves, which stripped him of his raiment, and wounded him, and departed, leaving him half dead.

And by chance there came down a certain priest that way: and when he saw him, he passed by on the other side.

And likewise a Levite, when he was at the place, came and looked on him, and passed by on the other side.

But a certain Samaritan, as he journeyed, came where he was: and when he saw him, he had compassion on him,

And went to him, and bound up his wounds, pouring in oil and wine, and set him on his own beast, and brought him to an inn, and took care of him.

And on the morrow when he departed, he took out two pence, and gave them to the host, and said unto him, Take care of him; and whatsoever thou spendest more, when I come again, I will repay thee.

Which now of these three, thinkest thou, was neighbour unto him that fell among the thieves?

And he said, He that shewed mercy on him. Then said Jesus unto him, Go, and do thou likewise. (Luke 10:29–37)

The narrator then analyzed this parable through the fictional character. This character realized that the priest and the Levite, both holders of the priesthood, had crossed over to the other side of the road, not wanting to be burdened with the "messy" situation. However, the Samaritan not only crossed over to the man who was beaten, but also bound his wounds, poured antiseptic into the wounds, and helped him on his donkey. None of this was convenient. The Samaritan then took the man to an innkeeper, paid for the expenses, and expressed his willingness to incur additional debt on behalf of the injured man.

Like a bolt of lightning, the characters became real to me. The man on the side of the road became the young woman who had called asking for my help. Her "little pink bike" was broken and she needed someone to help inflate the tires, lube the chain, and

> oil the bearings. I was the high priest who felt I was being imposed upon by the inconvenience of a call from the hospital. I had been very willing to stay on my own side of the street and not get my hands dirty, not wanting to let anyone else in my family suffer the same inconvenience. I recalled the long-term help my son had provided to this young woman, and the parallel between him and the Samaritan hit me forcefully.
>
> Hot pangs of guilt flooded over me as the Holy Ghost taught me of a better way. I felt selfish and in need of repentance. Tears poured down my face as the Spirit placed new characters into the setting of that ancient parable.

Each of us, at some point in our lives, encounters difficulty and discouragement, where we feel we are riding our own little pink bike. Some have life-long struggles with particular issues. A leader's ability to recognize these individual needs and attend to them builds trust and confidence in the leader's ability to serve everyone.

Part Four: Remain Flexible

At the conclusion of what must have been a long but transcendent day, the Savior is ready to ascend back to the presence of His Father. He invites all who were with him to return to their homes, and to "ponder upon the things which I have said, and ask of the Father, in my name, that ye may understand, and prepare your minds for the morrow, and I come unto you again. But now I go unto the Father, and also to show myself unto the lost tribes of Israel, for they are not lost unto the Father, for he knoweth whither he hath taken them." But the people were not ready to have Him leave. They had experienced something remarkable and didn't want the experience to end. Jesus then "cast his eyes round about again on the multitude, and beheld they were in tears, and did look steadfastly upon him as if they would ask him to tarry a little longer with them." Jesus had an agenda. He had responsibilities to fulfill. But He recognized His greatest responsibility in that moment was to attend to the needs of the one. He therefore responds: "Behold, my bowels are filled with compassion towards you" (3 Nephi 17: 3–6). Jesus stays, and what follows is one of the most remarkable vignettes in all recorded scripture as He prays for the people, heals their sick, and blesses their children—again, one by one. Angels come and minister as the children are encircled by fire, while the multitude witnesses this event and is overcome. Jesus' compassion is so deep and so profound, He weeps in response to the experience. Words are inadequate to describe the magnificence of this event, which, initially, was not on the schedule.

Leadership Lesson: Are we, in our leadership responsibilities, willing to set aside the prescribed, planned events in order to attend to the needs of others who are not on the schedule? How about the needs of the one? Are we open to the extraordinary events that will follow? Are we flexible and willing to adjust when we see a need? Do we recognize that people are more important than programs?

President Thomas S. Monson lived a life of seeking out the one. He developed a keen sensitivity to the Spirit by consistently acting on promptings he received to visit those in need. It was a practice prompted by an experience he had when he was a twenty-three-year-old bishop, as related by Elder Jeffrey R. Holland, then president of Brigham Young University:

> [Bishop Monson] was uncharacteristically restless as the stake priesthood leadership meeting progressed. He had the distinct impression that he should leave the meeting immediately and drive to the Veterans' Hospital high up on the Avenues of Salt Lake City. Before leaving home that night he had received a telephone call informing him that an older member of his ward was ill and had been admitted to the hospital for care. Could the bishop, the caller wondered, find a moment to go by the hospital sometime and give a blessing? The busy young leader explained that he was just on his way to a stake meeting but that he certainly would be pleased to go by the hospital as soon as the meeting was concluded. Now the prompting was stronger than ever: "Leave the meeting and proceed to the hospital at once." But the stake president himself was speaking at the pulpit! It would be most discourteous to stand in the middle of the presiding officer's message, make one's way over an entire row of brethren, and then exit the building altogether.

Painfully he waited out the final moments of the stake president's message, then bolted for the door even before the benediction had been pronounced. Running the full length of the corridor on the fourth floor of the hospital, the young bishop saw a flurry of activity outside the designated room. A nurse stopped him and said, "Are you Bishop Monson?" "Yes," was the anxious reply. "I'm sorry," she said. "The patient was calling your name just before he passed away." Fighting back the tears, Thomas S. Monson turned and walked back into the night. He vowed then and there that he would never again fail to act upon a prompting from the Lord. He would acknowledge the impressions of the Spirit when they came, and he would follow wherever they led him, ever to be "on the Lord's errand."[6]

Part Five: Seek Those Who Are Missing

After Jesus beholds the multitude and determines to stay and bless them further, He asks: "Have ye any that are sick among you? Bring them hither. Have ye any that are lame, or blind, or halt, or maimed, or leprous, or that are withered, or that are deaf, or that are afflicted in any manner? Bring them hither and I will heal them." (3 Nephi 17:7). His immediate invitation to those who had experienced the marvelous events of that day is for them to go find others who were not there, but who also might need His healing influence, and to bring them to Him.

Leadership Lesson: Do we, in our leadership and ministering efforts, seek those who are missing? Do we look beyond our comfortable circles, beyond those who naturally fit in to seek out and include those who, for whatever reason, are not always with us, those who are "afflicted in any manner"?

I love the lyrics by Scottish hymn writer, Elizabeth Cecilia Clephane:

> There were ninety and nine that safely lay
> In the shelter of the fold,
> But one was out on the hills away,
> Far off from the gates of gold—

Away on the mountains wild and bare,
Away from the tender Shepherd's care,
Away from the tender Shepherd's care.

Lord, thou has here thy ninety and nine;
Are they not enough for thee?"
But the Shepherd made answer:
"This of mine has wandered away from me,
And although the road be rough and steep,
I go to the desert to find my sheep,
I go to the desert to find my sheep.[7]

Are we willing to go to the desert to find the one who is lost? Are we willing to travel the rough roads, to invest in an arduous, steep climb in order to serve the one?

Elder John R. Lassiter related the following experience he had visiting Morocco as part of an official United States government delegation. His group was invited to travel a significant distance into the desert to view some ruins. He shared:

> Five large black limousines moved across the beautiful Moroccan countryside at considerable speed. I was riding in the third limousine, which had lagged some distance behind the second. As we topped the brow of a hill, we noticed that the limousine in front of us had pulled off to the side of the road. As we drew nearer, I sensed that an accident had occurred and suggested to my driver that we stop. The scene before us has remained with me for these many years.
>
> An old shepherd, in the long, flowing robes of the Savior's day, was standing near the limousine in conversation with the driver. Nearby, I noted a small flock of sheep numbering not more than fifteen or twenty. An accident had occurred. The king's vehicle had struck and injured one of the sheep belonging to the old shepherd. The driver of the vehicle was explaining to him the law of the land. Because the king's vehicle had injured one of the sheep belonging to the old shepherd, he was now entitled to one hundred times its value at maturity. However, under the same law, the injured sheep must be slain and the meat divided among the people. My

interpreter hastily added, "But the old shepherd will not accept the money. They never do."

Startled, I asked him why. And he added, "Because of the love he has for each of his sheep." It was then that I noticed the old shepherd reach down, lift the injured lamb in his arms, and place it in a large pouch on the front of his robe. He kept stroking its head, repeating the same word over and over again. When I asked the meaning of the word, I was informed, "Oh, he is calling it by name. All of his sheep have a name, for he is their shepherd, and the good shepherds know each one of their sheep by name."

It was as my driver predicted. The money was refused, and the old shepherd with his small flock of sheep, with the injured one tucked safely in the pouch on his robe, disappeared into the beautiful deserts of Morocco.

As we continued our journey toward the ruins, my interpreter shared with me more of the traditions and practices of the shepherds of that land. Each evening at sundown, for example, the shepherds bring their small flocks of sheep to a common enclosure where they are secured against the wolves that roam the deserts of Morocco. A single shepherd then is employed to guard the gate until morning. Then the shepherds come to the enclosure one by one, enter therein, and call forth their sheep—by name. The sheep will not hearken unto the voice of a stranger but will leave the enclosure only in the care of their true shepherd, confident and secure because the shepherd knows their names and they know his voice.

The words of the Master Shepherd rang loudly in my ears:

"But he that entereth in by the door is the shepherd of the sheep.

"To him the porter openeth; and the sheep hear his voice: and he calleth his own sheep by name, and leadeth them out.

"And when he putteth forth his own sheep, he goeth before them, and the sheep follow him: for they know his voice.

"And a stranger will they not follow, but will flee from him: for they know not the voice of strangers" (John 10:2–5).[8]

A shepherd loves his sheep. He sacrifices for them. Amid a chorus of continuously competing voices, the shepherd calls to his sheep and they recognize his voice. Jesus is the Good Shepherd and He declares, I "know my sheep, and am known of mine" (John 10:14).

One by one leadership requires us to be shepherds by following the example of the Good Shepherd. President Spencer W. Kimball noted, "Jesus said several times, 'Come, follow me.' His was a program of 'do what I do' . . . He walked and worked with those he was to serve. His was not a long-distance leadership. He was not afraid of close friendships; he was not afraid that proximity to him would disappoint his followers. The leaven of true leadership cannot lift others unless we are with and serve those to be led."[9]

Andrew Skinner, former dean of religious education at Brigham Young University, shared an experience he had with a group of students while he was serving at the Jerusalem Center: "I have seen in my mind's eye, many times on field trip sites, the Savior teaching and preaching and performing miracles. I well remember being with a group of students as we went to Shepherds' Field. They were singing the songs associated with Jesus' birth in Bethlehem. On this particular occasion, they were singing "O Little Town of Bethlehem" as the sun was setting and the church bells across the valley in Bethlehem were chiming. Then, as if on cue, one of the Bedouin family members who lived in that area walked up the west slope of the hill on which we were sitting with a flock of sheep trailing behind him. He walked past us. The cameras were flashing as he walked his sheep down the east side of the hill. As if staged, there was a straggler, a lamb that had become separated from the flock because of the camera flashes. As he stood in front of this crowd of photographers—I don't know what fear feels like from a sheep's point of view, but it sure looked like fear to me—he was clearly confused, looking to the right, to the left, and behind, but he could not find the flock. Then from over the hill came the voice of the shepherd, calling to this little sheep. The ears of the lamb perked up, and he looked in that direction as the shepherd came, picked him up, cradled him in his arms, and said a few words, in Arabic I suppose. I don't know, but I believe that the shepherd was offering some calming and comforting sentiments . . . I will never forget the very real feeling that came over me as I thought of the Savior's voice in place of the Bedouin herder's, the voice of the One who is not just a good shepherd but the Good Shepherd.[10]

Elder Joseph B. Wirthlin reminded us, "This instruction [to seek after the one] applies to all who follow Him. We are commanded to seek out those who are lost. We are to be our brother's keeper. We cannot neglect this commission given by our Savior. We must be concerned for the one."[11] Dag Hammarskjold, the former U.N. Secretary-General said, "It is more noble to give yourself completely to one individual than to labor diligently for the masses."[12] And Mother Theresa sums it up thus:

> I never look at the masses as my responsibility. I look at the individual. I can love only one person at a time. I can feed only one person at a time. Just one, one, one. . . . So you begin—I begin. I picked up one person—maybe if I didn't pick up that one person I wouldn't have picked up 42,000. The whole work is only a drop in the ocean. But if I didn't put the drop in, the ocean would be one drop less. Same thing for you, same thing in your family, same thing in the church where you go. Just begin . . . one, one, one.
>
> —Mother Theresa[13]

This is how Jesus loves us. This is how He leads us. He sets the pattern and expects us to follow. This is how we are to love and lead those we serve.

Some things to consider doing:

1. Prayerfully approach the Lord and ask which "one" needs your specific help today.
2. Who might feel isolated and on the fringe of social acceptance or who stands in need of friendship? Initiate a relationship.
3. Who, outside your immediate circle, could you reach out to and serve?
4. Carefully study the book *One by One*, by Elder David A. Bednar

CONCLUSION

Shall we not go on in so great a cause? Go forward and not backward. Courage, brethren; and on, on to the victory! Let your hearts rejoice, and be exceedingly glad. Let the earth break forth into singing.

—D&C 128:22

God does notice us, and He watches over us. But it is usually through another person that He meets our needs.

—Spencer W. Kimball[1]

Abram (soon to be Abraham) and his nephew, Lot, both had significant holdings. Combined, their flocks and herds and tents were so vast and "their substance so great" (v7) the two men and their households could not be accommodated in one consolidated area. Tensions between the two men's herdsmen began to arise as they all vied for land to sustain their cattle.

This conflict was troubling to Abram. They were brethren who shared both familial and spiritual bonds. Because of this bond, as they discussed separating, Abram offered Lot his first choice of land. Lot surveyed the area and selected the verdant, green Jordan plain (which included Sodom and Gomorrah) as his new home, leaving Abram with the more arid land of Canaan.

But Sodom and Gomorrah were wicked and therefore were without the protection and blessing of the Lord, and thus vulnerable to attack from other kingdoms. After Lot is settled and his family established, a great battle ensued between the kings of Sodom and Gomorrah and other kingdoms (known as the Battle of the Vale of Siddim or the War of Nine Kings) wherein Lot, his household and all his goods are taken captive. Thankfully for Lot, one from his household escaped and reported his predicament to Abram.

It could be argued that Lot's circumstances are purely a function of his choices—he placed himself in this position. He selected Sodom as his new home and chose to associate with the people of both decadent cities. Perhaps he should have known better. Perhaps his capture is of his own doing. Certainly, there are consequences to choices.

None of that mattered to Abram. Lot was his brother's son, and no lengths were too great to save him. Abram gathered his very best trained servants, armed them—all of them, totaling 318, the size of a large ward—and went to go after the one person, who, because of his choices, placed himself in this position. Abram and his 318 faithful servants prevail against the armies of Lot's captors, and Lot, his household, and all his goods are returned to their homes unscathed.

Who is worth saving? To what lengths will we go to save them? Who needs to be involved? What resources do we need to marshal? Sometimes we jump in to serve individually. And sometimes it requires the efforts of others (like an entire ward). In Abram's case with Lot, it was a significant undertaking, requiring extreme efforts and intense sacrifice of many, including Abram and his finest and best trained servants—all 318 of them.

What if you don't feel up to the demands of the calling? What if you feel the task is too great? If you feel you are too insignificant to make a difference, you have never, as the Dalai Lama once said, tried sleeping with a mosquito. Your unique contribution is vital. You can make a difference, and the Lord has called you to do just that.

When Enoch received his assignment to preach repentance to a wicked world, he responded, "Why is it that I have found favor in thy sight, and am but a lad, and all the people hate me; for I am slow of speech; wherefore am I thy servant" (Moses 6:31)? The reader can feel his angst and can likely relate in a very personal way. But the Lord's confidence in His chosen leader is clear as he admonishes His new prophet to "Go forth and do as I have commanded thee, and no man shall pierce thee. Open thy mouth, and it shall be filled, and I will give thee utterance, for all flesh is in my hands, and I will do as seemeth me good. Say unto this people: Choose ye this day, to serve the Lord God who made you" (Moses 6:32–33). Enoch trusted in the Lord, he exercised faith, and he got to work. "And so great was the faith of Enoch that he led the people of God, and their enemies came to battle against them; and he spake the word of the Lord, and the earth trembled, and the mountains fled, even according to his command; and the rivers of water were turned out of their course; and the roar of the lions was heard out of the wilderness; and all nations feared greatly, so powerful was the word of Enoch, and so great was the power of the language which God had given him" (Moses 7:13).

My friend, Reed, travelled a stony path for much of his life. He had grown up with the benefit of loving parents who taught him and nurtured him with Christ-like kindness and provided a gospel-centered home environment. But as he entered young adulthood, he pursued different values and priorities than those of his parents and church leaders. For years he sought happiness in what the world offers but found only emptiness. One bad choice led to another, until he found himself, like the prodigal son, isolated, destitute, and without a belief in any kind of future. But several factors sparked a rekindling of a hope for something better. He remembered the consistent counsel from his father, who patiently but lovingly persisted in his parental admonitions. Like the prodigal son, when Reed was still "a great way off" but making his way back, his father saw his efforts, "and had compassion on him, and ran, and fell on his neck, and kissed him" (Luke 15:20). Reed experienced the loving and never-ending patience of his mother, who had served faithfully every week as a temple worker as part of her efforts to seek divine help for her boy. His bishop refused to lose sight of him. His stake president, likewise, engaged in important ministering efforts, and both leaders marshalled the help of others in the ward and stake to assist. Slowly, but surely, Reed's life and priorities changed. He began to feel the warmth of the Spirit once more.

He found joy in serving. His spirit began to long to come home. And he did.

At a Saturday evening session of stake conference, Reed recounted the efforts that so many leaders had been put forward on his behalf, and with tears in his eyes and a quivering voice, he did his best to share his nearly inexpressible joy at receiving his patriarchal blessing, the Melchizedek Priesthood, and in obtaining a temple recommend.

Reed had many powerful examples to draw upon throughout his difficult journey back. Certainly his parents and grandparents played a prominent role, as did his formal church leaders. He had extended family that were unrelenting in their faith in him and for him. And he had the example of others who had gone before him whose influence he felt and whose example of leadership and devotion to those they served inspired him. Here is one example, in his own words:

> My great-great-grandmother lived to be 102 and I knew her well as we lived very near her. She would often talk about her life and its challenges during our visits. She was widowed in her early twenties and was left with two little girls to raise on her own. One of her two daughters left the church at a very young age and it was a source of disappointment and sorrow for my great-great-grandmother throughout her long life. I remember her talking about how much she wanted her daughter, my great aunt Sally, to come back to the gospel. I know that up to her death at 102 she still was praying for her eighty-one-year-old child to embrace her Savior and the church our ancestors sacrificed so much to help establish.
>
> Nine years after her mother's death, my wayward Aunt Sally at age ninety, had a wonderful home teacher assigned to her. He, himself, was in his eighties when he became her home teacher. He went above and beyond in service and commitment to his calling. He became just the right person to reintroduce the gospel to her after seventy-five years away from activity. She started reading the Book of Mormon. She began going to church. At ninety-two she qualified for a temple recommend and received her endowment in the Salt Lake Temple.[2]

Reed will forever be grateful for the persistent faith and prayers of his great-great-grandmother, who refused to give up on her efforts. And he will also be eternally indebted to an eighty-year-old home teacher, whose name he does not know, but whose faithful and diligent service blessed his life with an assurance that the gospel plan does, indeed, work, and that Jesus Christ's atonement reaches far enough for him, despite the distance from the path he had travelled.

Your leadership, regardless of your age, your role, your family circumstance or whatever calling you may have, can make a profound and lasting difference in the lives of those you love and serve. And while that impact may not always be immediately known, it can have lasting consequences beyond your immediate purview, a ripple that can extend into eternity. This is a transcendent work, a work directed by a loving Savior, who knows what needs to be done and knows how to magnify His leaders to accomplish His purposes.

President Russell M. Nelson declared:

> You were sent to earth at this precise time, the most crucial time in the history of the world, to help gather Israel. You are among the best the Lord has ever sent to this world. You have the capacity to be smarter and wiser and have more impact on the world than any previous generation! This is the mission for which you were sent to earth. Set a standard for the rest of the world. Embrace being different. Be happy that your light is shining brightly in this ever-darkening world. I testify that this is the work of almighty God, He lives! Jesus is the Christ! This is His church. You are the hope of Israel![3]

The leadership mandate is clear. We cannot lose sight of it. Our part is critical in these days of the final gatherings. We will most certainly face opposition. We'll have days when we feel we've lost the bigger picture or when we feel our individual part isn't necessary. To paraphrase the writer Ambrose Redmoon: courage to lead is not the absence of fear, but rather the judgment that something else is more important than one's fear. The timid presume it is lack of fear that allows the brave to act when the timid do not. But to take action—to lead—when one is not afraid is easy. To refrain when afraid is also easy. To lead regardless of fear is brave.[4]

Leadership is a choice. And it's a choice you must make, for the Lord is counting on you to carry His kingdom to your families, to the Church, and to all His children.

One of the great examples of the character of Christ's leadership is in Jacob's recounting of Zenos' allegory of the olive tree—or, in other words, the story of the House of Israel and of God's unfailing and unrelenting love for His children.

The allegory covers an extensive period of human history. We learn of the gathering and scattering of Israel, and its subsequent gathering . . . again . . . and again—from the early foundations of the House of Israel to the time before Christ's birth, then to the time of Christ and His apostles, and later through the great apostasy. Finally, the time comes for the gathering and restoration, where our role as leaders and fellow vineyard laborers becomes central alongside the Lord of the vineyard. What follows is a glorious time of peace and joy—the millennium—which ends with the Lord's final gathering and salvation and exaltation of his people.

Zenos provides rich leadership lessons over the course of this long journey through history. We learn of a God who refuses to give up on his people. We learn, after His constant digging and pruning of his trees (or his people), his people become corrupt. He sorrows: "It grieveth me that I should lose this tree." This tree—this people—this person. We learn that leaders prune—which can hurt. Sometimes His guidance comes in the form of dung—it can be uncomfortable, it can be unpleasant, it can stink, both figuratively and literally! But throughout this process we are constantly developed.

The Lord of the vineyard nourishes his trees. Leaders nourish their people. Zenos uses this word 20 times throughout his allegory. The Lord works diligently to preserve his people—Zenos uses this word 15 times—which means to guard, to keep, to rescue, to deliver. And the Lord is unrelenting in His efforts to do so. Again, and again and again the Lord returns to his vineyard to nourish and preserve. If it doesn't work one time, He comes back. He perseveres. Again. And again. His leadership isn't once and done. He doesn't give up if no one responds or if He is rejected a first or second or third time. He goes again.

Sometimes we, the trees of the vineyard, are placed in a poor spot of ground. To that, the Lord declares, "I knew that it was a poor spot .

. . wherefore . . . I have nourished it . . . and behold . . . it hath brought forth much fruit" (Jacob 5:22). That statement reminds me of the well-known phrase: "If it were easy, they wouldn't need me (or you) to do it."

The restoration of the Lord's church is an ongoing process. He didn't simply restore everything all at once, somewhere between 1820 and 1844. It continues. Too often, we think of "restoration" as applying only to the tenants, doctrines, and structure of the church. And certainly, that is true. But the whole purpose—the summum bonum of the restoration of the church is so that people—you and I—can be restored to God. He is restoring each one of us—personally and individually. And it is a messy, on-going, and lengthy process. He works with us, he nurtures us, he believes in us, he sees us for what we can be and for who we really are.

As leaders, we are enlisted alongside Him. The Lord invites, "Let *us* take of the branches" (v. 52), "*We* will nourish again" (v 58), "Wherefore, go to, and call servants, that *we* may labor diligently with *our* might" (v 61), "Wherefore, let *us* go to and labor" (v 62).

The Lord of the vineyard doesn't give up. He takes the long view. This is His character. This is His leadership. Therefore, we can't give up. We must keep trying. Again. And again. And again. See the patience of the Lord. And go and do likewise.

ACKNOWLEDGMENTS

This project has been incubating for many years, and over the course of that time, I've had the privilege of discussing it with and gathering input from many sources. For me, at least, my writing initiatives tend to be highly interactive. I am intensely grateful to so many who have been willing to engage with me in bantering ideas back and forth, sharing experiences, and offering wisdom and thoughtful insights, as well as reading chapters and drafts and providing important feedback. Many, though not all, are members of The Church of Jesus Christ of Latter-day Saints. All of them volunteered significant time, as well as their faith, vulnerability, authenticity, and encouragement. Special thanks goes to the following for their willingness to participate: Jeanette Bennett, Tracy Radmall, Alan Radmall, Sherri Hymas, Ben Hulme, Tanner Ainge, Jeff Acerson, Kristin McQuivey, David M. R. Covey, William Shupe, David Bennion, James Stone, Von Orgill, Stephen M. R. Covey, Reed Shupe, Joshua Chase, Eric Stats, Robert McKee, Jodi Orgill Brown, Thomas Worthlin McConkie, Timothy Taggart, Greg Brimhall, David Rutter, Steven McGhie, A. Roger Merrill, John Harding, Larry Radford, Lori Seely, Breck England, Amy Feisthamel, Craig Christensen, Lincoln Jacobs, Larry Gelwix, Preston Luke, Jessica Gledhill, Gaylord Karren, Ann Takasaki, Randy Boothe, and Patrick Leddin.

Many thanks also for the professional guidance of wise editors, graphic designers, and other leaders at Cedar Fort. It is always a delight to work with this team!

My children have the unfortunate position of being both the subject of several stories in this book as well as convenient audiences for quick feedback on a sentence or concept. Their willingness to help anytime, despite whatever else they might have been working on is much appreciated. Love and thanks to Brittney, Ryan, Emily, Mallory, Jacob, Matthew, and Megan.

A special call-out to my oldest son, Cameron, who engaged his heart in this project and enthusiastically offered many hours on its behalf. He volunteered stories, called former leaders to gain their perspective, and acted as a sounding-board at every step along the way. His contributions to this book have been monumental!

As always, I express my appreciation to Michele, the love of my life and my partner in everything I do. I am grateful for her support and encouragement, especially during the times when I'm not able to see the next step in front of me. She helps bring perspective and illumination to everything I do.

Finally, many thanks to all the leaders in my life—some of whom have been in formal leadership roles, and some in informal leadership roles. I have been richly blessed by my association with each of them. Whether business leaders, colleagues, Church leaders, mission presidents, parents, family members, and friends, my life is better because of their leadership and their impact on me, and those they serve is deep and profound.

BIBLIOGRAPHY

Introduction

1. Welch, Jack. *Winning.* Harper Business; 1st edition (March 26, 2013).
2. Published by TrainingIndustry.com, https://trainingindustry.com/wiki/outsourcing/size-of-training-industry/.
3. Kimball, Spencer W., "Jesus, The Perfect Leader," from an address given to the Young Presidents Organization, Sun Valley, ID, January 1977.
4. Ibid.
5. Quoted by J. Lawrence Richards, "Just for Today," at an address presented at LDS Business College, January 8, 2013.

Chapter 1

1. Eyring, Henry B., "Watch with Me," *Ensign*, Apr. 2001, 38.
2. Otterson, Michael, "On Faith: Great Voices: Gordon B. Hinckley: 1910–2008, *Washington Post*, January 29, 2008.
3. Quoted by Pappus of Alexandria in *Synagoge, Book VIII.*
4. Uchtdorf, Dieter F., "The Greatest Among You," Ensign, May 2017.
5. Rowling, J. K., *Harry Potter and the Deathly Hallows*, Arthur A. Levine Books, January 1, 2009.
6. Hinckley, Gordon B., "Whosoever Will Save His Life," *Ensign*, August 1982.
7. Dew, Sheri L. "You Were Born to Lead, You Were Born for Glory," from an address given at Brigham Young University, December 9, 2003.
8. Roosevelt, Eleanor, https://www.goodreads.com/quotes/142537-to-handle-yourself-use-your-head-to-handle-others-use.
9. *Teachings of Presidents of the Church: John Taylor* [2001], 164.
10. Quoted by Tricia McDermott, "Ronald Reagan Remembered," https://www.cbsnews.com/news/ronald-reagan-remembered/.
11. Wilson, Woodrow, https://www.passiton.com/inspirational-quotes/4241-you-are-not-here-merely-to-make-a-living-you.
12. Emerson, Ralph Waldo, https://www.brainyquote.com/quotes/ralph_waldo_emerson_130588.
13. Quoted by Megan Bailey, "7 Quotes by Inspirational Leaders," Mother Teresa, https://www.beliefnet.com/inspiration/quotes/7-quotes-by-inspirational-leaders.aspx.
14. Quoted by Robert Allred, "The Persuasive Leader," http://allred10.com/?p=539.
15. Tolkien, J.R.R., *The Fellowship of the Ring*, Mariner Books.
16. Truman, Harry S., *More Plain Speaking*, Berkley Books; 10TH edition (January 1, 1973).
17. Givens, Terryl & Fiona, *The God Who Weeps.* Salt Lake City: Deseret Book, 2017.
18. Quoted by Jim Lara, "Do I Have What it Takes to be a Transformational Leader," https://www.graystoneadvisors.com/transformational-leader/.
19. Quoted by Manukurizingal, ""Vision of Leadership," https://manukurizingal.wordpress.com/2015/06/24/vision-of-leadership/.
20. Quoted by David Van Rooy, https://www.inc.com/david-van-rooy/15-timeless-presidential-quotes-for-presidents-day.html.
21. Quoted on https://ldsquotations.com/author/harold-b-lee/.
22. Quoted by Rodger Dean Duncan and Ed J. Pinegar, *Leadership for Saints*, Independently Published, March 27, 2017.
23. Ibid.
24. Ibid.
25. Hinckley, Gordon B. "Be a Leader in Honorable Causes," *Ensign*, Jan. 1998, 72.
26. Quoted by Rodger Dean Duncan and Ed J. Pinegar, *Leadership for Saints*, Independently Published, March 27, 2017.
27. Quoted on: https://internetpoem.com/henry-ford/quotes/i-am-looking-for-a-lot-of-men-who-have-an-infinite-34393/.

28. Quoted by Charles Swigart, https://www.linkedin.com/pulse/being-powerful-like-lady-you-have-tell-people-arent-van-heerden, December 11, 2015.
29. Kimball, Spencer W., "Small Acts of Service," *Ensign*, December 1974.
30. Covey, Stephen R., *The 8th Habit: From Effectiveness to Greatness*, p. 98, Simon and Schuster, 2003.

Chapter 2

1 Covey, Stephen R., "Stephen R. Covey Quotes," https://quotefancy.com/stephen-r-covey-quotes.
2. Packer, Boyd K., "The Mantle is Far, Far Greater Than the Intellect," from an address to religious educators at a symposium on the Doctrine and Covenants and Church history, Brigham Young University, 22 August 1981.
3. Wilcox, Brad. *Born to Change the World.* Salt Lake City: Deseret Book, 2019.
4. Sheler, Jeffery L., "The Mormon Moment," *US News and World Report*, November 2000, Cover Story.
5. Dew, Sheri L. *Go Forward with Faith: The Biography of Gordon B. Hinckley* (Salt Lake City: Deseret Book, 1996) 592–93.
6. Woodruff, Wilford., Journal of Discourses, Volume 18. September 12, 1875, 110.

Chapter 3

1. Hale, Edward Everett, "Pass It On," https://www.passiton.com/inspirational-quotes/3660-i-am-only-one-but-still-i-am-one-i-cannot-do.
2. Eyring, Henry B., "That We May Be One," *Ensign*, May 1998.
3. https://www.churchofjesuschrist.org/study/ensign/1998/05/that-we-may-be-one?lang=eng.
4. Nelson, Russell M., "The Love and Laws of God," from an address given at Brigham Young University, Sept. 17, 2019.
5. Kimball, Spencer W., "Jesus, The Perfect Leader," From an address given to the Young Presidents Organization, Sun Valley, ID, January 1977.
6. Barker, Joel. *Future Edge* (New York: W. Morrow, 1992).
7. Elias, Ric, "Thee Things I Learned While My Plane Crashed," from Ted2011.
8. Monson, Thomas S., "Duty Calls," *Ensign,* May 1996, 44.
9. Emerson, Ralph Waldo, https://www.inspirationalstories.com/quotes/ralph-waldo-emerson-every-great-and-commanding-movement-in-the/.

Chapter 4

1. Lorenz, Stephen R., *Lorenz on Leadership, Lessons on Leading People, Teams and Organizations*, (Air Force Research Institute, Air University Press, 2021), 7.

Chapter 5

1. Hinckley, Gordon B., from an address given at Brigham Young University, September 17, 1996.
2. Smith, Joseph. "The Wentworth Letter," March 1, 1842.
3. Bornstein, David, *How to Change the World: Social Entrepreneurs and the Power of New Ideas* (New York: Oxford University Press US, 2004), 291.
4. "On Poetry," *Dead Poets Society*, DVD, Directed by Peter Weir, 1989, Touchstone Home Video, Inc.
5. Quoted by Amos Lee Collins, https://slideplayer.com/slide/10955646/.
6. Schweitzer, Albert. *Out of My Life and Thought*, JHUP; 60th Anniversary edition (July 1, 2009).
7. Holland, Jeffrey R., "Unless You're a Mormon," from an address given at Brigham Young University, September 9, 1986.

Chapter 6

1. Lewis, C. S., *The Weight of Glory and Other Addresses* (New York, MacMillan Publishing Co., 1980), 92.
2. Hinckley, Gordon B., *Standing for Something* (The Crown Publishing Group, 2000).
3. Brooks, Arthur C., "More Love, Less Contempt," from an address given at Brigham Young University, April 2019.
4. See George A. Smith, JD 3:283–84.
5. Hinckley, Gordon B., "Small Acts Lead to Great Consequences," *Ensign*, May 1984.

6. Quoted by James E. Faust, in Conference Report, Apr. 1996, 6; or *Ensign,* May 1996, 7.
7. Holland, Jeffrey R., http://mormonchannel.org/ces-devotionals.

Chapter 7

1. Bushnell, Nolan. https://www.brainyquote.com/quotes/nolan_bushnell_130640.
2. Goethe, Johann Wolfgang. https://www.quotes.net/quote/1138.
3. Craig, Michelle, "Avoid Being in the Thick of Thin Things," from an address given at BYU Women's Conference, May 2018.
4. Lewis C. S., *The Screwtape Letters* (New York: Harper Collins, 1996) 139.
5. Goethe, Johann Wolfgang. https://www.brainyquote.com/quotes/johann_wolfgang_von_goeth_150560#:~:text=Johann%20Wolfgang%20von%20Goethe%20Quotes&text=Plunge%20boldly%20into%20the%20thick%20of%20life%2C%20and%20seize%20it,will%2-C%20it%20is%20always%20interesting.
6. Bell, Alexander. https://www.brainyquote.com/quotes/alexander_graham_bell_387728.
7. Monson, Thomas S., "What Have I Done for Someone Today," *Ensign*, November 2009.

Chapter 8

1. Holland, Jeffrey R., "The Best Is Yet to Be," from an address given at Brigham Young University, January 13, 2009.
2. "Master, The Tempest is Raging," *Hymns*, no. 105.
3. Ibid.
4. Calone, Charles Alexander de, https://www.encyclopedia.com/humanities/dictionaries-thesauruses-pictures-and-press-releases/difficult-done-once-impossible-takes-little-longer.
5. Collins, Jim, *Good to Great* (New York: Harper Collins Publishers Inc., 2001), 109.
6. Quoted in "Just What Are You Trying to Say?," by Joel Peterson, November 13, 2012: https://www.forbes.com/sites/joelpeterson/2012/11/13/just-what-are-you-trying-to-say/?sh=72505d67370c.
7. "Where Can I Turn for Peace," *Hymns*, no. 129.
8. Holland, Jeffrey R., "However Long and Hard the Road," January 18, 1983.
9. Robinson, John S., "A Complete Look at Perfect," from an address given at Brigham Young University, July 13, 1999.
10. McConkie, Bruce R., "The Probationary Test of Mortality," from an address given at the University of Utah, January 1982, p. II; See JD 1:6.
11. Holland, Jeffrey R., "The Best Is Yet to Be," from an address given at Brigham Young University, January 13, 2009.
12. Malloch, Thomas, https://small-courage.com/good-timber-douglas-malloch/.
13. Oliver, Mary. https://apoemaday.tumblr.com/post/175408809725/i-worried.
14. Wirthlin, Jospeh B., "Sunday Will Come," *Ensign*, November 2006.
15. Watterson, Bill. https://www.google.com/search?q=it%27s+funny+how+day+by+day+nothing+changes+calvin+and+hobbes&tbm=isch&hl=en&sa=X&ved=2ahUKEwj_8cmIzbT1AhVYA50JHdavA2sQrNwCKAB6BQgBEMkB&biw=1440&bih=821#imgrc=4ooxaNDfjBWOKM.
16. Uchtdorf, Dieter F. "Come, Join with Us," *Ensign*, November 2013.
17. Renland, Dale G. "Consider the Goodness and Greatness of God," *Ensign*, May 2020.
18. Thayne, Emma Lou Warner. *The Place of Knowing.* Bloomington, IN: iUniverse, 2011.
19. Quoted by Tom Brady, https://boston.cbslocal.com/2016/01/06/tom-bradys-inspirational-playoff-quote-i-didnt-come-this-far-to-only-come-this-far/.

Chapter 9

1. McConkie, Bruce R., Mormon Doctrine. 2nd ed. Salt Lake City: Bookcraft, 1966, p. 121.
2. Emerson, Ralph. https://www.goodreads.com/quotes/595590-that-which-we-persist-on-doing-becomes-easier-not-that.

3. Holland, Jeffrey R., remarks at the 2020 Mission Leadership Seminar.
4. Top, Brent L. *(https://rsc.byu.edu/healing-his-wings/perfect-balance-justice-mercy./.*

Chapter 10

1. Smith, Joseph, *Teaching of the Prophet Joseph Smith.* Selected by Joseph Fielding Smith. Salt Lake City: Deseret Book, 1976, p. 257.
2 Kimball, Camilla, https://www.ldsliving.com/When-a-Loved-One-Leaves-the-Church-4-Mistakes-to-Avoid/s/80170.
3. Smith, Joseph, *Teaching of the Prophet Joseph Smith.* Selected by Joseph Fielding Smith. Salt Lake City: Deseret Book, 1976, p. 321.
4. Journal Discourses, 11:215, London: Latter-day Saints' Book Depot, 1854–86.
5. Hinckley, Gordon B., remarks at the Jordan Utah South Regional Conference, March 2, 1997.
6. Faust, James E., "The Greatest Challenge in the World—Good Parenting," *Ensign*, November 1990, 35.
7. Packer, Boyd K., "Our Moral Environment," *Ensign*, May 1992.
8. Nelson, Russell M., "Children of the Covenant," *Ensign*, May 1995, 33–34.
9. Holland, Jeffrey R., *https://www.calledtoshare.com/2021/03/02/elder-hollands-message-to-those-who-struggle-with-idea-of-traditional-family-eternal-family/.*
10. Personal interview, Thomas Wirthlin McConkie. Used with permission, April 15, 2020.

Chapter 11

1. Nichols, Morgan Harper, https://morganharpernichols.com/blog/a-few-notes, June 3, 2020.
2. Thoreau, Henry David, http://www.literaturepage.com/read.php?titleid=walden&abspage=6&bookmark=1.
3. Maxwell, Neal A., "Brim with Joy," Brigham Young University Devotional, January 23, 1996.
4. Wilson, Keith J., "In Times of Discouragement, Remember the Widow of Nain," *Ensign*, April 2019.
5. Ibid.
6. Quoted in "Lessons Learned in the Journey of Life," *Ensign*, Dec. 2009, p. 9
7. Ibid.
8. Covey, Stephen R., https://www.google.com/search?sxsrf=AOaemvKX2Z1qBrr81RhnKgJGO0jrrP2c2w:1642210436546&source=univ&tbm=isch&q=the+deepest+need+of+the+human+heart+is+to+be+understood&fir=RhiBGmvDofcMNM%252Cs6Mi9GX1g0h26M%252C_%253B3cT8NF-beLIH2M%252CrObn0-xhursc7M%252C_%253B0Qj_sK0lII6iEM%252CWdMRYz81Cvd8cM%252C_%253BqxteOIR1lQrlXM%252CqejqIdqjupoi8M%252C_%253BX0GbSPr04W3ekM%252CJER53Z_IezK4YM%252C_%253BZuNQu_KUMyz24M%252CnXIkWlrkf2mdpM%252C_%253BeWulLOQv41jaMM%252CTpMl1FqtOnUKnM%252C_%253B0nK8cYhasSlWcM%252C3h4svunDcNJqsM%252C_%253BTGXMeRp8BJ6f_M%252C26PD719MtXPzcM%252C_%253BouSqx__5KqXcfM%252CRNtEBucxFMryJM%252C_&usg=AI4_-kTH0_G_j9nOMtWTjlaCVPm7iSPf3Q&sa=X&ved=2ahUKEwi5k93NzrL1AhUcJ0QIHf4pD1gQjJkEegQIIxAC&biw=1440&bih=821&dpr=2#imgrc=X0GbSPr04W3ekM
9. https://www.merriam-webster.com/dictionary/empathy#note-1.
10. McQuivey, Kristin, shared in talk given September 29, 2019, in the Lindon 15th Ward.
11. Freeman, *Emily, Don't Miss This,* https://www.youtube.com/watch?v=B_YxYiepQ5I.
12. Parkin, Bonnie D., "Personal Ministry: Sacred and Precious," *BYU Magazine*, Sept. 2007.
13. Hepburn, Audrey, https://libquotes.com/audrey-hepburn/quote/lbf1k2r.
14. Personal interview, Jodi Orgill Brown, Used with permission, Nov. 29, 2020.
15. Ibid.

Chapter 12

1. Bednar, David A., " 'Hear Him' in your Heart and in Your Mind," https://www.

churchofjesuschrist.org/inspiration/hear-him-in-your-heart-and-in-your-mind?lang=eng. April 21, 2020.

2. Packer, Boyd K., "The Light of Christ," from an address given on June 22, 2004 at a seminar for new mission leaders, Missionary Training Center, Provo, Utah, 2004.
3. Bednar, David A., "Receive the Holy Ghost," *Ensign*, November 2010.
4. Smith, Joseph, *Teachings of the Prophet Joseph Smith*, selected by Joseph Fielding Smith, Salt Lake City: Deseret Book, 1976, p. 97.
5. Scott, Richard G., "How to Obtain Revelation and Inspiration for Your Personal Life," *Ensign*, April 2012.
6. Hemp, Paul. "Death by Information Overload," *Harvard Business Review, https://hbr.org/2009/09/death-by-information-overload.*
7. Bulao, Jacquelyn. "How Much Data is Created Every Day in 2021," *https://techjury.net/blog/how-much-data-is-created-every-day/#gref, January 4, 2022.*
8. Coleridge, Taylor. https://www.poetryfoundation.org/poems/43997/the-rime-of-the-ancient-mariner-text-of-1834.
9. Kimball, Spencer W., "When the World Will Be Converted," *Ensign,* Oct. 1974, 10–11.
10. Nelson, Russell M., https://www.churchofjesuschrist.org/media/video/2020-02-4600-president-nelson-hear-him-personal-revelation?lang=eng&collectionId=eef65c6a216243dd8670af9eadf53f70.
11. Butler, David. *Don't Miss This*, JSH 1:1–26.
12. Bednar, David A., *https://www.churchofjesuschrist.org/media/video/2020-02-2030-how-i-hearhim-elder-david-a-bednar?lang=eng&collectionId=eef65c6a216243dd8670af9eadf53f70.*
13. Benson, Ezra Taft, "The Power of the Word, *Ensign*, May 1986.
14. Holland, Jeffrey R., #HearHim blog post on ChurchofJesusChrist.org, November 8, 2020.
15. Bednar, David A., "The Spirit of Revelation," *Ensign*, May 2011.
16 .Bednar, David A., "Receive the Holy Ghost," *Ensign*, November 2010.
17. Maxwell, Neal A., *The Enoch Letters*, Salt Lake City, Deseret Book, 1975.
18. Renland, Dale, "Consider the Goodness and Greatness of God," *Ensign*, May 2020.
19. Packer, Boyd K., "The Candle of the Lord," *Ensign*, January 1983, pp. 54–55.
20. Scott, Richard G., "How to Obtain Revelation and Inspiration for Your Personal Life," *Ensign*, April 2012.
21. Wirthlin, Joseph B., "The Law of the Fast," *Ensign*, May 2001.
22. Smith, Joseph F., Conference Reports of The Church of Jesus Christ of Latter-day Saints, April 1916, pp. 2–3. See also *Gospel Doctrine*, 5th ed. 1939, 430–31.

Chapter 13

1. Wesley, John, quoted in "Forbes Quotes: Thoughts on the Business of Life:, https://www.forbes.com/quotes/5542/#:~:text=com-,Do%20all%20the%20good%20you%20can%2C%20in%20all%20the%20ways,long%20as%20ever%20you%20can.
2. Uchtdorf, Dieter F., "Lift Where you Stand," *Ensign*, October 2008.
3. Ibid.
4. Benson, Ezra Taft. *The Teaching of Ezra Taft Benson*. Salt Lake City: Bookcraft, 1988, pp 451, 52. See also: "Provo Tabernacle Rededicated," *Ensign*, December 1986, p. 70.
5. Personal interview, Von Orgill, Used with permission, August 8, 2021.
6. Ballard, M. Russell, "Strength in Counsel," *Ensign*, October 1993.
7. Dalton, Elaine S., "Now Is the Time to Arise and Shine!," *Ensign*, April 2014.
8. Quoted by Robin Gordon-Farliegh, https://www.manaraglobal.com/in-focus-news/2019/5/7/leadership-is-the-capacity-to-translate-vision-into-reality.
9. Holland, Jeffrey R., comments shared at Mission Leader Seminar, June 27, 2017.

10. Aristotle, quotes in "Forbes Quotes: Thoughts on the Business of Life:, https://www.forbes.com/quotes/678/.
11. Drucker, Peter F., "Peter F. Drucker Quotes," https://quotefancy.com/peter-f-drucker-quotes.
12. Picasso, Pablo. "Famous Pablo Picasso Quotes," https://www.pablopicasso.org/quotes.jsp.
13. Morley, Curtis. *The Entrepreneur's Paradox*. Coral Gables: FIU Business Press, pp 53–54.
14. Young, S. Dilworth, "Brigham Young: The Early Years," *Liahona*, June 1989.
15. Personal correspondence, Cameron Moon, July 10, 2020.
16. Richards, Stephen L., Conference Reports of The Church of Jesus Christ of Latter-day Saints, Oct. 1953, p. 86.
17. Ballard, Russell M., "Counseling with our Councils," *Ensign*, April 2004.
18. Ballard, Russell M., "Keeping Covenants," *Ensign*, November 1993, p. 77.
19. Merrell, V. Dallas, "Will You: Implementing the Mission of the Church," from an address given at the Church Educational System Symposium at Provo, Utah, on August 12, 1997.
20. Erying, Henry B., "God Helps the Faithful Priesthood Holder," *Ensign*, November 2007.
21. Book of Mormon Author Team, https://bookofmormoncentral.org/qa/how-could-lehi-travel-from-jerusalem-to-the-red-sea-in-3-days.

Chapter 14

1. Hinckley, Gordon B., "How to Be a Teacher When Your Role as a Leader Requires You to Teach," General Authority Priesthood Board Meeting, Feb. 5, 1969.
2. Eyring, Henry B., "A Witness," *Ensign*, October 2011.
3. Mason, Patrick, *Restoration*, Faith Matters, p. 7.
4. Santayana, George, https://www.forbes.com/quotes/3588/#:~:text=Fanaticism%20consists%20in%20redoubling%20your%20efforts%20when%20you%20have%20forgotten%20your%20aim.
5. Saul, Joshua, "Barnacles Destroy Boats, But Getting Rid Of Them Destroys The Sea—Until Now," https://www.popsci.com/science/article/2011-06/barnacles-destroy-boats-getting-rid-them-destroys-sea-until-now/.
6. Covey, Stephen R., *The 8th Habit: From Effectiveness to Greatness*, p. 98, Simon and Schuster, 2003.
7. Lewis, C. S., *The Weight of Glory*, HarperOne, 2001, pp. 45–46.
8. Smith, Joseph. *Teachings of the Prophet Joseph Smith*, selected by Joseph Fielding Smith. Salt Lake City: Deseret Book, 1976, p. 137.

Chapter 15

1. Dew, Sheri L., "You Were Born to Lead, You Were Born for Glory," Speech presented at Brigham Young University, December 9, 2003.
2. Condie, Spencer J., "Some Scriptural Lessons on Leadership," *Ensign*, May 1990.
3. Conca, James, "Uranium Seawater Extraction Makes Nuclear Power Completely Renewable" https://www.forbes.com/sites/jamesconca/2016/07/01/uranium-seawater-extraction-makes-nuclear-power-completely-renewable/?sh=18a9220a159a.
4. Monson, Thomas S., "Duty Calls," *Ensign*, May 1996, 44.
5. Eyring, Henry B., "Rise to Your Call," *Ensign*, Nov. 2002, 76.
6. Monson, Thomas S., *Favorite Quotations from the Collection of Thomas S. Monson*, Deseret Book, 1985.
7. Joseph Smith, address to the elders assembled in Kirtland, in Young, *History of the Organization of the Seventies,* 14.
8. Quoted in Leonard J. Arrington, *Brigham Young: American Moses*, 1985, 45–46.
9. Wilford Woodruff (December 12, 1869), Journal of Discourses 13:158.
10. Smith, Joseph, *History of the Church*, 2:124.

Chapter 16

1. C. S. Lewis (1971). "The Four Loves," p. 77, Houghton Mifflin Harcourt.

2. *Hamilton*, Original Broadway Musical, Lin-Manuel Miranda, 2015.
3. Holland, Jeffrey R., "Keeping Covenants: A Message for Those Who Will Serve a Mission," *New Era*, January, 2021.
4 Lewis, C. S., https://www.spiritualsmoothies.org/2016/05/11/god-has-infinite-attention/.
5. Maxwell, Neal A., Conference on the Doctrine of Covenants and Church History, Aug. 2002, Brigham Young University.
6. Holland, Jeffrey R., "President Thomas S. Monson: A Man of Action, Man of Faith, Always on the Lord's Errand," February, 1986.
7. Clephane, Elizabeth Cecilia, https://hymnary.org/text/there_were_ninety_and_nine_that_safely, public domain.
8. Lassiter, John R. "Shepherds of Israel," *Ensign*, April 1988.
9. Kimball, Spencer W., "Jesus, The Perfect Leader," from an address given to the Young Presidents Organization, Sun Valley, ID, January 1977.
10. Skinner, Andrew C., "Faculty Perspectives and Experiences at the Jerusalem Center," https://byustudies.byu.edu/article/faculty-perspectives-and-experiences-at-the-jerusalem-center/?utm_source=BYU+Studies&utm_campaign=d1a6789b4c-EMAIL_CAMPAIGN_2019_10_04_03_05_COPY_01&utm_medium=email&utm_term=0_e4342d96b2-d1a6789b4c-73888457.
11. Wirthlin, Joseph B., "Concern for the One," *Ensign*, May 2008, 17–20.
12. Quoted by Stephen R. Covey, *The 7 Habits of Highly Effective People* (New York: Simon and Schuster, 1990), 201.
13. Susan Conroy, *Mother Teresa's Lessons of Love and Secrets of Sanctity* (New York: Our Sunday Visitor Publishing, 2003), 205.

Conclusion

1. *New Era*. Salt Lake City: The Church of Jesus Christ of Latter-day Saints, 1981/03.
2. Personal conversation, used with permission.
3. *New Era*. Salt Lake City: The Church of Jesus Christ of Latter-day Saints, 2019/03.
4. *Chicago Tribune*, Julia Keller, March 29, 2002.

ABOUT THE AUTHOR

For over thirty years, Shawn D. Moon has worked with clients across the globe, from Fortune 500 to governmental organizations, bringing his first-hand experience in leadership and management to help them achieve remarkable results. His deep knowledge and robust experience inspire others to become leaders through personal effectiveness and execution.

Shawn is an experienced executive and *Wall Street Journal* best-selling author. He has been featured in *Forbes* and *Inc.* and is the author or coauthor of several books. He is a highly sought-after speaker, having addressed leaders across the world.